Saddlery

SADDLERY

Elwyn Hartley Edwards

J. A. ALLEN
London

© *Elwyn Hartley Edwards 1963, 1992, 2007*
First published in Great Britain in 1963 by J.A. Allen
This edition 2007

ISBN 978 0 85131 931 5

J.A. Allen
Clerkenwell House
Clerkenwell Green
London EC1R 0HT

J.A. Allen is an imprint of Robert Hale Limited

A catalogue record for this book is available from the British Library

Design by Nancy Lawrence
Line illustrations by Maggie Raynor
Edited by Martin Diggle

Printed in Singapore

Contents

Acknowledgements

My thanks are due to all those manufacturers who have provided illustrative material and given permission for its use.

I am particularly grateful to Nick Creaton B.H.S.I., for his generosity in providing me with illustrations of saddles in his collection and to Mary Herbert who photographed them.

As ever, I am indebted to Julie Thomas for her collation of an unusually difficult MS and for unravelling the intricacies of an ever burgeoning technology.

I have also to express my thanks to Cassandra Campbell of J. A. Allen and her editorial staff who have displayed great patience with a complex text.

Foreword to the First Edition

By Lieut. Colonel F.W.C. Weldon, L.V.O., M.B.E., M. C.

The late Frank Weldon, captain of the British Gold Medal Olympic event team at Stockholm in 1956 and for many years the iconic Director of Badminton Horse Trials, wrote this foreword to the first edition of Saddlery published in 1963 and it is re-printed here in full.

EHE

It is remarkable how ignorant most of us are about the saddlery and equipment we use every day – which is just as indispensable as the horse himself to our favourite recreation or sport – how it is made, what it is made of and how to get the best out of it.

I have been using it as much as anyone for forty years, yet from this book I have learned much that I did not know, and some of the bits and appliances, whose function and use are explained, were little more than romantic names before. It is not that I despise 'gadgets' on principle, be they martingales, nosebands, the more severe bits or other contrivances. I take the view that if we ride for pleasure, it is plain stupid not to employ any device which undeniably improves our safety, confidence or ease of control in times of stress. However, it would be wise to heed the author's warning in his introduction to The Principles and Mechanics of Bitting before clutching gratefully to some ingenious device which in less skilled hands may only produce a worse problem in the end. There is no short cut to success at anything to do with riding, no lasting good ever came out of the use of force, and there is no substitute for sympathy, patience or tact; so the simplest, most direct means of communication will probably be the best in the long run.

Undoubtedly the greatest contribution to the art of equitation in the last twenty years has been by the saddlers who have developed the modern, spring-tree saddle. Not only does it put the rider willy-nilly into the most convenient position for the horse to bear his weight and understand his signals, but it is infinitely more comfortable to sit in and, above all, almost impossible to fall out of. I would no more dream of using a conventional hunting saddle in preference to a modern general-purpose one for hacking, hunting, jumping or cross-country riding than I would pick a kitchen stool rather than a well-upholstered armchair for a Sunday afternoon nap

If this book only serves to encourage some of its readers to ride better and get more pleasure out of riding, then in this respect alone it will have succeeded admirably; but it will do much more. Never before has any-one attempted to explain in simple language the use and purpose of the bewildering variety of equipment and clothing which has been devised for the comfort and protection of the horse both in the stable and at work. Pray Heaven that we shall never have to buy all of it at once, but how convenient to have such a reference book handy and to be able to look up the best solution to the crisis of the moment.

Introduction

Saddlery was first published in 1963 and has been in print ever since, being extensively revised in 1991. But, of course, the world has changed dramatically, even in the last decade, and the saddlery industry, with the sports and leisure pursuits it supports, is no exception.

From being a near-parochial trade it has developed into a global industry with much of the equipment used and designed in Europe and America being manufactured in the Far East.

There is, also, a significant South American input and the increasing participation of eastern European countries, where costs of production, as in the Far East, are no more than a fraction of those pertaining in the Western world.

Naturally, such a situation has led to the decline of the traditional centres of the industry. The West Midlands town of Walsall, England, for example, for long the virtual epicentre of the equestrian goods trade, has lost its pre-eminence in the world scene, although, supported by the inherited skills of its work force, it remains the world leader in innovative design, particularly in saddle technology.

Indeed, the Walsall product at its best, like the Saville Row suit, is probably superior to any other, but is necessarily expensive in relation to the out-sourced article. (Today, a suit can be measured and cut in England from English cloth, and then finished in one of the Shanghai workshops, while a good number of books, like this one, are printed in the Far East.)

In recent years an American influence has also become evident in the European market, along with the 'horse-whisperers' and the slick gurus of 'natural horsemanship'. The powerful pharmaceutical market apart, it is pretty well confined to the area of bitting, control halters, etc. and, as might be expected, is skilfully promoted and vigorously marketed.

Additionally, and inevitably in the twenty-first century, fashions have altered radically as well as the attitudes and perceived needs of a new generation of horse-owners and riders, many of them inexperienced in horse management. Meanwhile, the variety of activities that can be followed increases commensurately, each creating a market for new or adapted items of equipment.

Indeed, it would seem that the one constant factor in the developing history of equitation and horse equipment is the base element itself, represented by the horse.

Certainly, in terms of basic physiology and structure the horse has not altered in the 6,000-odd years of domestication. Nonetheless changes in the physical character have come about as a result of selective breeding and improved management techniques. As an example, there is the Warmblood of mainland Europe, founded, largely, on coaching and light carting blood. There is little evidence of that foundation in the often elegant modern Warmblood, which has benefited from Thoroughbred outcrosses (hot-blood) made over the past twenty to thirty years.

Similarly, the Arab horses brought to England by the Blunts in the nineteenth century to form the renowned Crabbet Stud were, on photographic evidence, almost common when compared with the highly refined Arabian of today.

Necessarily, the results of upgrading are reflected in the design and manufacture of equipment and they are one of the reasons for undertaking this extended revision.

The occasional interpolation in the main text of bracketed material in italic type is included for three principal reasons: to emphasise points made in the original book and retained in this edition; to provide additional comment in the light of recent development, or as a reflection of changing attitudes within the equestrian field.

The stated object of the original *Saddlery* was 'to give as comprehensive an account as possible of the range, scope and variety of articles available …' putting them in perspective within the context of their use. The objective remains unchanged for this new edition.

E.H E. Chwilog 2007

1   Leather

'There is nothing…like leather.'

The first basic material of the saddlery trade is leather, and although increasing use is made of synthetics in the production of protective boots, headcollars and even girths, leather remains pre-eminent in the manufacture of saddles and bridles. Of course, both saddles and bridles are also made from synthetics – it is, after all, a plastic age – but leather is a 'living' substance and has particular qualities not found in the man-made materials.

The cow or, more correctly, the bovine species, is the source of as much as perhaps 95 per cent of the leather used in saddlery. Otherwise, there is sheepskin, used for backings, etc.; some goatskin and calf; a small quantity of doeskin and finally, pigskin, a commodity now in fairly short supply and not used nearly to the extent that it was in the past.

Traditionally, pigskin was used to make the saddle seat and its use for this purpose was pretty well universal up to comparatively recent times. Pigskin is a light leather of little 'substance' (the word used to describe the thickness of leather) but it has great strength and a peculiarly elastic property. It was fitted to the prepared saddle tree after being well soaked. In that condition it could be stretched over the tree and when it dried a neat, tight seat was produced that was free from the suspicion of a wrinkle. Moreover, it was incredibly hard-wearing and there can be little doubt that it was the best material for the purpose.

The very best English saddles, less than a handful, still have a pigskin seat with the cowhide flaps and skirts embossed or printed to match the unique grain of the pigskin, in which the bristle markings are clearly visible as groups of three.

Otherwise, modern saddles, the seats of which, in the interests of economy, are no longer 'set' or built by hand in the old way, employ a panel hide (a supple oxhide 'shaved' to a light substance) or, less frequently, a calfhide and only very occasionally a doeskin. All these are

1

less hard-wearing than pigskin, there is a tendency for them to sag in use and sometimes the very light leathers will split.

Pigskin has fallen out of favour because of the additional manufacturing costs involved; the shortage of suitable skins, most of which are now imported from Asia, and the influence of the German industry which produces by economically viable production-line methods excellently finished and popular saddle ranges with never a pigskin seat in evidence.

Some of the best leather of fifty years ago was imported largely from South America, while the best of all was considered to be from mature Aberdeen Angus cattle. Today's leathers, less mature and of an inferior quality in comparison, are produced in various European and Scandinavian countries, particularly in Germany, Switzerland, Austria and even in Norway, whilst a considerable trade is being built up in Asia, the source of the red buffalo hides. There are advantages to these leathers. It is claimed that the substance of the hides is more consistent and for that reason less wastage is incurred in the cutting. They are also free from warble marks and scoring from barbed wire, both of which weaken and blemish the finished hide, and they are very carefully dressed to give a particular soft, clinging feel when used in saddle construction.

These 'novelty' hides provide an obvious promotional platform. One German firm, for instance, has developed a 'secret tanning process' to produce a thick, shrunk leather which is said to stretch and expand to give a particularly soft, instant-comfort feel. A famous French firm announces the use of Norwegian Cow as though its saddles were built from the hide of the 'sacred cow' itself. An English firm advertises saddles employing Schrumpf and Mokko leathers, which are slightly 'tacky' and, according to the copywriters, 'increase the security of the rider's seat', whilst another uses a combination of thick German doeskin for the seat, and stout, flabby buffalo hide for the flaps.

(The same tendency is apparent in modern breeches which have their seats made from a variety of light, 'grip-fast' leathers. One Australian firm actually advertised 'sticky bum' breeches, whilst in America a special type of glue can be obtained to apply to the saddle seat to increase the rider's security!)

Again, in the interests of sitting tight, the majority of modern saddles incorporate soft knee-pads which can be covered with doeskin (a suede leather made from deerskin); goatskin, which is probably as good as anything, or a simple reversed cowhide in which the underside of the leather (the 'flesh' side) is scuffed up by machine to give a rough, suede finish. In years gone by the ultimate saddle was one covered in doeskin, the thinner doeskin being used for the seat and being laid on top of the usual oxhide skirts and flaps. Doeskin, or buckskin, is very expensive: there are, however, 'mock' doeskins – mutton, dressed not in this case as lamb but deer – which are cheaper and must be described correctly as 'mock doeskin'. The relevant characteristic of doeskin is its soft feel and its peculiarly clinging property, even though the latter is relatively short-lived. Neither doe nor mock doe should be confused with reversed hide. Saddles are frequently made in this 'scuffed up' leather. Such a surface affords considerable grip in the early years of its life and is often helpful for either small children or for those of us who require every possible assistance to stay in the plate. In time the rough surface will wear smooth but this final stage can be delayed by repeated applications of a wire brush or even a little sandpaper. (Doeskin, of course, is naturally smooth and an assault by a wire brush would not be appropriate.) Reversed hide is no more expensive than an ordinary finish.

Dressing the Hide

Left to its own devices a hide would simply putrefy and rot away, a fact appreciated very early in human history, when primitive peoples made use of animal skins for clothing, footwear, water containers and so on.

Men of the Ice Age delayed the onset of total decay by scraping away the flesh from the skin with sharp flints. In the course of a good few hundred years they learnt to peg out the cleaned skins in the sun to dry them. To soften the skin again it was rubbed with the brains of animals, which contain quantities of grease and oil, but it remained a skin that would perish in a relatively short period of time; it was not *leather*.

By definition, 'leather is a hide or skin which retains the original fibrous structure and has been treated so as to be imputrescible even after treatment with water' (*B.S.I. Glossary of Leather Terms*).

Hides are converted into leather and become to all intents an imperishable substance by the process of *tanning*, a word that has its origin in the Amoric word *tanu*, meaning oak. Oak bark, particularly, as well as parts of other trees and shrubs, contains tannin or tannic acid. Skins treated in a solution (known as a *liquor*) made from those vegetable substances are rendered imperishable and take on the properties of *leather*, although, of course, additional dressing processes are involved in the finished product.

In brief the tanning process begins with the washing of the hides in water. They are then soaked in a solution of limewater which loosens the hair so that it can be removed easily. Peculiarly, the lime has first to be used on other skins before it is effective for this purpose. The used lime absorbs bacteria from the skins on which it has been used previously. It is these bacteria which destroy the hair roots and allow the hair to be taken off without difficulty. Once the flesh and hair have gone the hides are immersed in *liquors* of progressively greater strengths so that the leather is tanned right through its substance.

Thereafter, the hides go through the *currying* (dressing) process. After being taken out from the liquor pits the hides are further cleansed in revolving drums of acid and are dried. They are then dressed by a process involving the application of oils, usually of fish and marine mammal origin, and tallows (animal fat mostly obtained from sheep). The white film sometimes apparent on the leather is due to the tallow content and is nothing more than the 'spewing out' of surplus fat. (It follows that the greater the substance of the hide, the greater will be its capacity to absorb the preservative oils, etc. used in the currying process and there will on that account be a corresponding improvement in its flexibility and wearing properties.)

Oak bark tanning is still carried out extensively today although the process has now to be condensed to maintain economic viability. Gone forever are the days when hides could be matured in the pits for up to two years and when the finished product would be kept in store for many weeks to complete the maturing process. You will see, principally on stirrup leathers, the words 'oak bark tanned'. They indicate that the hide is of the best quality, and has undergone this special and lengthy treatment.

(It is a sad but inescapable fact that modern leathers do not approach in quality those available forty or, more particularly, fifty years ago. On the other hand, the very excellence of the product was, in a sense, counter-productive. It contributed to the inherent and not very intelligent conservatism of horsy people, many of whom expected any item made from leather to be indestructible

and to give good service over at least two lifetimes – a most presumptuous attitude.)

In countries where the oak tree is not indigenous, other sources of tannin are used. *Sumach*, a shrub found in Italy and Spain, is used in the tannage of light leathers. South American tannage is based upon *quebracho* bark; Australia and South Africa rely upon *wattle* and India makes use of the bark of the *babu* tree. The latter two produce leathers that are characteristically pinky-red in colour and unless great care is taken in the tanning they can be prone to excessive stretching.

Whatever the base material used, these are all examples of *vegetable tannage*, the most usual method employed in the production of saddlery leathers.

However, some leathers are produced by *mineral tannage*. Alum (an aluminium-based sulphate) and salt are used for the famous soft, white leathers (goat and split horsehide) of Cordova, Spain, from which city the English Guild of Cordwainers (shoemakers) derives its name. The blue-grey 'chrome' or helvetia leather, from which field headcollars and girth straps are often made, is the result of a mineral tannage involving chromium salts, the leather then being softened by a dressing of soap and oil. Chrome leather can be produced more quickly and therefore at less expense than other saddlery leathers because of the mineral tannage process. (Chrome-tanned leather should not be confused with *rawhide*, properly called *split rawhide*. This is an oxhide subjected to a special form of vegetable tannage. It can be recognised by an untanned central layer which appears as a line of lighter colour running through the centre of the leather, like the filling of a sandwich, when viewed edgewise. It is a stiff, very strong leather which used to be employed in making stirrup leathers, girth straps, etc. but is now only rarely seen.) Red buffalo hides are also chrome tanned.

Colour

Colour is applied by pad staining or spraying the *grain* side (outside) of the leather in the final stages of dressing when the outer surface is sealed and made nearly waterproof, and it demands great skill on the part of the operator if the colour is to be even and the dye fast. (South American, Australian, South African and Indian leathers often fail in both these respects.)

The traditional colour for saddlery leathers was an orangey-yellow known as London colour. Properly cared for it could be toned down to a rich and very attractive mahogany shade. Less new in its appearance was Havana, the colour of a good cigar, and Warwick, which was much darker. Today, the call is for soft, unprinted, well-greased hides in dark browns, black, grey and even green, whilst bridles may be backed with shiny white patent leathers (or even plastics) on nosebands and browbands.

Parts of the Hide

A full hide is divided into sections according to the purposes for which it is used and saddlers do not necessarily buy a whole hide. The best part is on either side of the backbone and it is from the butts and in some cases the full back that the best bridles and stirrup leathers are made. A pair of butts will be sufficient to produce just four top-quality bridles, a matter which accounts for the high cost of such items. Saddle flaps and skirts are also cut from the butts. Cheaper saddles make use of the coarser shoulder leather, which is also used for headcollars. The leather deteriorates in quality and substance (thickness) lower down the flanks, the 'bellies' being used for linings, etc. since they are too thin for work requiring a substantial leather.

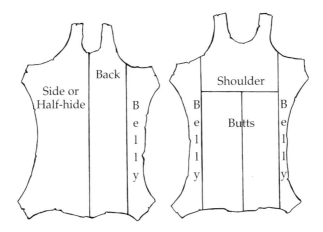

Fig. 1 A full hide showing the possible divisions.

Substance depends on the purpose for which the leather is required and, of course, on the quality and character of the individual beast. (Leathers from Third World countries are often of poorer quality in comparison with those from other sources because of the size and relatively poor condition of the cattle.) The substance, appropriate to one purpose or another, is determined by the leather being passed through a 'shaving' machine after the tanning process.

Leather, Good and Bad

In the first and subsequent editions of *Saddlery* I expressed my views on leather in the following terms and there seems no reason to change them now.

'While most horse people (by divine right?) consider themselves competent to criticise the quality of leather, or at least to qualify their criticisms by saying, "Well, I'm not an expert, of course, but I do know a good piece of leather when I see one", I will, for the benefit of those in whom the precept of divine right may not be so firmly entrenched, give a few pointers as to what I think they should look for in a piece of leather.

'First, good leather has plenty of *substance* or thickness. The greater this is, the greater is the possible fat content which is its lifeblood.
'Secondly, the *flesh* side (the inside) should be smooth in texture and there should be no rough, loose fibres visible.

'Thirdly, the leather should feel slightly greasy and should in no way be dry.

'Fourthly, it should be firm and not soft or pappy to the touch.

'Lastly, when the leather is bent in the hand, neither side should form bubbles on the skin.'

In addition I would add a note of warning about leathers which are noticeably reddish in colour and which in some, but not all, instances may give off a faint odour of paraffin. They are usually of Asian origin and the complexion is almost always accompanied by a particularly loose and rough fibre structure. They should be avoided. In fairness, there are other leathers of Eastern manufacture which are stout and reliable and have the advantage of being less expensive than the European hides.

Buffalo hide, which is both distinctively red on its surface and also of Asian origin, is another matter altogether. Its principal use is in the manufacture of stirrup leathers, although it may also be used for other items of equipment. To all intents it is almost unbreakable, but it does stretch very considerably. It is easily recognised by the body of the leather; when viewed edgewise it is grey in colour.

A last word on *substance*; this will vary according to the requirements of the finished article, a body roller, for instance, requires a greater degree of substance than a bridle. A show bridle, where the object is to produce an elegant article, will be made from leather of a lighter substance than a hunting bridle, which will be expected to stand up to harder usage. Similarly, the flaps of a jumping saddle may be lighter and of less substance than those of a general-purpose saddle.

A moral here – if you want a show bridle and intend to use it for hunting as well, let the saddler know and effect a compromise. If you ask for the lightest possible bridle, and then use it as an everyday one, do not be surprised if the saddler is not entirely sympathetic when you complain that it has not worn very well.

Even today there are people who like to have their saddle flaps made in a very light substance, so that there is little resistance to the leg positioning. The quality of leather dressed to meet this requirement remains unaffected, but obviously it will not wear for as long as flaps of a heavier type. For my part, I would prefer to have light, supple flaps (providing they were not so light as to roll under my leg) and to renew them every few years, rather than to have the longer-lasting but uncomfortably rigid flap of the stronger variety.

The Care and Cleaning of Leather

I have previously referred to leather as (a) having two sides, a *flesh* side and a *grain* side and (b) as having a fat content which is its 'lifeblood'. If we appreciate these two points we are halfway to looking after our tack so that it will give us the best possible service.

Let us deal first with the fat content. Leather loses a percentage of this constituent every day of its life, and just as we need food to replace our used energy so leather needs constant replenishment of its particular 'lifeblood' if it is to continue to lead a useful life. In its fight for survival *water*, *heat* and *neglect* are the three main enemies with which leather has to contend and which deprive it of this vital commodity. Water, particularly if it is hot, melts and removes the fat, whereas heat dries it out. Every time a bridle or girth is used, for example, it loses some of its fat content on account of heat and sweat from the horse's body, and this results in the leather becoming dry and brittle. It is not necessary, however, to throw a bridle into a bucket of hot water after use – a damp sponge is by far the best thing to use. It is equally stupid to hang a wet bridle over the kitchen range or to drape it over a radiator; in both cases, for reasons which I have described, the leather will become dry, brittle and dangerous.

There are, however, a whole legion of preparations on the market that will keep leather supple, but, before applying them, it is essential to remember the differences between the two sides of leather – the flesh and the grain. The grain side has been waterproofed and the pores have been sealed, whereas the flesh side has not received this sealing to any extent and the pores are therefore open and ready to receive (and to lose) the nourishment that leather requires.

If then we appreciate this point and, when cleaning tack, first make sure of removing the sweat deposits which will have formed on the flesh side, thus blocking the pores, we will accordingly apply the nourishment more to this side than to the grain side. Then, when the bridle is clean and dry, the preparation of our choice can be rubbed in with the fingers on the flesh side and the bridle subsequently finished off with saddle soap, preferably of the glycerine variety, applied with a *slightly* damp (not wet) sponge. Polished with a chamois leather, the bridle should acquire a sheen combined with a good supple feel. (It is always better when using a bar of soap to dip the end of it in the water and use it with a dry sponge, rather than to wet the sponge itself.)

Saddles should be treated with saddle soap on the outside and with one's chosen preparation on the flesh side, or underside, of the flaps so that the grease will work through and keep them soft. Too much grease applied to the outside of your saddle will not be absorbed, and a very stained pair of breeches will be an indication of your zeal! ('Jockeys', those little black blobs of obstinate grease that collect on the panel and sweat flap, can be removed with a ball of horsehair made up from the tail-pullings.)

Saddle soap should be used regularly every day and a dressing of grease given perhaps once weekly. Needless to say, you cannot clean a bridle properly without taking it to pieces first. Any saddlery being stored for a long period should be treated modestly with a grease or cream, and buckles, etc., should be smeared with it to prevent corrosion. Do not store saddlery in polythene bags. They cause condensation and the moisture will do the contents of the bag no good at all. Use a bag or cover of cotton or linen, made up, perhaps, from an old summer sheet.

The chief cause, as we have seen, of deterioration in leather is loss of fat content as a result of neglect, but it is possible to go too far in the other direction and overfeed the leather. Leather preparations used in this way will just make the tack unpleasantly greasy, and should you be a devotee of neatsfoot oil, the result will be even more serious. If this is used to excess (and many people with new tack soak it in neatsfoot oil) the leather, being unable to absorb the surfeit of nourishment, will lose its tenacity, becoming flabby and greasy and in fact ooze oil at every opportunity. Just as the human body loses its efficiency if it over-indulges itself in high living, so leather will suffer in the way I have indicated for somewhat similar reasons.

Occasionally show headcollars and the like are polished with boot polish, but I would not recommend this treatment for articles in every-day use because boot polish tends to seal the pores of leather which will, in time, make it prone to crack. If it is used on a saddle you will slide from front to rear quite beautifully!

The chances of well-looked-after, supple leather breaking in normal use are not very great, but neglected leather will give one day and the fault will be its owner's. Leather, or bridle leather anyway, is not unbreakable and if you allow your horse to tread on his rein or if you tie him up with a rein and he runs back, it is more than likely it will snap. The point I wish to make is that under those circumstances do not blame the leather ('It must have been poor quality leather') or the saddler, but indeed yourself.

These are the general rules for tack cleaning *but there are exceptions*. Beware aniline! Many of the soft, instant-comfort hides used in modern saddle manufacture are produced with an aniline finish (i.e. a finish involving an aniline dye), which is splendid but does not conform to the instructions for cleaning given in the manuals of equitation, most of which have yet to catch up with this relatively recent development.

Aniline leathers cannot be cleaned with spit, sponge and soap – not, that is, soap containing glycerine. Instead, one must use, sparingly, a gentle cream or a wax-based product. Most saddle-makers affix swing tickets to their products giving advice about how the leather should be treated prior to use and thereafter, and they also warn about the possibility of colour loss. Modern leathers, dressed to the colours demanded by the market, are not colourfast and they can be easily marked by rain unless preventive measures are taken. For these reasons it is absolutely essential that the saddle should be treated according to the maker's instructions before it is used. The application of a recommended cream will help fix the dye, discourage discoloration and save breeches from being marked beyond redemption. It should be noted that black dyes are the least reliable of all and equipment made up from leathers of this colour should be treated with care and respect.

Many manufacturers create a soft feel to the saddle flaps by inserting a layer of foam between a necessarily thin outside hide and a somewhat stouter leather on the inside. It works very well until the flap is cleaned with an oil preparation. The latter soaks through the thin hide and reduces the interlaid plastic foam to a most unpleasant 'gunge' which destroys the stability of the flap.

2 Metals and Materials

'All that glisters is not gold.'

The second basic material connected with the production of saddlery is metal. In our grandfathers' day bits and stirrup irons were made from steel, either hand-forged or drop-forged, and produced in far greater variety than is possible today. These bits were of exceptional strength, beautifully made and finished. They were not, however, rustless, but with cheap and plentiful labour this hardly mattered. To clean them a burnisher and a little sand were employed; the curb chains were placed in a stable rubber with a mixture of coarse sand and oil and then swung vigorously, a method that was very effective. Today all bits and irons are rustless, but few can compare with the workmanship displayed in these old bits.

Traditionally, there were three principal metals, four if aluminium is included, and, of course, there was also brass which was confined to the manufacture of buckles.

The first of the three was *solid nickel* and it was employed extensively. It was, and is still, rustless, cheap and otherwise without virtue. It turns yellow quickly, it will bend and it is easily broken. A sharp knock on a gatepost is enough to break a nickel stirrup and even a sudden application of weight may be enough to cause a fracture; while a strong-pulling horse can easily bend the ring of a nickel bit and, indeed, there are numerous instances of the bit having broken in the mouth. In short, there is nothing to recommend it. Indeed, I am told that horses may develop allergies as a result of contact with nickel bits, although I have no experience of that. Why it should be graced with the bastion-like prefix 'solid' is, one supposes, a last-ditch marketing ploy. Thankfully, the metal is far less prevalent in today's stirrup irons, bits and spurs.

There are then what may be termed the *named nickel mixtures*, specifically alloys containing nickel, which are in an altogether different category. Bits and stirrups made of these metals will be stamped with a trade name, like Eglantine, Kangaroo or Premier, for example and, usually, have faint bluish colour. They are good and reliable; they are also rustless and breakages are very infrequent.

Probably the most popular metal that still occupies a prominent place in the market is *stainless steel* used in the manufacture of bits, stirrup irons, spurs, the best buckles and, of course, the all-important stirrup bars.

Articles made from these metals are cast in a mould and then finished by machine and hand. The variety of bits and stirrup irons, etc. is, therefore, dependent on the number of pattern moulds held by the manufacturer.

Hand-forged stainless steel, the aristocrat of all metals, was still obtainable in the years immediately following World War II, but is now unobtainable. Hand-forged bits, stirrup irons and spurs were, indeed, the apogee of the loriner's art. They could be made in any shape or size and they lasted indefinitely – today, they could be classed as collectors' pieces.

Materials for Bitting

Horsemen have long appreciated the need to encourage salivation in the mouth as a means of producing relaxation in the lower jaw, hence the plethora of dangling keys and rollers which were often a feature of bits used in the classical Renaissance period. It is generally accepted that a 'soapy' mouth, with froth visible round the lips, is a sign of a relaxed horse, happily mouthing his bit. Conversely, a 'dry' mouth is taken to be an indication of tension, discomfort and a generally stiff, unhappy animal.

Between the two World Wars, when the riding public appears to have been even more obsessive in its attitude to bits and bitting than the riders of the twenty-first century, bit patterns proliferated. In fairness, while most were concerned to give the rider greater control, they also sought to afford a high degree of comfort and it is certain that far greater emphasis was given to 'making' the mouth. The thick revolving wooden mouthpiece of the Kerro bit was an example of bits designed to that end. However, it was something of a nine-day wonder and is now pretty much a museum piece. Vulcanite, and leather-covered mouthpieces were popular and it was by no means unknown for horsemen to wrap the mouthpiece with a bandage soaked in honey or treacle so as to encourage acceptance and relaxation as the horse mouthed the bit. It may have been effective in that respect but it was a very messy business.

Today, the fashion in bitting is for the use of 'sweet metal' alloys, copper, iron and the synthetic polyurethane. One prominent German manufacturer of high quality bits, in terms of finish and design, markets an extensive range using 'golden' oxidised metals.

If the manufacturers and distributors of bits in this new category have one thing in common it is the use of extravagant hyperbole in the marketing of their products, along with claims which are difficult to substantiate. The bits described are not necessarily any the worse for the efforts of the catalogue compilers but it is as well to regard them, and the copy matter, with a degree of objectivity.

One company, asserting that 'nickel allergies' are 'more and more prevalent these days', (a statement for which there is absolutely no factual foundation), claims that its golden oxidised metal 'produces the distinctive and pleasant taste that horses love. This particular taste encourages horses to chew and produce saliva which promotes rapid acceptance ...' etc. Objective scrutiny suggests that the chewing and salivation may indeed occur, stimulated by a chemical reaction with the metal of the bit, but whether the horse *considers the* taste 'pleasant' is open to question – it actually seems to have a bitter taste – try it yourself in comparison to stainless steel. The chewing and salivation, therefore, are not necessarily accompanied by happy relaxation. It may be so, but the reaction could just as likely be *'a fake or artificial version of the desired sign of relaxation'*. (The words are those of Dr Debbie Marsden, *How Horses Learn*, J. A. Allen 2005.)

A carefully chosen and fitted bit *contributes* to relaxation in the mouth and the whole horse; it does not of its own produce that desirable state – there's a lot more to it than that.

In practical terms, 'sweet metal' bits do not wear as well as stainless steel and can develop irregularities as a result. Similarly, polyurethane mouthpieces are not 'resistant to chewing', although, if proper attention is paid to the horse's teeth, they give acceptable service. (One famous make goes so far as to introduce an apple flavour into the plastic. From observation it does appear that horses like apples!)

Materials for Saddle Construction

The use of leather has been discussed in Chapter 1. The traditional wooden tree is usually made from strips of beech laminated in moulds with a urea-formaldehyde resin (see Saddle Trees, Construction and Panels, Chapter 16.) Steel or the lighter Duralumin are the materials used for reinforcement. Nylon and fibre-glass trees in racing saddles have been commonplace for some years and many modern saddles now use moulded polymer trees that are both light and entirely symmetrical. (Synthetic materials are also used in the manufacture of stirrup irons and spurs.)

3   The Bridle

*'It is not a question of how to use the
reins but how to do without them.'*

This chapter concerns the component parts of the bridle and the methods
of attachment to the bit. The principles involved in bitting and an explanation of the action of various bits are discussed in subsequent chapters.
Every type of bridle can be classified under one of five groups or families. These are:

    a. The snaffle
    b. The Weymouth/Ward Union double bridle
    c. The pelham
    d. The gag
    e. The bitless bridle.

Recent years have seen the introduction of *multi-ringed* bits which come
close to constituting an additional group rather than another sub-
division of the five conventional families. In simple terms, the action of
such bits combines that of snaffle and a curb without incorporating a
curb chain. (The Kimblewick (p.90) did the same thing but with the help
of a curb chain and considerably less pressure on the poll.) Indeed, with
some justification the battalions of the multi-ringed might be considered
as the Mr Bossom of the bit groups. Mr Bossom was that gentleman of
whom Winston Churchill famously remarked: 'Bossom? Bossom? Huh,
neither one thing nor the other!'

    Nor is the nomenclature of individual patterns anything but
confusing. Some are described as 'elevators', which patently they are not,
others as American or Dutch 'gags'. They may be American, Dutch, or
Hottentot, but gags, by definition, they are most certainly not. The action
of some of these misnamed bits is discussed later in this chapter.

    Certain parts of the bridle are common to all these groups even if they
do not take the same form. They are:

1. The head, in which is incorporated the throatlatch (pronounced, as is our English custom, throatlash). The throatlatch is there to prevent the bridle slipping off the horse's head when emergencies which might render this a possibility arise, and it should be adjusted to allow two fingers to be easily inserted between it and the animal's throat. A throatlatch adjusted too tightly throttles the horse and would effectively prevent flexion at the poll. *(There are bridles, designed originally for the older type of thick-jowled Warmbloods, that have the throatlatch adjustable on both sides of the head so as to allow for the fleshy conformation of the throat.)*
2. The cheeks, to which the bit is secured and which buckle on to the points of the head.
3. The browband, or front, as it is termed in the trade.
4. The cavesson or noseband.
5. The reins.

In the case of the double bridle the bradoon, or snaffle, is secured by a secondary strap and one cheekpiece (together known as the sliphead), which is passed through the slot of the browband. In a double bridle, the slot should be larger than in the snaffle bridle to allow for the extra thickness of this strap. The head strap of the noseband is positioned last and therefore next to the animal. The cheek of the sliphead is fastened to the offside bit ring so that the buckle corresponds to that of the noseband head, which is fastened on the nearside.

In both the double bridle and the pelham two pairs of reins are used and there is the addition of a lipstrap. The purpose of the latter is (a) to keep the curb chain in its place in the curb groove, and (b) to prevent a possible, if unlikely, reversal of the bit in the horse's mouth. The lipstrap is fitted with the buckle piece on the nearside of the bit in the loop provided on the cheek of the bit for that purpose. The return strap is fixed in the same loop on the offside, this latter strap passing through the centre link of the curb chain before being attached to the buckle.

(Present day riders, encouraged by the example of the dressage fraternity, appear to have dispensed with the lipstrap – one must suppose out of ignorance of its purpose within the overall action.)

Years ago it was fairly common to see a snaffle fitted with two pairs of reins, presumably for those who put their trust neither in princes nor in one rein. This practice has now largely disappeared and the snaffle bridle has only one pair of reins to the bit. *(Two pairs of reins were also used in the past in conjunction with a snaffle bit and a running martingale. The lower rein, passing through the martingale rings, could be used independently of the top rein as a check or as a mild form of draw rein.)*

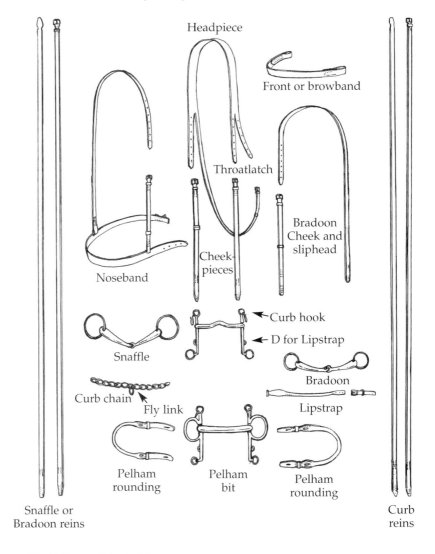

Fig. 2 Parts of the bridle.

Now we will look at those parts of the bridle which, although serving the same basic purpose, vary in design. First the browband, which for general purposes should be in plain leather. For showing or for racing, it is permissible and attractive to have a browband covered in silk or in plastic in the owner's colours. Plastic has the advantage of being easily cleaned, whereas silk has not; plastic in my opinion never looks so correct, though doubtless I am prejudiced in this respect. *(Did I really think this was so and what on earth was meant by being 'correct'. Mind you, a silk browband does have more 'style'.)*

An important feature of the bridle is the noseband, without which a horse looks almost undressed. It came into fashion towards the end of the nineteenth century and while, in many cases, the noseband is merely an ornament it is not entirely so. Apart from being the most convenient place to which a standing martingale can be attached – and I am now speaking only of the plain cavesson type, not the drop noseband – it can also, if adjusted fairly tightly and slightly lower than usual, effect a partial closure of the mouth; the opening of the mouth being one of the more common evasions of the bit. Obviously this closure does not approach that created by the drop noseband (the types and action of which are dealt with in Chapter 5 Auxiliaries to the Action of the Bit), as it is adjusted well up on the jawbones – but it can be helpful.

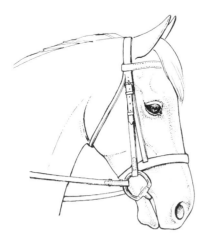

Fig. 3 A plain noseband (cavesson) with the headpiece slotted through the nosepiece.

The plain leather noseband is correct for hunting and I prefer it to be made as it is in the illustration (Fig. 3) with the headpiece slotted through the nosepiece and not sewn directly on to it. This ensures that the noseband does not droop or lose its shape and is also the only practical method to adopt when using a standing martingale. An ordinary stitched-on head will very quickly give way under the considerable strain imposed on it by a standing martingale, whereas the loop-through method will not. *(If the 'plain leather noseband' was ever 'correct' for hunting it is certainly no longer so. At least half the average field ride in drop nosebands of one kind or another. I use a noseband which, for want of a better reason, I have called the Grandstand noseband after Mr. Keith Luxford's famous champion cob who used to wear one. The modern nomenclature is for a 'crank' noseband. It allows for a closure of the mouth without what is to my mind the less acceptable practice of tying the jaws together below the bit with the conventional drop noseband. Standing martingales are largely out of fashion except in polo, although one is beginning to see a few returning to the hunting field. Their demise was due, largely, to an uninformed 'establishment' element who held that the martingale restricted the extension of the neck, but that, providing the martingale is properly adjusted, is absolute rubbish!)*

For showing and racing the lighter and more elegant stitched noseband (Fig. 4) is popular and there is no reason why it should not appear

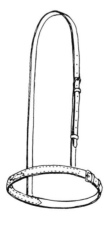

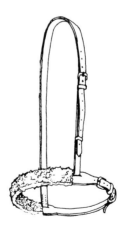

Fig. 4 The stitched and raised lightweight noseband often used in the show ring.

Fig. 5 A sheepskin-covered noseband, deriving from the 'anti-shadow' or 'anti-shying' noseband used in harness racing.

on the hunting bridle also. It would, of course, be unwise to use a standing martingale with this type as it is not designed to withstand the possible strain.

For showjumping, or more particularly polo, where a standing martingale is used which imposes considerable pressure on both the noseband and the horse's nose, I would recommend a very stout noseband, padded with chamois round the nosepiece and possibly made of rawhide. Occasionally a roundedleather nosepiece is fitted to intensify the pressure on the nose when used in conjunction with a standing martingale. Again, if this device is really necessary, I would recommend that a thick piece of rounded rawhide or helvetia leather should used in the nosepiece (not a thin one, which might cut).

Last of all is the sheepskin-covered noseband (Fig. 5) made popular by French trainers and now a familiar sight on our racecourses, in showjumping circles and, of all places, on children's ponies! It originated as an 'anti-shadow' or 'anti-shying' noseband for trotting horses in the United States and, in that sphere, I can see it has certain merits, which might possibly be extended to the racecourse provided the noseband is adjusted high enough up the face. Even so a surprising number of trainers hold divergent opinions as to its function. Personally I think its importance is exaggerated, although I admit it is a good way of spotting your horse if he happens to be the only animal running in one. For showjumping, if its aim is to prevent chafing, I would condone it; otherwise it is just another unnecessary appendage. For children's ponies it is both ridiculous and a needless expenditure.

The Reins

Reins, to those who look upon them as lifelines, are an even more important item on the bridle. They are made in considerable variety with the object of giving a better grip. Apart from the normal plain leather rein, which in wet weather or on a sweating horse does become slippery, there is the *rubber-covered* rein. Invariably used for racing, frequently for showjumping, and quite often in the hunting field, it does afford an excellent grip. In Britain the length of rubber is 76 cm (30 in) and it begins some 25 cm (10 in) from the bit end of the rein. In America, where a much shorter hold is taken by race jockeys, the length of rubber is only 46 cm (18 in) and it begins closer to the bit. Incidentally,

Americans seem to prefer a very much thicker rein for race riding than we do, the width often being as much as 2.5 cm (1 in), whereas 1.6 cm (⅝ in) for flat racing and 1.9 cm (¾ in) for chasing are normal in Britain.

There are two points to bear in mind when buying rubber reins. First, if they are to be used for chasing or point-to-pointing, it is essential that there should be sufficient length in the buckle end of the handpart (all good-quality reins should have a buckle in the handpart, i.e. the last 20–25 cm [8–10 in] at the buckle end of the rein, and not be sewn together) for you to tie a knot, so that in the event of your slipping a rein to its full extent, possibly when everything has gone wrong and you are performing extraordinary acrobatics to maintain some sort of affinity with your mount, you will not be exerting any undue pressure on the buckle fastening but rather on the knot and will thus avoid the disaster usually associated with the buckle-fastening parting. *(Many modern reins do not have sufficient length in the buckle end of the handpart, but then very few modern riders seem to appreciate the need to tie a knot in them. In fact, of course, other than for the sake of convenience, a buckle in the handpart is something of an anachronism in the same mould as the 'safety' catch on the stirrup bar, which is never, I hope, used, or that ridiculous lash appended to the end of a dressage, polo or cutting whip. There is a very good reason for attaching a lash to the thong of a hunting or lunge whip, but none whatsoever for putting one on any other form of whip. So, why is it there? The time-worn and very unsatisfactory answer given by whipmakers is because: 'It has always been made like that'.*

The buckle in the handpart, like the cavesson noseband (Fr. caveçon = a halter) and its recommended fitting, has its origin in military practice. The buckled rein was divided, primarily, to connect horses to their neighbours on either side and in the interests of uniformity the buckle was always on the right (offside) rein and the point on the left, the latter lying under the left thumb.)

Secondly, the rubber covering should be stitched by hand with a large spot stitch down the centre of the rein it encloses. Close machine stitching may be quicker, but reduces the leather's strength with its line of close perforations. In time and with continued use the rubber handparts will wear smooth and will have to be replaced. This is not an unduly difficult job and any saddler should be able to undertake it for you. *(The rubber covering should still be stitched by hand, but it is not, and today it would make the rein impossibly expensive.)*

Two reins somewhat similar in appearance and often confused are the *plaited* rein and the laced rein. In the former the rein is split in strips, usually five, and then plaited, and in the latter a lace is inserted and passed over and through the rein in V-shapes down its length. Both give excellent grip, but the plaited rein does tend to stretch; I once saw one that had attained the remarkable length of 2.4 m (8 ft). Of the two I prefer the laced one, which has the added advantage that the labour and expense involved in its making is less than that required for the plaited variety.

There is a group of reins all of which are not made entirely from leather. Among these is the *web* rein, which is sometimes a tubular web, with or without finger slots of leather placed at intervals of 10 or 12.5 cm (4 or 5 in) along the handpart. Made with finger slots they are used for showjumping, and, when made of a plain, tough, ribbed web without slots, they are relatively inexpensive and very hard-wearing exercise reins affording a good grip in all conditions. I am always surprised that web is not more popular, particularly among racing trainers who spend much time and money having rubber reins re-covered. Trainers are, however, notoriously conservative where tack is concerned.

Also in this category are the ubiquitous and, to my mind, quite ineffectual *nylon-plaited* reins. Apart from being too long in most cases for their intended purpose, i.e. showjumping (a shorter rein to correspond with the shorter hold taken being desirable), they achieve, when wet, a degree of slippery sliminess which is horrid and, when dry, become so hard and the edges so abrasive as to remove the skin from even the most calloused finger. You will gather that I do not approve of them and would put them well down my list of practical reins, although *linen-corded* reins (flat woven cord of linen strands) do a reasonably effective job.

The length of a normal size rein is 1.5 m (5 ft) or thereabouts; for showjumping, to conform with the shorter hold taken, 1.4 m (4 ft 6 in); and in the case of small children, 1.3 m (4 ft 3 in) or shorter is quite sufficient because anything over that length hangs down where they can most easily catch their feet in the festoons of loop. The width will depend upon personal preference and upon the width of the bridle, the measurements of which are discussed later in this chapter. Normally, however big a front your horse may have, you will not get a leather rein to measure more than a little over 1.5 m (5 ft), for the simple reason that the back from which the rein is cut does not exceed that length, and it is unlikely that a breed of long-backed animals will be evolved purely to overcome this. *(In fairness, a great many of the hides originating in mainland Europe are of ample size to provide reins of 1.5 m (5 ft and more.)*

Attachment to the Bit

(I have deliberately retained the following passage describing methods of attaching bit to bridle to show how quickly opinions, and fashions, can change. Not all of it is outdated but a new generation of riders could be forgiven for thinking it somewhat 'old-fashioned'.

Largely because, for a time, hook-stud fastenings imported from the Far East proved to be unreliable and, therefore, unsafe, there has been a noticeable increase in the use of a strong buckle fastening, once the anathema of the conventional horseman. The loop fastening, too, has become more popular, with the loops often being made of metal.

Distance riding has produced its own preferred methods of attachment including a variety of snap and trigger hooks, which are certainly practical if less than aesthetically pleasing. Sewn bridles are out, of course. As always, brass buckles on a riding bridle are for gypsies and soldiers and remain almost as great an abomination as bridles and fastenings studded with diamante.)

The next step to be considered in the making up of a bridle is concerned with its attachment to the bit. There are five methods.

First, the bridle can be sewn to the bit, which used to be always the case with a race bridle, a race exercise bridle and often with a showing bridle also. At one time this method was also *de rigueur* in the hunting field, but times change and this is not so now. Nothing looks so neat as a sewn bridle and providing proper care is taken, it is safe. It does, however, have disadvantages. For one thing you cannot remove the bit when cleaning the bridle and it is important, therefore, to see that where the leather turns over the bit and where friction, and consequently wear, are greatest, it is kept well cleaned and greased to prevent the leather from drying out and becoming brittle. Then again it is inconvenient for those who belong to the 'key to every horse's mouth' brigade and who find the key to be an elusive one. Constant changing of the bit in a sewn bridle is both bad for the bridle (the cutting out and restitching weakening the leather), and hard on the pocket in terms of labour costs. *(I have two sewn bridles, each between sixty and seventy years old. If I could buy another I would not, and I suspect I could not.)*

Secondly, one can employ the now firmly established *stud* fastening (Fig. 6), which can be either in the shape of a hook or a round stud. The fastening is always on the inside and looks neat and workmanlike. It is a joy to the 'searchers for the key' and is nearly 100 per cent safe, although

I think I would personally prefer a sewn bridle if I were to ride in a steeplechase. Because the bridle is so easily dismantled the turns of leather where they come in contact with the metal of the bit can be cleaned regularly and so kept soft and supple. The danger in this fastening, if there is one, is that people will try to use force to fasten and more particularly unfasten these studs. The correct and easiest way to fasten a stud billet is to put the loose end round the bit ring, then pass it through the first keeper over the top of the stud, making no effort at this stage to push the stud through the slot, then well through the second keeper. Now press the leather in front of the stud down with your thumb and ease it in the reverse direction, when the stud will slip into the slot. To undo the fastening, push the turn of leather encircling the bit ring forward again with one thumb, while the other thumb restrains the loose end. A loop will then be formed over the stud and it will slip out quite easily. On the whole, hook-stud fastenings are among the more practical methods of attachment and have now found acceptance with all but the staunchest diehards.

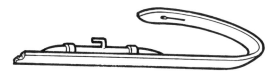

Fig. 6 The common hook-stud fastening, which is in general use.

A third method which one occasionally comes across is the *loop* fastening sometimes called 'monkey up the stick' (Fig. 7), a name which I find difficult to understand. This is generally found on showjumping reins and can also be seen on American and Australian racing reins. I have rarely seen this fastening on the bridle cheeks as well, but there is no reason why this should not be so as it is very convenient and workmanlike. It consists simply of a leather loop sewn on the bit end of the cheek and rein, the actual loop being on the reverse side. Cheek and rein are then passed round the bit ring and through the loop to make a neat, secure and very safe fastening which is easily kept clean and supple. For an exercise bridle, either in a racing stable or otherwise, I think this rather neglected method would be admirable, and if one condones the hook-stud for other bridles, then I see no reason why the more easily made loop fastening should not be equally acceptable.

Fig. 7 The safe and neat loop fastening.

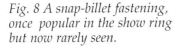

Fig. 8 A snap-billet fastening, once popular in the show ring but now rarely seen.

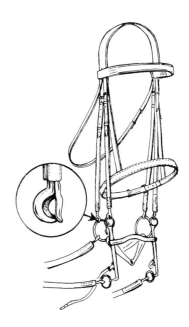

Another fastening now seldom seen is the *snap billet* type (Fig. 8) which used to be employed for showing bridles. This consisted of a neat snap billet or hook set into the leather of the cheeks and reins which clipped onto the bit. Undoubtedly it was very neat and unobtrusive and the fact that metal was moving against metal and not against leather did improve the free action of the bits. It was, however, limited in its application to show bridles only and it would be inadvisable, if not dangerous, to use it for any other form of equestrian activity. The trouble, of course, was that the hooks could so easily be overstrained when they were put on the bits and, once forced in this way, they became unsafe.

Even if you were very careful with these hooks, it was still advisable to know that your horse was not going to take off with you, otherwise you might find yourself in the same predicament as the lady who, some years ago, showed an ex-racehorse at one of the principal shows in just such a bridle. It was a class for hacks and the racehorse, having begun his canter safely enough, decided to enliven the proceedings by showing how fast he could go if he really tried. Horse and rider careered round the ring, both pulling hard, until such time as the little snap billets had had enough and, on their giving up the unequal struggle, the bits just fell out of the horse's mouth. Fortunately, the horse was stopped and no great harm was done.

I have purposely left the *buckle* fastening to the last because as a means of attachment it is in that order also that I would employ it. Buckles are to my eye a clumsy form of fastening and can, by their propensity for getting caught up in almost anything that is to hand, be dangerous as well. In addition, most cheap bridles tend to go in for this type of fastening and a man who makes or sells a cheap bridle is naturally going to use a cheap buckle. Buckles have tongues, and cheap buckles have tongues which bend, corrode and ultimately break. I would excuse a strong buckle on a stout exercise bridle, but under no other circumstances. The American market does call for a buckle on its race bridles and these are usually very strong and well made, but even so they spoil what to my mind is an otherwise eminently practical article.

On the subject of buckles, which form a part of all bridles, and the weakest part at that, two types will be found; a square buckle which I personally prefer, or a rounded buckle, known as a 'fiddle' buckle. Provided they are the best obtainable – and the only way to ensure this is to buy a bridle of top merit from a reputable firm – a user will find little difference between the two. I do think, however, that the square buckle follows the shape of the point better, whereas the 'fiddle' tends to pinch the edges of the leather, but it is really a matter of individual preference.

Bridles and Their Scope

This is an appropriate place in which to mention the differences between bridles and the scope of each. I would divide them into hunting (showjumping, cross-country, etc.), showing and racing, and exercising.

Hunting bridles should be made from leather having plenty of substance and the width of the cheek will probably be 1.9 cm (¾ in) with the rein, of whichever type you prefer, either the same width or a little wider. In a double bridle (or a pelham where two reins are employed) the bradoon or snaffle rein will be 0.3 cm (⅛ in) wider than the curb rein. An ordinary hunting bridle has reins of 1.6–1.9 cm (⅝–¾ in) respectively.

A show bridle, particularly in hack or pony classes, will be a lighter affair altogether and will be made from leather of a thinner substance. In this case the width of the cheek may well be 1.6 cm (⅝ in) or even 1.25 cm (½ in) with correspondingly narrow reins.

Many showing people, principally in pony classes, demand reins so thin that after a little use they must assume an appearance similar to that of a bootlace. While I appreciate that a child may find a thick rein difficult to hold, it is well to remember that too thin a rein encourages clenching of the hand and, with the consequent tightening of the forearm muscles, it becomes easy for the child (or adult) to develop a pair of 'mutton fists'.

Racing men are obsessed with the idea of weight, as indeed they have to be, with jockeys having to count every gram, and race bridles, particularly flat-race bridles, are therefore very light, the cheek not exceeding 1.25 cm (½ in) in width and the reins (rubber-handparted) 1.6 cm (⅝ in). Chasing bridles are stouter, with a 1.6 m (⅝ in or 1.8 m (¾ in) cheek and a 1.9 cm (¾ in) rein, unless, of course, the owner has a particular preference for a wider rein.

Exercising bridles on the other hand should be stout and of good substance. The tougher the better, for race-exercise bridles get more rough treatment than any other form of bridle, and they can either be sewn to the bit, or possibly fastened by the loop method. A good type of exercise bridle is the old 'dealer's' bridle (Fig. 9), with a single buckle adjustment on

Fig. 9 A practical, everyday bridle, often called a dealer's bridle.

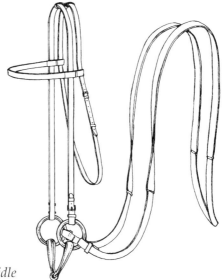

*Fig. 10 American pattern bridle
with separate throatlatch.*

the poll. I have often wondered why they are not more in demand by
trainers as they are certainly cheaper and I would have thought more
practical where labour is such that tack is the last thing to get cleaned.

I have always admired the American-pattern bridle (Fig. 10) and,
although its appearance may seem a little odd, it is undeniably strong
and has so much adjustment that it would be difficult to find a horse it
would not fit. The bridle is always double-sewn, sometimes being lined
with rawhide, and the head and the throatlatch are made separately,
being joined by three double loops. A noseband is not usually worn with
this bridle. My illustration shows a buckle fastening, but the bridle
would be an ideal subject for a loop-type fastening.

Bridles are usually made in three general sizes: pony, cob and full size.
Personally I find these names annoying and confusing because there are
numbers of ponies with enormous heads that would never fit into a pony
bridle, and 'cob' is an extremely vague term covering too great a multi-
tude of equine sins. However, as a general guide they will continue to be
referred to thus. Personally, I would much rather know the size and type
of pony and, if in doubt, have a measurement taken from lip to lip over
the poll.

Bit sizes can also cause difficulty, and when measuring a bit with a straight mouth – that is, an unjointed one – the measurement taken should be the inside measurement between the cheeks or the rings. For a jointed bit, measure it between the rings laid flat. As a rough guide the inside measurement of a Weymouth or pelham bit corresponds to the size of the animal as follows:

> 14 cm (5½ in) = Full-size hunter
> 13.3 cm (5¼ in) = Blood horse, or between 15 h.h. and 16 h.h.
> 12.5 cm (5 in) = 14.2–15 h.h.
> 12 cm (4¾ in) = 13.2–14.2 h.h.
> 11.5 cm (4½ in) = 12–13 h.h.

It is interesting to note that bit sizes have decreased during the past century. Bits with 17.5 cm (7 in) and even 20 cm (8 in) mouths were at one time quite common. Today, with so much more Thoroughbred blood having played its part in producing a finer-bred horse, 14 cm (5½ in) is rarely exceeded.

4 The Principles and Mechanics of Bitting

'Half of riding is seat, the other half is legs.'

As a first step towards a better understanding of bitting and use of the bit we should appreciate that while the bit assists us by suggesting the head position to give maximum control over the speed and direction, it is not in itself the *originator* but rather the *extension* of the process.

The origin of the head position lies in the early training of the horse, which should induce suppleness and a proper rounded outline, thus enabling the motive power of the horse – the loins and the hocks – to become engaged. The bit is the last item in the chain and to attempt to obtain any form of advanced head carriage by the agency of the bit alone

Fig. 11 Plain snaffle bridle with jointed mouth and wire rings.

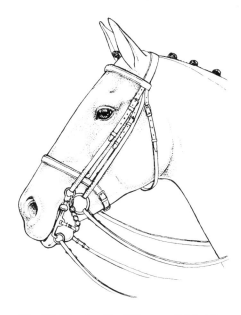

Fig. 12 The double (Weymouth) bridle with correctly adjusted throatlatch.

Fig 13 Fixed-cheek curb bit and bradoon of the double bridle.

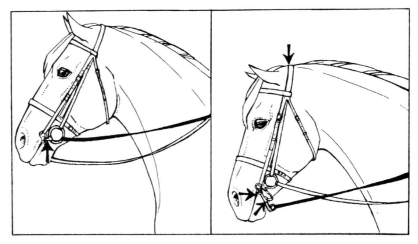

Fig. 14 Left: action of the bradoon in the double bridle.
Right: action of the curb bit in the double bridle.

results only in stiffness and a restricted action. The motive force, which is behind the saddle, is controlled by the action of our legs and seat, and the bit, through the agency of our hand, becomes an extension of these forces.

It is nevertheless essential that even if we appreciate and practise these concepts, and more particularly if we do not, we should understand the action of the bits we use.

All bits and bitting systems can be placed in one of the five principal bitting groups (with the possible inclusion of a sixth comprising the multi-ringed bits), which can be described as a cross between a snaffle and a curb.

The five groups are:

   a. The snaffle
   b. The double bridle, either a Weymouth or a Ward Union
   c. The pelham
   d. The gag
   e. The bitless or nose bridle (also known, incorrectly as a hackamore).

Occasionally we shall find marriages between the families, resulting in a part combination of the characteristics of the two, or we shall find one whose construction has been altered to accentuate a particular characteristic, but basically all types can be so divided.

(a)   (b)

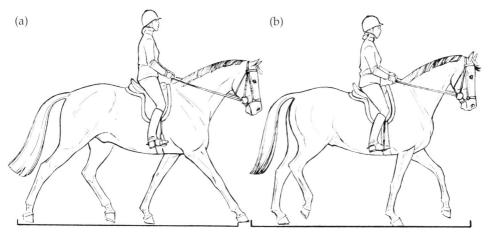

Figs. 15a & b The leg, preceding the hand, used to lengthen and shorten the outline.

All these groups impose control by operating on one or more of the seven parts of the horse's head upon which pressure is applied by the bit. The seven parts are:

   a. The corners of the mouth
   b. The bars of the mouth
   c. The tongue
   d. The poll
   e. The curb groove
   f. The nose
   g. The roof of the mouth.

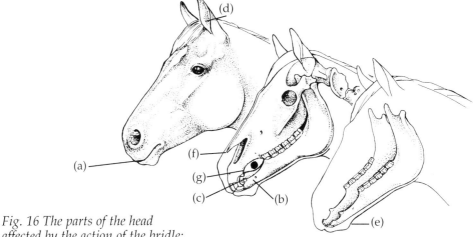

*Fig. 16 The parts of the head
affected by the action of the bridle:
(a) the lips; (b) the bars; (c) the tongue;
(d) the poll; (e) the curb groove; (f) the nose; (g) the roof of the mouth (not acceptable).*

When used, martingales and nosebands, particularly those of the drop variety, are an integral part of bitting, and, being auxiliaries to the bit, either intensify and/or alter its action. For this reason they are included in the series of chapters connected with bitting.

The pressures applied through the bit to the head vary in intensity and character in accordance with four factors:

    a. The construction of the bit.
    b. The conformation of the mouth.
    c. The angle at which the mouth is carried in relation to the hand.
    d. The type and fitting of any accessory to the main bit action that may be used.

The action of the bit and the subsequent result become more or less effective in relation to the rider's ability to use the supporting aids within the aid combination. In short, *the bit is only as good as the rider*.

The Snaffle

The snaffle family, consisting of one mouthpiece either jointed in the centre or unjointed in a half-moon shape known as a mullen mouth, is the simplest form of bridle, and in both cases the action, so far as the young horse moving in extended outline is concerned, is essentially an upward head-raising one acting on the corners of the mouth. The jointed mouthpiece produces a squeezing or nutcracker action on the mouth, which is lacking in the mullen mouth variety, making it more direct than the latter. In the mullen mouthpiece more bearing is taken upon the tongue, as is the case with all such mouthpieces. These pressures and the overall action are governed by the position of the head and are, in consequence, dependent upon the latter. When the horse assumes a working outline, with the nose a little in advance of the vertical, the action of the bit is more over the lower jaw than upwards against the corners of the lips. In the advanced outline, with poll, neck and shoulders raised and the face carried in the vertical plane, the action is almost wholly across the lower jaw and the emphasis is to the rear rather than upwards, as it would be when pressure is applied to the corners of the lips.

The addition of the drop noseband assists the action across the lower jaw since it can be instrumental in lowering the head. It can, therefore, be said to change the character of the snaffle.

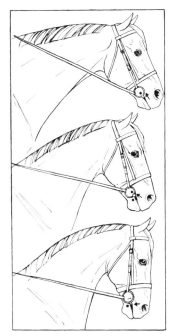

Fig. 17 The action alters according to the position of the head.

Top: In the early stages of schooling the action is upwards against the corners of the lips.

Centre: In the working outline the action comes more across the lower jaw and less against the corners of the lips.

Below: The action is almost entirely across the lower jaw in the advanced outline, the emphasis being to the rear on a near-horizontal plane rather than upwards.

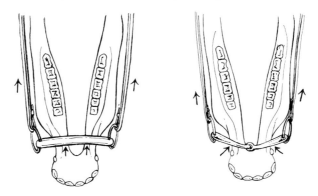

Fig. 18 The action of the snaffle across the lower jaw.
Left: a mullen or half-moon mouthpiece. Right: a jointed mouthpiece.

The Double Bridle

The Weymouth or double bridle (in this latter designation I include any type of curb bit used in conjunction with a bradoon), contrary to the snaffle, is the most advanced form of bitting and employs many more of our seven parts of the head to achieve its object. Because it is the most advanced bridle, its use should be confined – and it is not always so – to the educated horseman and to the horse who has achieved a more advanced stage of training. The bridle consists of the bradoon or snaffle, below which is placed the curb bit fitted with a curb chain, thus giving us two bits in the mouth.

The bradoon is lighter than the conventional snaffle and is normally jointed. The mouthpiece of the curb is a straight bar, in the centre of which is an upward bend known as the port.

In this bridle the positioning of the head is encouraged by (a) raising the head with the snaffle by upward pressure on the corners of the mouth and (b) by lowering the head and bringing the nose inwards to a virtually vertical plane by means of the curb bit. To achieve this position-ing, the curb operates first on the bars of the mouth (the port of the mouthpiece, allowing room for the tongue and removing pressure from it, enables the mouthpiece on either side of the port to bear downwards on to the bars of the mouth). The degree of this bearing on the bars depends, accordingly, upon the size and shape of the port. A mullen (half-moon) mouthpiece in a curb bit would transfer the pressure from

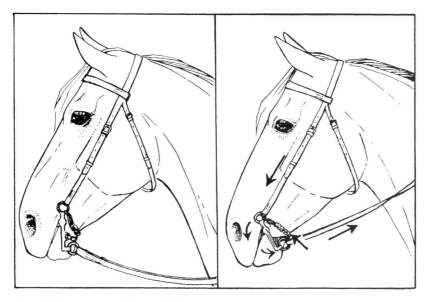

Fig. 19 *The action of the curb bit, exerting pressure downwards and to the rear.*

the bars to the tongue, the intensity varying according to the depth of the tongue groove and its ability to accommodate that organ. Conversely, a deep and wide port would allow greater bearing surface on the bars by allowing more room for the tongue, which would be drawn up into the port and would in consequence be less likely to lie over the bars.

Secondly, the curb bit operates on the poll by means of an increased downward tension on the cheekpieces of the bridle, when sufficient feel on the curb rein places the cheek of the bit at an angle of 45 degrees or more.

Finally, on assuming this angle the curb chain tightens in the curb groove, applying a downward and backward pressure on the lower jaw.

With a curb bit where the port was unusually high, the last of the seven parts – the roof of the mouth – would be brought into play and the increased leverage would intensify the downward force. Fortunately such bits are rarely found today and the use of the roof of the mouth to assist in obtaining the correct head carriage would not normally be regarded as legitimate or humane.

Given a horse, therefore, whose elementary training in the snaffle has been properly carried out, and a rider of equal calibre, the combination of forces brought into play by this bridle will result in the production of a head carriage most conducive to maximum control. The head will be carried fairly high with the nose virtually in the vertical plane and the poll and lower jaw bending and relaxing in accordance with the indication of the hand. From the opposite viewpoint it requires no great flight of imagination to envisage the damage and discomfort that could be caused by the inexpert horseman.

In Britain it is usual for the bradoon rein to be held on the outside of the little finger and outside the curb rein, thereby accentuating the action of the bradoon. Mr Henry Wynmalen, however, in his book, *Equitation* (Country Life), as well as many other authorities, recommends the French way whereby the bradoon rein is held between the third and fourth fingers and the curb rein under the little finger, with consequently more emphasis on the curb bit than on the bradoon. In this position the reins are held to correspond with the position of the bradoon and the bit in the mouth, so it would seem to be logical, and certainly many well-known instructors advocate this method. It is only fair to say, however, that there are others who use the former method equally satisfactorily.

Until World War II and perhaps for a short while after, the double bridle was regarded in Britain as the hallmark of the schooled horse, who graduated to this most articulate means of control and communication through the snaffle or, perhaps, the Rugby Pelham (p.89). In the right hands the double bridle completed the making of the mouth, finalising the head carriage and contributing to the balanced outline.

In the twenty-first century, when there is less awareness of 'good hands' in everyday riding, it has to be acknowledged that the double bridle is very much out of fashion and that there is widespread ignorance of its purpose and potential; which is hardly surprising since it is doubtful whether nine out of ten riders have ever ridden in one or received instruction in its use. The modern preference is for the combination of snaffle and tightly fastened Flash or drop noseband, the equivalent, all too often, of a blunt instrument when compared with the double bridle.

The shift away from the double bridle in Britain came in the immediate post-war years when the British, in the forefront of eventing, were, of necessity, discovering dressage. Increasingly, emphasis was placed on the snaffle as British riders learnt that horses had to be stretched, or lengthened, as a prelude to collection. The noseband, the continental 'reit-halter', arrived at about the same time and became immediately fashionable.

Sixty years on it is difficult to realise that the double bridle was so widely used between the World Wars as a means of effective control made through the positioning of the head and neck. It was the accepted bridle in the hunting field; it was widely-used in polo with, of course, the obligatory standing martingale; while in India the pigstickers galloped with scant regard for their necks over broken ground covered in tall '*jhow*' grass in pursuit of the wild boar, putting their trust in the horse, the Almighty and the same bitting arrangement.

The Pelham

Our third group of bridles is the pelham, which is a halfway house between the snaffle and the double bridle. It tries to achieve the same result as the double bridle, but with the employment of only one mouthpiece. Theoretically, and I believe practically also, this is impossible; nevertheless, it is a useful bit in which many animals go exceedingly well. Its success is probably due to the fact that it is a sloppy, kind bit which many horses seem to appreciate. In its most common form the mouthpiece is a mullen one of either metal or vulcanite, but there are numerous variations, discussed later, by which its action is changed.

Generally speaking, however, the pelham's action is achieved by pressure on the corners of the mouth when the snaffle rein predominates,

Fig. 20 Pelham fitted with vulcanite mullen mouthpiece.

Fig. 21 The pelham bridle – a single mouthpiece operated by two reins.

and on the poll and curb groove when the curb rein is the stronger. When a mullen mouthpiece is used, pressure is upon the tongue and not on the bars. Inevitably these pressures are ill-defined and the action can never be the positive one of the double bridle. In this, too, may lie part of its success. The reference to the position of the reins in the hands made in connection with the double bridle is likewise applicable to this bit.

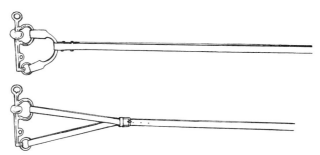

Fig. 22 Top: The pelham rounding allowing the bit to be used with a single rein. Below: The more effective divided rein, which is adjustable.

In addition, the pelham will often be seen used, particularly by children, with a leather rounding, or couple, joining the snaffle ring to the curb ring so that only a single rein, attached to this coupling, is employed (Fig. 22). Apart from the fact that one rein for children is easier to manage than two, I have never been able to make sense of this device. If the leather of the rounding and the turn of the rein around it is well greased – and it usually is not – and if the rounding is as short in length as possible – and it rarely is – then I will concede that with a lowered hand the rein will move slightly down the rounding and some curb and poll pressure will be induced. On the other hand, if these conditions are not fulfilled, I cannot see that any very positive action is likely to ensue. The divided rein, with the rein being bifurcated some 30 cm (12 in) from the bit (Fig. 22), is rather more intelligent since it is possible to adjust the lower strap so as to deliver a more consistent curb pressure as a result of fixing the attitude of the bit.

In general terms the pelham is best suited to horses with a short jaw formation, like Highland Ponies, Welsh Cobs and sometimes Arabs. Such mouths do not easily accommodate both bit and bradoon but they do allow for the curb chain to lie in the curb groove. Thoroughbred-type horses, on the other hand, will often have a long jaw formation, and if the pelham is adjusted high enough in the mouth to be both comfortable and effective, the curb chain will be compelled to rise upwards, out of the curb groove, and to bear upon the unprotected jawbones.

The Gag

The fourth group is the gag family. Really an exaggerated snaffle, the rings of the gag bit have holes set in them at top and bottom and through these rings is passed a cheekpiece of rounded leather or cord, to which the rein is attached. The upward head-raising action is, therefore, accentuated by the rounding sliding through the holes in the bit ring, the action thus becoming a clear indication to the horse that he should raise his head smartly.

This bridle is of particular use on those unpleasant animals who persist in approaching their fences at great speed and with their noses held uncomfortably close to ground level. Logically, of course, one might argue that the gag might also lower the head because you cannot exert an upward pressure on the corners of the mouth in this way without a consequent downward pressure being brought to bear on the poll. It is, therefore, something of a contradiction in opposing forces, with the head being compressed between them through the pressure on the poll and the corners of the mouth,. However, for practical purposes we can assume that the gag does raise the head, although continued and inexpert use will result in a very stiff head carriage. Furthermore, it will impose some overall restraint on a strong-pulling horse across country.

In this respect it is always advisable to have two reins on a gag bridle, the one connected to the rounded cheekpieces and the other attached to the ring itself in the normal way. The horse can then be ridden on the latter while he is carrying his head correctly and the former need be brought into play only as the necessity arises. Used in this fashion the gag remains an effective instrument, whereas continual riding on the gag rein alone will lead to a stiffened head carriage and may ultimately result in the horse finding further evasions.

A gag with a small ring, such as the Cheltenham, or a Duncan gag, is sometimes used to replace the bradoon of a double bridle, thereby

Fig. 23 A gag bridle used with a second rein attached to the bit ring.

accentuating the upward action of this article, and occasionally one will see a sharp twisted gag of the overcheck variety in use.

The rounded cheekpieces of a gag bridle are made of leather rounded on to a piece of cord, and while the initial appearance is good, the constant friction with the metal of the bit ring causes wear in a very short time. I would much prefer to use a strip of buffalo hide or helvetia very well greased, or even more satisfactorily a strong cord, which would last far longer even though its appearance might not be so good. In any case, of course, it is essential that the rounding should be kept well greased to assist the sliding action.

(In days when the niceties of bitting were more appreciated it was usual for the gag cheeks to befitted with 'stops' so as to limit the upward movement of the bit in the mouth.)

The Bitless or Nose Bridle

(The last of our bridle groups is that which I term the nose or bitless bridle. It is, I admit, more usually known as a hackamore, but this is really one of our many equestrian misnomers and although well established by common usage that is no reason why I should compound the error. The word hackamore (la jaquima) *belongs to the sophisticated school of the Californian reinsman and*

has its origin in the system of horse schooling that evolved on the Iberian Peninsula during the Moorish occupation of the seventh and eighth centuries.)

These bridles rely upon our one remaining part of the head, the nose itself, in order to achieve control. They have no concern with the mouth at all and therein lies their strength. Most varieties of bitless bridles combine pressure on the nose with pressure on the curb groove, and in Blair's pattern (see Fig. 24), one of the most common, the cheek-pieces, although not nearly so long as in the older types, are sufficiently long to give considerable leverage. Other patterns are made without cheeks of this type and the simplest 'do-it-yourself' variety would be a drop noseband with a couple of rings on it to which the reins could be attached.

Fig. 24 Blair's pattern bitless bridle.

The various types of bitless bridles are discussed in more detail in Chapter 10, but their advantages can be seen clearly when dealing with a horse whose mouth has sustained so much damage as to render the use of a bit impractical, or with a horse who, through bad management, will not go well in any normal bridle.

While a horse can be ridden safely in these bridles (their stopping power is more than ample), it is obvious that school movements and particularly anything calling for lateral movement would not come easily within their scope.

Segundo's System of Bitting

It is interesting to observe, if only from an academic viewpoint, that as long ago as 1832 one Juan Segundo produced a system of bitting which, although entirely mechanical, was meticulous in its study of those seven parts of the head and the action of various-shaped mouthpieces upon them. Segundo, in his study of the horse's mouth, divided horses into six groups: very hard mouthed, hard mouthed, good mouthed, etc., basing his classification to some extent on the size and shape of the bars and tongue – that is, a horse with broad, flat and heavily fleshed bars would be hard mouthed, one with sharply accentuated lightly covered bars would be soft mouthed. He produced six curb bits with varied mouthpieces and length and shape of cheeks to be used with a combination of curb chains, which he claimed as a panacea for all equine bitting problems.

Fig. 25 The system of related but interchangeable mouthpieces, cheeks, curb chains, etc. which were at the heart of the Segundo system.

His system never achieved success in Britain, although, in his treatise, many highly coloured letters praising it appeared over the names of various continental cavalry commanders of the period.

Today, apart from a purely mechanical standpoint, his bits would be considered severe and much of his theory and recommendations as to the mouthpiece best suited to accommodate the tongue would be questioned. There are, however, still a few Segundo bits used in this country at the present time by skilled horsemen of, perhaps, a previous generation. The removal of the tongue into the heart-shaped port allows a very definite bearing on the bars, but demands excellent hands.

Segundo's treatise was included in what is believed to be the only loriner's book published. This book, entitled *The Loriner*, was produced with a large number of illustrations by Benjamin Latchford in 1883 (Latchford was a famous loriner with premises in London) and the well-known saying 'There is a key to every horse's mouth' originated from a passage in his book. Personally, I would rather think of the key as lying not only in the bit but in the training of the horse and in the application of the rider's seat, legs and hands as well. I am also very fond of quoting another of his assertions that of every twenty bits he made, nineteen were for men's heads and one for the horse's!

(In recent years, the Segundo mouthpiece has made a modest comeback and has been incorporated into snaffles, pelhams and curb bits. Sometimes the port is inclined forward with the suggestion that this attitude will discourage the habit of putting the tongue over the bit. The modern curb and pelham versions do not, however, use Segundo's independently revolving cheeks. There is something to be said for the Segundo mouthpiece, but I suspect that the modern makers are not very sure of what they are trying to achieve.)

General Observations on Bitting

To conclude this section, one or two general observations might be helpful. The first of these concerns the thickness of the mouth-piece in any bit; as a rule it is true to say that a broad, thick mouthpiece is more comfortable for the horse and gives greater control to the rider. A thin mouthpiece concentrates the pressure on a small area and bad hands will quickly remove all sense of feeling from the affected parts, resulting in a dead mouth or in a horse who cannot be stopped – probably both. Horses pull *against* pain and a sharp bit encourages this practice. A broad mouthpiece is softer in its action and spreads its pressure over a larger area of sensory nerves, the resultant comfort experienced by the horse rendering him more amenable to control.

Mouthpieces of rubber or, if this is too mild, vulcanite, are all relatively thick and are kind to the mouth. The practice of some trainers of covering a bit with soft leather on either side of the mouthpiece is also conducive to comfort. It is a mistaken kindness that rejects a broad-mouthed bit for a narrow pencil of a mouthpiece on the grounds that the former is too heavy for the horse to carry comfortably; the horse has more than enough strength in his head and neck to carry the additional gram or so involved.

Secondly, it will not require any great thought to realise that in the case of curb bits (including pelhams) the degree of severity will depend upon the length of the cheek; a long cheek giving considerably more leverage than a short one.

Bridle Fitting

The rules of fitting (excluding bridles employing nosebands other than a plain cavesson) are based firmly on military practice established over nearly 200 years, and they are none the worse for that. Their object is to ensure that the horse suffers no discomfort. The degree of control produced by the bridle is not an issue in this context.

The two critical points concerning the bridle parts other than the bit itself are (a) the *browband*, or 'front' and (b) the *throatlatch*.

Too short a browband pulls the bridle head forward so that it presses against the back of the ears. This is a source of irritation to the horse, particularly if he is one of the thin-skinned sort, and it will frequently give rise to the habit of head-shaking, a frustrating resistance that will often be continued long after the cause of the irritation has been eliminated. Horses who have contracted the habit are to all intents out of control, since any proper action of the bit is made impossible. If the browband is fitted so high as to come up against the base of the ears it, too, may cause head-shaking. (There are, of course, physical conditions concerned with the ear or the sinuses, for example, that encourage head-shaking, but it is surprising how often this problem is associated with a thoughtlessly fitted bridle.)

As a guide: allow for the insertion of one finger between the browband and the forehead and position the browband 2.5 cm (1 in) below the base of the ears.

A throatlatch adjusted too tightly causes discomfort resulting in resentment and resistance. It restricts the breathing and discourages flexion at the poll. Allow for the insertion of three fingers between the throatlatch and the gullet.

The cavesson is less of a problem. The instruction given in the manuals is that it should be fitted just below and clear of the cheekbone projection and should allow for the insertion of two fingers. This was the military rule and very applicable when the cavesson was, in fact, a halter. It is irrelevant, other than in the cosmetic sense, in the modern context unless a standing martingale is to be worn. Otherwise, if it is thought necessary, the noseband can be dropped a hole and fastened snugly to effect a partial (but quite satisfactory) closure of the mouth.

The buckles of the cheekpieces lie level with, or just below, the eyes. The buckle fastening the headpiece of the noseband is similarly positioned on the nearside of the head. The buckle of a double bridle sliphead lies level with that of the noseband on the opposite side.

Poll Pressure

In recent years 'innovative' bridlemakers have focused attention on the relief of poll pressure, a matter that has concerned horsemen for upwards of 200 years. Indeed, our forebears, aware of the problems that might arise, were at pains to avoid excessive poll pressure, preferring to rely on a meticulously fitted bridle and the delicate balance between bradoon and curb to obtain a finished head carriage.

Today, there are a number of bridles of excellent quality, purporting to reduce poll pressure, that feature carefully designed padded headpieces, and most of them reposition the narrow head of the noseband to avoid any concentration of pressure from that source.

Inevitably, modern marketing may sometimes support the product with a deal of pseudo-scientific babble, but the bridles are, nonetheless, to be welcomed as an effort to provide greater comfort and also because they serve to highlight the existence of some very badly fitting and poorly constructed bridles, for which both riders and manufacturers can share responsibility.

Nonetheless, while poll pressure may be mitigated by the reconstruction of the bridle head it will not be eliminated. Poll pressure is the result of the eye of the bit moving on a downward arc in response to rein action. Pressure is then transmitted via the bridle cheek to the bridle head and thence to the poll.

Samuel Chifney (1753–1807) understood that very well when he designed his Chifney curb bit over 200 years ago. His bit had the eye fitted independently of the curb cheek. It did, indeed, eliminate poll pressure but, of course, the curb action was proportionately more severe. Chifney's bit achieved little acceptance among his peers, so one must presume that they preferred to put up with a little poll pressure applied by sensitive hands rather than risk the potential increase in the severity of the curb chain.

(Samuel Chifney was a noted jockey of the eighteenth century, winning the 1789 Derby on Skyscraper. Otherwise he seems to have been a mightily conceited fellow: 'I can ride horses in a better manner in a race to beat others than any person ever known in my time' and later, 'I can train horses for running better than any person I knew in my time.' After becoming involved in a number of racing scandals Chifney died in poor circumstances – but he did have the answer to eliminating poll pressure.)

Moderate poll pressure is integral to the action of the curb bit and many thousands of horses over the centuries have accepted it without experiencing any notable problem. In general terms, so long as the cheek of the bit above the mouthpiece is kept short – not more than 44 mm (1¾ in) and in proportion to (not more than half the length of) the cheek beneath the mouthpiece, i.e. 88 mm (3½ in) – no difficulties should arise other than in very rare circumstances.

We need to make use of the poll in exerting control over the horse in a variety of instances, when it is infinitely preferable to control by the application of a little pressure on the poll than by hauling away at the animal's mouth. The padded headpiece is to be welcomed certainly, but otherwise to give undue emphasis to the possible or imagined evils of poll pressure is the equivalent of emphasising the dangers inherent in swallowing an orange pip.

The Snaffle

Whatever the type employed, the snaffle should correspond as nearly as possible to the width of the mouth (see Fig. 26 for an illustration of a simple, homemade mouth measure).

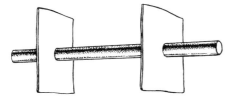

Fig. 26 A simple, homemade piece of equipment with which the width of the mouth can be measured accurately.

The bit should fit closely to the cheeks, the butt-end of a loose-ring snaffle projecting by no more than 1.25 cm (½ in) on either side. (It is, of course, easier to obtain a snug fit with an eggbutt or full-cheek snaffle.)

Too narrow a bit will obviously pinch the cheeks, but most are too wide and cause their own problems as a result. Too wide a bit slides across the mouth, prohibiting the central action and exaggerating the pressures on one side. Almost invariably it causes bruising to the tongue, bars and lips on the side affected.

A bit adjusted too low – which is a common enough fault at places which should know better – may knock against the incisor teeth, particularly if it is also too wide. If a drop noseband is used, which by closing the mouth prevents the horse from evading the discomfort, it is likely that the central joint of such a bit will bear painfully on the roof of the mouth.

The snaffle is correctly fitted when there is a slight but definite wrinkle at the corners of the lips. Since the gag is to all intents an accentuated version of the basic snaffle, the same observations apply to its fitting.

The Curb Bit

The curb bit in the double bridle lies below the bradoon, the latter being fitted, like the snaffle, as high as the mouth permits. A curb should fit as closely to the outside of the lips as possible without actually pressing on them.

If it is too wide (and most of them are too wide) it will be displaced to one side or the other and cause significant damage to the bars and the tongue. The action is then uneven and will be reflected in the head carriage and the movement, which becomes noticeably unlevel.

Too tight a bit bruises the inside of the lips and causes corresponding difficulties.

Fixed-cheek bits can be fitted much more closely than the far less acceptable slide-cheek types, which reflect a very incomplete understanding of the mouth and the bit action. Fitted closely a slide-cheek increases the chances of the lips being pinched by the movement of the mouthpiece in the cheek.

Modern bits, made mostly in the Far East by gentlemen who know nothing about the application of their product to a living being, and may care even less, have inevitable, built-in failings. Principal among them is the vertical construction of the cheeks, which makes no allowance for the face swelling outwards above the lips, consequently most modern curb bits press more or less severely into the face according to the conformation of the individual. The deficiency can be made good by bending the cheeks outwards a little in the jaws of a small vice.

The mouthpiece of the bit, if it is to be effective without causing discomfort, should lie over the bars and be equidistant between the tushes (of a gelding) and the molars. The old ruling, still applicable since the horse has not changed, is 'one inch above the tush of a horse and two inches above the corner incisor of a mare'. Obviously, there has to be some tolerance in the fitting to accord with individual peculiarities.

The other, invaluable guide is, 'place the mouthpiece on that part of the bars exactly opposite the chin groove'.

The curb chain adjustment is made by tilting the bit in the mouth until it reaches a 45-degree angle. The chain, if the length adjustment is correct, should then be brought into effective contact with the curb groove. Should you have a horse who resents anything other than a minimal poll pressure the angle may be reduced. There will then be a more immediate response to the curb rein and a greater need for the gossamerlike touch of an angel's hands.

The Pelham

Compromises are never entirely satisfactory and the pelham is very much a case in point. In most patterns the longer length of the cheek above the mouthpiece causes the curb chain to be pulled upwards out of the curb groove, particularly when the bit is fitted high enough in the mouth to be effective and comfortable. The only exception, and the only really acceptable pelham in terms of action and comfort is, to my mind, the Rugby pattern with its loose bradoon ring. Otherwise one must follow as nearly as possible the military rule regarding placement in the mouth; fit a curb chain with a rubber guard or, better still, use an elastic curb, and make sure the cheeks above the mouth are inclined away from the face. (In many instances it is advisable and certainly more effective if the curb chain of the pelham is passed through the bradoon rings.)

The Nose Bridle

This has to be fitted very closely if the nose is not to be chafed, with the nosepiece never less than 7.5 cm (3 in) above the nostrils. It is necessary to alter the placing of the nosepiece very frequently (every day perhaps) to avoid continual pressure causing the nose to become calloused. Both the nosepiece and the backstrap, as well as the area in contact with the sides of the face must be well padded to avoid rubbing the skin.

5 Auxiliaries to the Action of the Bit

'It takes two to pull.'

(The original opening to this chapter reflected the horse world of forty or fifty years ago when the use of the drop noseband was, almost unbelievably, still a controversial issue, and when it was the showjumpers who were under constant criticism for the severity of their bitting systems. Today, if there have to be villains of the piece it would probably be the polo players, who do use some pretty fearsome combinations on their ponies. As for the drop noseband, its use has become commonplace, even if its action is sometimes still less than perfectly understood.)

Nosebands and martingales are regarded as auxiliaries to the bit, emphasising and sometimes changing its action. In this chapter these auxiliaries are dealt with in some detail to show the ways in which they assist, and in some cases counteract, certain evasions by helping the bit to position the head so that the horse becomes more obedient to the hand.

The Drop Noseband

There are a number of patterns of drop noseband. All of them succeed in closing the mouth (opening of the mouth or crossing of the jaws, thereby sliding the bit through the mouth and so avoiding the correct action, being common evasions). Even more important is the fact that the drop noseband, used in conjunction with a snaffle, alters the whole conception of the snaffle bit. The noseband imposes pressure on the nose, following pressure on the bit through the reins, and the resultant position of the head (i.e. lowered because of the nose pressure) allows the bit to bear more directly across the lower jaw, exerting a downward and inward force as opposed to the normal upward pull when the bit is acting purely on the corners of the mouth. Briefly, therefore, it is possible to produce very adequate flexion of the lower jaw and the poll, not normally possible with the snaffle alone. The drop noseband, by positioning the head correctly, materially assists the rider's control, and although it qualifies as an accessory to the bit, it has its own place in the training of the horse. *(In fact, the noseband exerts a considerable degree of restraint by its action on the nose causing a momentary disruption to the breathing. The result is that the horse drops the nose, allowing the bit to act more decisively across the lower jaw and thus increases the rider's control over the immediate situation. A prerequisite of control is that the nose should be held a little lower than the hand. If the head and, in consequence, the mouth, is raised above this level, or if the horse gets behind the bit by over-bending so that his chin is tucked into his chest, the rider, quite simply, is out of control.)*

For those reasons the correct, even meticulous, fitting of the noseband is crucial if it is to operate effectively but without causing undue discomfort which might become counterproductive to the desired result.

The correct fitting of the drop noseband (Fig. 27) is for the nosepiece, which should be broad enough to avoid intense localised pressure, to lie some 6.25–7.5 cm (2½–3 in) above the nostrils just below the termination of the facial bones, with the rear strap fastening under the bit and lying in the curb groove. It should fit snugly but not too tightly and thus should have no excessively severe effect upon the wind.

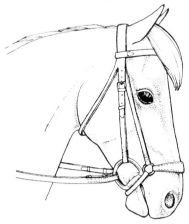

Fig. 27 The drop noseband adjusted correctly to lie on the lower part of the nasal bone. This noseband, formerly the continental reit-halter, is less popular than formerly, its position having been largely usurped by the almost ubiquitous Flash pattern.

Fig. 28 The spiked ring which ensures that the nosepiece is held in place and cannot drop.

The important thing when buying a drop noseband is to make sure that the nosepiece is fixed in such a way that it cannot drop downwards over the nostrils. This is done by either the use of a ring which has two projecting spikes which are sewn into the nosepiece and the head strap (Fig. 28), or by a connecting crosspiece of leather from the base of the head to the nosepiece, or by both. A common fault is for the rear strap to be made too short, causing the nosepiece to be positioned so low that it is bound to obstruct the nasal passages.

Other Types of Noseband

(The very popular Flash noseband, named after a now long-forgotten showjumper, was devised originally to combine the action of the drop with a noseband that would also provide a point of anchorage for a standing martingale – at one time an obligatory item of equipment for a jumping horse. Obviously, the attachment of a standing martingale to the usual type of drop noseband would result in an unacceptably severe action on the sensitive nose area. The Flash noseband, therefore, provided a proper solution to the problem.)

The Flash (Fig. 29) is no more than a very strong cavesson noseband with the addition of two crossing straps sewn to the centre of the noseband, or a single strap passing through a loop attachment sewn similarly at the centre of the nose.

The mouth is closed quite effectively by these means but the lowering pressure on the nose is reduced because the point of pressure is higher than in the case of the conventional drop pattern. *(The single-strap pattern is probably the most popular today and has an advantage in that the strap can be easily removed from the main noseband. It is, however, less effective than the crossover straps which allow a far better adjustment in the chin groove.)*

Fig. 29 *The popular Flash noseband, originally constructed to allow the fitting of a standing martingale to the nosepiece, the lower strap acting to keep the jaws closed.*

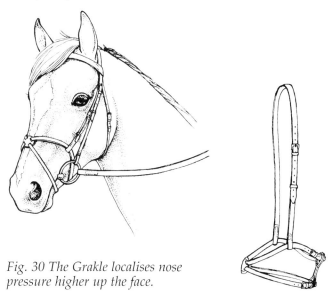

Fig. 30 *The Grakle localises nose pressure higher up the face.*

Fig. 30a *A correctly made Grakle, showing the rear retaining strap connecting the nose straps to keep them exactly in place.*

The Grakle noseband (Fig. 30), named after the 1931 Grand National winner who wore one, has the lower straps fastened under the bit and the top ones above, with, in the original patterns, a connection at the rear to keep them in place (Fig. 30a). The nose pressure is consequently localised higher up the face and can be considered as being less restrictive to the breathing than the usual drop noseband, and it will also allow a little more movement in the jaws. It will, nonetheless, prevent an evasion of the bit by the jaws being crossed. Properly made, the small nosepiece, through which the two intersecting straps are passed, can be adjusted up or down to increase or decrease the strength of the action.

In recent years the Grakle has been called the figure-eight or the crossover noseband, but these latter were not really shaped like the Grakle, although at the present time there is precious little difference between them.

The Kineton or Puckle noseband (Fig. 31) is named after its inventor who lived at Kineton, and is to be found in stables specialising in hard pullers, for its action is fairly severe and it is essentially designed for use with this particular type of horse. It differs from other members of the drop noseband group in that it does not close the mouth. It consists of two metal loops with a connecting nose strap which is adjustable at both ends. The centre of the nosepiece is usually reinforced with a strip of light metal covered with leather, the loops being fitted on the inside of the bit rings and behind the mouthpiece. Pressure on the bit and its consequent movement to the rear is then transmitted to the nose, effecting a lowering

Fig. 31 The Kineton; it is useful in the right hands.

of the head. The noseband should be adjusted so that the loops are in contact with the bit and it follows that the tighter the nosepiece is adjusted, the more salutary will be its effect upon the nose.

(In the past I confess to having dismissed the Kineton as a 'last hope' stopping device for the confirmed tearaway and to have expressed surprise that it should have been listed as a permissible piece of equipment for Pony Club cross-country and jumping competitions. The latter may still be a valid comment, but in the right hands and properly fitted I have come to appreciate its usefulness with certain ongoing horses.

The late Col. F. E. Gibson, founder of the Newmarket saddlery firm that bears his name and a contemporary of Pelham C. Puckle, who was responsible for the noseband, believed that it was never 'fully appreciated'. Gibson, like Puckle, was an accomplished horseman and recommended that the Kineton should be used with a mullen mouth snaffle rather than a jointed bit. The former, he held, allowed for a warning restraint to be put on the nose before the bit was brought fully into play and this, he argued, was why the Kineton could be so effective in the 'right hands'.)

A noseband now out of fashion is the Bucephalus (Fig. 32). It is also known as the Jobey noseband and is for use with either a pelham or the curb bit of a double bridle. It is just a swelled and padded strap tapering at the ends to a small dee. At the centre of the nosepiece is a small buckle and strap securing it to the cavesson noseband; the ends then pass round the jaws so that the offside dee fastens onto the bit's nearside curb hook and the nearside dee to the offside curb hook. In this way a further pressure point – that of the nose – is added to those already employed by the curb bit. *(Before polo players embraced the kitchen-sink style of bitting I used a Bucephalus with a Rugby pelham on one or two onward-going Indian country-breds and later on a similarly enthusiastic hunter. It worked beautifully and I regret its demise as a thoroughly practical device.)*

Fig. 32 The little-known Bucephalus or Jobey noseband which can be used to some effect in conjunction with either a pelham or the curb bit of a double bridle.

As mentioned in Chapter 3, an ordinary cavesson noseband adjusted a hole or two lower than usual and fastened tight will have the effect of both closing the mouth and lowering the head, although the action is not so well defined as that of the drop noseband.

Martingales

The purpose of martingales in all cases is to achieve a lowering of the head, thereby giving the rider more control by preventing the evasion of the bit which would occur if the head were thrown up. In the negotiation of any obstacle it is desirable, and much safer, if the horse's head is held low and the neck stretched; he then jumps with a rounded, supple back. Although when racing the parabola of the leap may be flatter, the jumping of any obstacle at speed with a head flung up high so as to cause the back to stiffen and hollow can be attended by some very unpleasant results.

The purist will say that the horse's early training should make him sufficiently supple in his neck and back so that there is no need for any contrivance to get his head down – and he is undoubtedly right. Unfortunately, we return again to the fact that horses are not always so trained and also that some of them, who may well be good performers, have their heads and necks so placed on their bodies as to make it difficult if not dangerous to ride them without some form of martingale.

Years ago the most common form of martingale was the *standing* one (Fig. 33), sometimes called a 'fast' martingale, and it was the simplest in its action. It consisted in basic form of a leather body with a loop at either end, one of which fastened on to the girth through the forelegs and the other on to the noseband. In common with all martingales, it had a neckstrap to keep it in position and possibly to act as a lifeline and a source of great comfort to those whose seat was, on occasions, likely to be less than secure.

The downward force it exerted on the nose achieved the object of keeping the head down. Clearly the tighter the martingale the greater was the control obtained, and it was certainly abused occasionally by being adjusted so tightly that the horse lost all freedom of his neck. While this position gave the rider more control it affected the animal's powers of extension, for to jump effectively, particularly over spread fences, the horse must be able to stretch his head and neck. Adjusted to a reasonable length it does not affect the animal's jumping capacity, because a horse

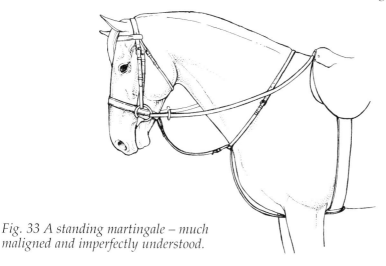

Fig. 33 A standing martingale – much maligned and imperfectly understood.

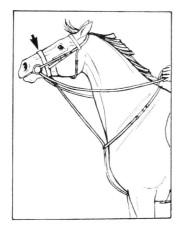

Fig. 33a The effect of the standing martingale – an accessory which saved many a bloody nose.

does not require to throw his head and neck up when he jumps (if he does, he should be stopped quickly) but rather to stretch them outwards and downwards.

The best type of standing martingale was one with a buckle adjustment at the top (Fig. 34) rather than at the girth, and with the top strap lined with rawhide and fastened with a stout buckle. This pattern was far easier to fit correctly than the one where the adjustment was on the loop to the girth. This sort of martingale is still a necessary piece of the polo pony's equipment, otherwise it is rarely seen.

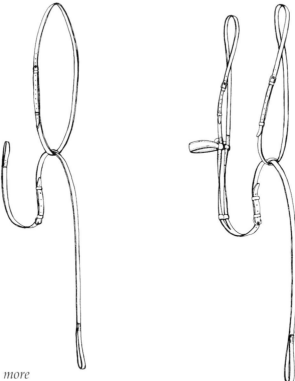

*Fig. 34 The more
convenient buckle adjustment
at the top of the standing martingale,
a practice favoured by polo players.*

*Fig. 35 The controversial
Grainger-pattern martingale.*

An interesting mixture of noseband and martingale was the Grainger pattern (Fig. 35) where the martingale was attached directly and permanently to the noseband, this being adjusted midway between the positions adopted by the drop noseband and the ordinary cavesson, pressure being consequently more on the nose than is usual. This device was used on very strong horses, often in conjunction with a gag bridle (this aspect of the gag is discussed Chapter 9, which is devoted to that bit). The sliding fitment on the two branches of the martingale could be altered to make the pressure on the nosepiece either more or less severe. I can appreciate that a horse so tied down would be more amenable to discipline, but I would hold that his powers of extension over spread fences must necessarily be restricted as a result.

Before World War II, and in the years immediately after, when showjumping was somewhat different, a popular variant was a standing martingale fitted with a quick-release device situated at the breast and operated by pulling a leather tag, a performance which could be achieved without dismounting. On release of the device, the martingale, until then pretty tight, could be lengthened by some 15 cm (6 in), the idea being that, after having cleared the upright fences with the head well tied down and at whatever pace you liked, you extended the martingale in order to give the horse more freedom when you set sail for the water jump, which was usually the last fence. With the change in showjumping rules and methods (that mad gallop at the water was never necessary and rarely successful), the quick-release martingale became obsolete.

Another variation, which has also largely disappeared, is the standing martingale made to fasten on to a ring on the cavesson with a stout snap hook incorporating a coiled spring. The spring allowed an inch or two of 'give' in the otherwise rigid martingale, which, I think, was helpful, particularly for the polo pony. *(This pattern, attributed to the Germans, is, I note, still offered in American catalogues together with the less acceptable Cheshire pattern which was attached directly to the bit rings.)*

The running martingale (Fig. 36) is a little more complex in its action, the reins passing through the rings of the martingale and restraint being imposed on the mouth when the horse raises his head beyond the limit allowed him by the adjustment of the martingale (Fig. 36a). It will be clear that the tighter this is, the greater will be the restriction on the upward movement of the head and the greater the rider's control (Fig. 36b). If the martingale is so tight as to make the rein form an angle between the mouth and the hand, its action, particularly with a jointed snaffle, will be severe. The basic action of the snaffle is again altered by the downward pull which brings the bearing of the bit more on to the bars and away from the corners of the mouth.

Properly adjusted (i.e. with the rings of the martingale in line with the withers), the running martingale is, I believe, a help to people with not so good hands, but if the adjustment is tight and low then good hands are very necessary if the horse is to be comfortable.

The bib martingale (Fig. 37b) comes within the province of the race-horse trainer, the centrepiece of leather between the branches being a sensible safety precaution against an excited horse getting himself

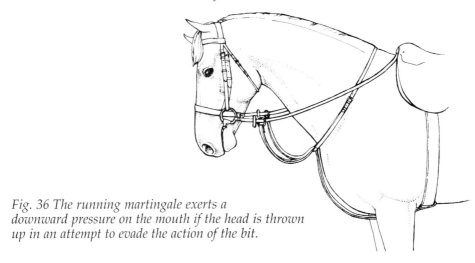

Fig. 36 *The running martingale exerts a downward pressure on the mouth if the head is thrown up in an attempt to evade the action of the bit.*

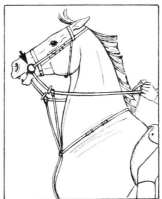

Fig. 36a *The action of the running martingale as a counter to the horse becoming above the influence of the bit.*

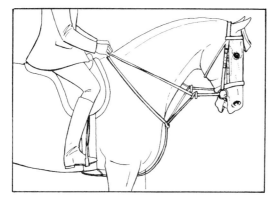

Fig. 36b *Adjusted two holes or so shorter than usual, the martingale can influence the head position and also increase the rider's control.*

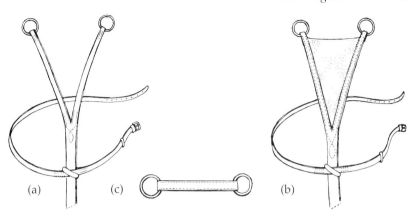

Fig. 37(a) A running martingale with a rubber ring fitted
across the body and the neckstrap to keep the latter in place;
(b) the bib martingale;
(c) an Irish martingale or 'a pair of specs'. It falls within the
category of Irish jokes.

caught up or even getting his nose between the branches. Its action is
otherwise exactly that of the running martingale.

Irish rings (Fig. 37c) are again a racing requisite and although sometimes called Irish martingales, they have no effect upon the positioning
of the head, their use being confined to assisting the correct direction of
the rein pull and to prevent the reins coming right over the head in the
case of a fall.

If a running martingale is used, an essential safety precaution is a pair
of rein stops, which consist of pieces of leather with slots in the centre
slid down the reins and possibly stitched some 25 cm (10 in) from the bit.
These will prevent the rings of the martingale sliding forward and
perhaps getting caught in either the rein fastening or even over a
tooth. Nothing will put a horse so quickly into reverse gear as this!
Otherwise stops made of rubber which can be slid over the rein are
satisfactory.

A pattern of martingale which I feel is unjustly neglected is the pulley
martingale (Fig. 38) where the rings are set on a cord which passes
through a pulley at the top of the body. Its advantage is that, for lateral
movement of the head and the quick changes of direction required
in modern jumping, it allows the horse to bend his head and neck

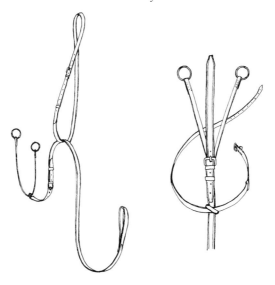

*Fig. 38 Left: the neglected but very logical pulley martingale.
Right: the combined martingale.*

in the required direction without the restriction against the opposite side of his mouth (i.e. the offside when making a left-handed turn and contrariwise), which must be exerted with an ordinary running martingale. The unrestricted up and down movement of the rings through the pulley adapts to the position of the reins without putting unwanted pressure on either side when turning sharply. It is a pity that this eminently practical training aid should have gone out of fashion.

For the showjumpers of yesterday the combined martingale (Fig. 38) did, as its name suggests, combine both running and standing martingale in one and it had the action of both.

If a running martingale is used with a double bridle (whether it should be or not is a matter of opinion) one either requires a smaller ring or, more satisfactorily, what is known as a triangle fitting with a roller which runs on the rein without either twisting it or getting caught up. At the same time, bearing in mind the action of a double bridle – i.e. the bradoon raising the head and the curb lowering it – the running martingale should be affixed in its logical place on the curb rein to assist the lowering action, which is the object of both the martingale and the curb bit. A martingale designed to lower the head put on to the bradoon rein, which is used to raise the head, is an illogical contradiction. *(When both reins of a double bridle are put through the martingale rings the bridle is reduced to a means of control by our old friend 'the blunt instrument'. A running martingale can be used to give something of the effect of a draw or running rein when used with a snaffle and two reins. The lower rein runs through the martingale rings, the martingale being adjusted tight enough to cause an angle in the rein between the mouth and the hand. When the lower rein is held shorter than its partner the bit exerts a greater downward pressure across the lower jaw. As the horse submits to the rein and drops his nose, control can be transferred gradually to the upper rein. The principle is really the same when a running martingale is used on the curb rein of either a double or pelham bridle.)*

The last martingale to discuss as an auxiliary is the much-maligned Market Harborough (Fig. 39), which in slightly different forms, all employing the same principle, is sometimes known, incorrectly, as the German rein. In Germany it is known as the English rein and elsewhere it may have other aliases. I class this as a martingale rather than as a rein because its action is primarily that of this group. Basically, it is a usual martingale body which ends at the breast in a ring to which are attached two strips of either rawhide or rounded leather, the former being the more satisfactory. These two strips pass upwards through the ring of the bit, are then connected to an otherwise normal rein with an adjusting buckle (or more satisfactorily with a small snap hook sewn to the end of

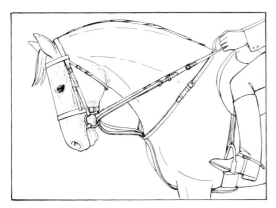

Fig. 39 The effective Market Harborough, a martingale which deserves more consideration than it receives.

the strip), and thence fastened on to one or other of four metal dees sewn along the actual rein. Either method allows the necessary adjustment required to impose more or less restriction on the upward movement of the head.

The action is a simple one and is operated not by the rider's hand, but by the horse's head. While the horse carries his head correctly, the strips passing through the bit rings are slack and inoperative; they tighten and exert their downward pull on the bit, and consequently across the lower jaw, only when the head is thrown upwards. There is absolutely no restriction on the extension of head and neck while jumping, and it is extremely good on a headstrong horse.

The Market Harborough, or anything else you like to call it, is in reality an improvement on the basic running rein which was fastened to the girth on either side, passing through the rings of the bit and back to the rider's hand. The effect of the running rein in less than expert hands, is likely to produce an overbent horse whose powers of extension are consequently limited. Why the Market Harborough should receive so much abuse, even today, I do not understand, as it cannot be any more harmful than either a running or standing martingale, and is considerably less severe than the former when that article is tightly adjusted and used perhaps with a twisted snaffle.

A further variation of the Market Harborough borrows something from the De Gogue (discussed in Chapter 13) and combines a piece of rounded leather running from the rein through a pulley fixed just below the ear and then back through the bit ring to a dee on the rein. This type employs, of course, poll pressure as well to induce the lowering of the head.

Used sensibly and very sparingly by educated riders, these auxiliaries can be helpful in certain instances. They should, however, be considered as means to an end and not an end in themselves.

6   Some Snaffles

*'Of every twenty bits I make nineteen are
for men's heads and one for the horse's.'*

The principal division in the snaffle group comes between the mullen mouth (half-moon) variety and the jointed types. However, these two groups have now been joined by snaffles fitted with ported mouthpieces, resembling those of a curb bit, and some of these feature the Segundo ports mentioned in Chapter 4. (Needless to say the saddlers' catalogues have a field day in the spelling of Señor Segundo's name, but then there are many who persist in referring to the snaffle which bears the name of James Fillis (1834–1913) as a *Filet* bradoon and that once popularised by François Baucher (1796–1873), which was to all intents the same thing, as *Butcher's* bradoon.)

The mullen mouth bits (Fig. 40), softer in their action than the jointed ones, are fewer in number, and variation occurs only in the material from which the mouthpiece is made and in the construction of the bit rings. The mildest form has a flexible India-rubber mouth with a chain through the centre for the sake of safety. It is useful for youngsters, particularly racehorses, who may be frightened of going on to the bit and may be very light mouthed. Conversely, it is recommended for pullers, the idea being that as the horse pulls against pain, it is reasonable to suppose that if the source of the pain is removed and something much softer substituted the animal will have nothing to pull against.

If you are only half convinced by this argument, a slightly stronger mouthpiece is available in vulcanite and an even stronger one in plain metal.

*Fig. 40 The mildest of all snaffles – a mullen
mouthpiece of either rubber or vulcanite.*

A further type of mullen mouthpiece of thick rolled leather, usually a soft rawhide, used to be made with the object of encouraging the horse to mouth his bit. I have never used one; nor, to be honest, have I ever had any great success with the other mullen mouthpieces. Apart from racing, I find that horses tend to hang on them, but this may be the fault of my hands and not of the bit. The modern functional equivalent of the old leather-covered mouthpiece is to be found in the ranges of German manufacture which employ mouthpieces made from polyurethane. These bits are sufficiently flexible to conform to the shape of the mouth and are often tapered to the centre so as to reduce the bearing on the tongue. At least one range of polyurethane bits marketed in America is claimed to be 'permanently apple flavored'. Whether or not this feature increases the acceptability of the bit is arguable, although it may encourage salivation and the consequent relaxation of the lower jaw. Another German firm, which produces nylon mouthpieces, also makes extensive use of copper, a material which has been 'rediscovered' in recent years and enjoys some popularity. Copper was incorporated into Spanish bits over 400 years ago and has been in general use throughout Mexico and South America since the days of the *conquistadores* who founded the first Spanish settlements. It is claimed that the metal is softer and warmer in the mouth than steel. It is said also that it encourages salivation, which allows the horse to 'mouth' the bit with the relaxed lower jaw that involves. Horsemen of the old school in England used to warm the mouthpiece of the bit in their hands before putting it in the horse's mouth. Whether it did much good to the horse or whether it was just another way of salving the conscience of the horsemaster determined to lavish every possible care on his charges is again a matter of conjecture. If horses appear to accept a copper mouthpiece happily that is as good a reason as any for using one – it will certainly do no harm. (Less understandable is the barbarous twisted wire mouthpiece, often produced as a double-wire mouthpiece with gag rings, which seeks, one imagines, to persuade us of its harmless nature by being made in copper, the soft, warm, acceptable metal!)

From America, also, come the so-called 'elevator' bits (Fig. 41). There may be a use for them but they certainly do nothing to 'elevate' the head carriage. They exert, in fact, a very powerful pressure on the poll, the leverage being enormously increased by the length of the cheek above the mouthpiece. Depressant, possibly; elevator, never.

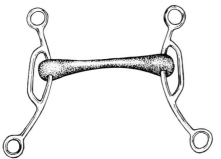

Fig. 41 The misnamed American 'elevator' bit,
which may lower the head but will never raise it.

The rings in any type of snaffle, where the bit rings are loose as opposed to being fixed like an eggbutt, are either rounded, when they are known as 'wire' rings, or flat in shape. The former are always preferable for the reason that they require a smaller hole in the mouthpiece through which to pass and there is consequently less danger of pinching the lips.

Fig. 42 The dee-cheek snaffle, preceding the eggbutt pattern, was derived from the plain cheek snaffle.

Fig. 43 A straightforward eggbutt snaffle with a jointed mouth.

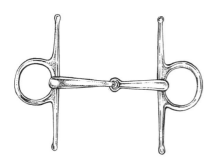

Fig. 44 A plain-cheek snaffle, a pattern very popular a century or more ago.

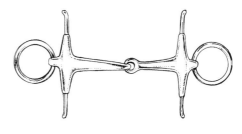

Fig. 45 The Australian (or Fulmer) loose-ring cheek snaffle, sometimes claimed to have originated at Vienna's Spanish Riding School – which it most certainly did not.

A second division in the snaffle group lies between those bits with loose rings, and those with fixed rings like the dee-cheek (Fig. 42), the eggbutt (Fig. 43), and the normal cheek snaffles (Fig. 44). The dee-cheek and the eggbutt developed, in that order, from the cheek snaffle. In Latchford's time all forms of snaffle mouthpieces were fitted with cheeks, as in Fig. 44. With the exception of the bit (Fig. 45) which I term an Australian loose-ring cheek snaffle (it was called this 100 years ago) and which is now better known as the Fulmer snaffle, there are not so many of them in use today, the eggbutt having replaced them in the popularity poll.

Eggbutt snaffles (or dee-cheeks or plain cheeks) have certain advantages, the first being that they cannot be slid through the mouth to evade the action. Secondly, they minimise the chances of pinching the lips. With this form of ring they are, however, fixed in the mouth with little play in the mouthpiece. Contrariwise, the mouthpiece fitted with loose rings affords considerable play, allowing the horse to mouth the bit and make saliva with a subsequent relaxing of the jaw. While normally the eggbutt suits many horses, it would not be a wise choice for a dry-mouthed animal who might be stiff in his jaw. Providing a wire ring is used and the hole through which it passes is not worn, there is little danger of a loose-ring bit pinching. As far as sliding through the mouth goes, a normal 8.75 cm (3½ in) diameter ring will make this habit difficult.

I used to prefer a loose-ring snaffle but now incline towards the eggbutt cheek which gives a more positive action, although initially I might still use a loose-ring on a young horse. In my view, if one accepts the relatively fixed nature of the mouthpiece, the bit is best fitted with a ring in which a slot has been punched for the attachment of the bridle cheekpiece (Fig. 46). Such an arrangement ensures that the bit is always carried in the same attitude in the mouth and it allows the mouthpiece to bear more over the bars than the corners of the lips.

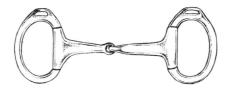

*Fig. 46 The eggbutt snaffle with slots punched
in the cheek is a rare expression of logical thinking.*

Fig. 47 Cursetjee's flat-mouthed snaffle, later called the Weedon snaffle, with, of course, slots on the rings.

Prior to the last war a very useful form of eggbutt snaffle with a slot in the ring and a broad, flat, curved metal mouthpiece was in vogue (Fig. 47). The slots in the ring placed the broad mouthpiece flat over the tongue and across the bars and lower jaw. Its width allowed a widely distributed surface pressure on the bars and the consequent downward action encouraged a degree of flexion not so easily obtainable with ordinary snaffles. This bit was marketed under the name of Distas, the pre-war company founded by Col. F. E. Gibson following his return from America after the Wall Street crash of the 1930s. Gibson had the bit made and patented for Major General Cursetjee, a Parsee officer in the Indian Medical Service. At one stage Cursetjee's bit was used in the British Army Cavalry School at Weedon, Northamptonshire, and for a time was known as the Weedon snaffle. Unfortunately, the bit has long since joined the ranks of the extinct species and it is unlikely to be seen again – unless, of course, like poll pressure, it is re-discovered by some bitting entrepreneur.

I have previously mentioned the importance of a good broad mouthpiece and today, even in the racing world, where the thinnest of mouthpieces were once to be found, the tendency now is for them to be fairly thick and comfortable. A good example of this trend was demonstrated by the growing popularity of the German snaffle (Fig. 48), introduced to Britain in the 1950s. It has a hollow, broad mouthpiece and is ideal for a young horse. The mouthpiece was also reproduced with an eggbutt ring and also in the Australian loose-ring snaffle – or Fulmer if you prefer. (The Fulmer School, run by Robert Hall, spearheaded the interest in dressage in the early 1950s and had an important influence on the development of British riding.) This latter bit, much used in the training of the young horse, obviates any objections to the usually fixed nature of this type of bit by having its rings set on independently of the cheek, thereby allowing some movement in the mouthpiece. As in all cheek snaffles, the cheeks facilitate the lateral movement of the head by being pressed up against one or other side of the face – a great help with a green youngster.

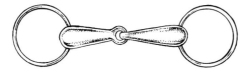

Fig. 48 Foremost among the snaffles of the post-war period was the German snaffle which features a broad, soft mouthpiece.

It is customary with this snaffle to secure the top of the cheeks to the cheekpiece of the bridle by means of a short connecting strap, known as a 'cheek retainer'. This has the advantage of keeping the cheek in an upright position, but to a certain extent nullifies the otherwise admirable loose ring by reducing the extent of the 'mouthing' movement that was previously possible. Nevertheless this bit, by whatever name it is called, is an exceedingly useful one.

Quite a number of snaffles depart from the usual central joint and are made with either a link in the centre as in the Dick Christian (Fig. 49) or with a spatula as in the French bradoon (Fig. 50). By the insertion of this link the nutcracker action is lessened and the link or spatula which rests on the tongue gives greater comfort. Such a construction also minimises the danger of the tongue being pinched in the joint. The former is named after the great hunting character of the nineteenth century, Dick Christian, and a version of this bit appears in Latchford's book under this name.

The French bradoon is available either as a bradoon for use in a double bridle, and as such is used by the famous Cadre Noir, or with

Fig. 49 Dick Christian's bit with a centre link reducing the severity of the nutcracker action.

Fig. 50 The excellent French bradoon has a curved spatula at its centre which lies easily on the tongue.

larger rings as a snaffle. These bits seem to suit horses who are inclined to be 'fussy' in the mouth and they are, of course, softer in their action than single-jointed snaffles.

Another bit of particular value, is the Fillis snaffle (Fig. 51), named after James Fillis, the English 'Master' who based his methods largely, but by no means entirely, on those of Baucher. Fillis, who demonstrated his art in the circuses of Paris held the post of Colonel and *Écuyer-en-chef* at the Russian Cavalry School for ten years until 1910, three years before his death. Fillis's *Manual of Equitation*, produced in his last years at the Russian School, had a profound and long-lasting effect upon Russian equitation.

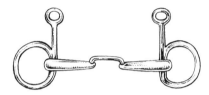

Fig. 51 The bit perfected by James Fillis, the English 'Master', famed for his ability to create the ultimate impulsion whilst the horse remained entirely light in the hand.

The Fillis bradoon, a refinement of Baucher's snaffle, is suspended in the mouth (as opposed to resting on it) and is jointed on either side of the central port, thus reducing the squeezing action. This port allows room for the tongue; a requirement that is not always generally realised or catered for. Some animals have a tongue that is almost too big for the mouth (possibly because the tongue channel is overly shallow), which can accordingly become an obstacle to comfortable bitting. With the tongue having sufficient room to lie normally, however, many of the difficulties encountered with this type of animal disappear, including the propensity for the tongue to be drawn over the bit causing, usually, a general stiffness through the spine. It is possible to use the bradoon independently or in conjunction with a curb bit.

(In the original edition of Saddlery *I deplored the disappearance of this bit which at that time was made only in hand-forged stainless steel. Happily, the bit is now available again along with some others which one had imagined to have been lost forever.)*

Strong Bits

Next there is the category of snaffle bits which I term 'strong', not always because they are excessively severe in their action but because their employment is generally confined to strong-mouthed animals.

Fig. 52 First of the 'strong' bits, the sharp, twisted-mouth snaffle.

Fig. 53 Rollers (or 'cherries') round the mouth are not so fearsome as they may appear.

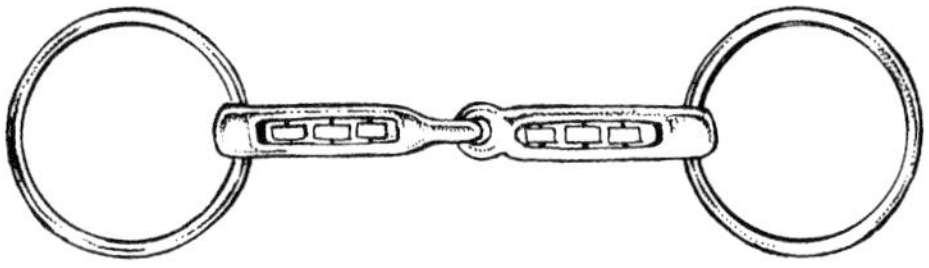

Fig. 54 The Magenis, with the rollers set across the mouth.

Fig. 55 The Dexter ring snaffle has its origins in harness racing but is now in common use for flat-racing. Not exactly a strong bit, it is sufficient to hold up an enthusiastic runner.

First, of course, is the once-common twisted snaffle (Fig. 52), made with either loose rings or a dee or eggbutt fitting; its accentuated action is obvious enough to require no explanation. Secondly, there are those bits with rollers set either round the mouthpiece (Fig. 53) or across it, like the Magenis (Fig. 54). Snaffles are not the only types of bit to have rollers round the mouth; they also occur among various members of the pelham family and could conceivably be incorporated in a curb bit. They are not nearly so fierce as they perhaps look at first sight, and their purpose is to distract the horse by encouraging him to mouth his bit, and so to make it difficult for him to seize hold of it and tear away like an express train. The addition of rollers to the mouthpiece does, therefore, give us far greater control without, I believe, the infliction of severe pain.

The Magenis (this is the correct name, although it has many others derived from those experts who have found it useful) has its rollers set across the mouth within the mouthpiece itself, the latter often being squared off at the edges. This is a stronger bit, but again is designed to give the rider greater control over a powerful horse and in particular over one who crosses or sets his jaw against the bit; rollers set in this fashion make it difficult for the animal to achieve this type of evasion.

I remember discussing this bit with a foreign competitor, whose name I cannot remember, at one of the London shows. He maintained that its greatest value was realised when the rider introduced a gentle sawing action by running the rollers to and fro across the mouth. A lowering of the head was thus induced and this, combined with the action of the leg, made collection of the horse and the 'giving' of the lower jaw quickly attainable. I am quite sure he was right but, of course, he had a pair of very active legs which he could use to some effect.

The Scorrier (Fig. 56), sometimes called the 'Cornish' snaffle, is yet another 'strong' bit. It varies from the usual run of riding snaffles by having four rings instead of two, such an arrangement being known as Wilson rings. The two inside rings are fixed in slots within the mouthpiece itself (the inside, or bearing, surface of the mouthpiece is grooved or serrated), these rings are then attached to the cheekpieces of the bridle while the outside rings are for the reins alone. The result of using the four rings in this way is to give a greater, direct effect to the rein, the inside rings on the cheeks of the bridle not giving the slight outward movement that mitigates the backward pull of the rein when both cheek and rein are fastened to one ring. When pressure is applied by means of the rein, the

Fig. 56 A 'stopping' bit, the Scorrier or Cornish snaffle.

inside rings of the Scorrier produce an inward squeezing action on the sides of the jaw, and this, together with the more powerful action of the rein and the serrated edge of the bit, can be fairly described as a strong restraining force.

The Y-mouth or W-mouth snaffle, with two mouthpieces (Fig. 57) set so that the joints are on either side, obtains its name from the shape it takes on when pressure is applied on the rein. This I regard as an unpleasant piece of ironmongery and one in which considerable pinching of the lips and probably the tongue, too, is possible. I cannot think that it is a very sensible bit. *(This type of mouthpiece made from twisted wire, whether of copper or not, is neither sensible nor humane.)*

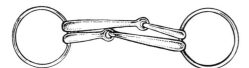

Fig. 57 '… an unpleasant piece of ironmongery', the Y- or W-mouth snaffle.

Fig. 58 A 'butterfly' clip, to be used occasionally on a headstrong subject.

Last of the more common bits in this category is the spring mouth (Fig. 58) or 'butterfly' bit, which is not really a bit but an attachment. It is clipped on to the rings of a snaffle to give a fairly strong additional action in the mouth and, although with good hands and used only occasionally, it may be effective on a headstrong subject, I do not like to see it inflicted on keen jumping ponies ridden by children who are overhorsed.

Multi-rings

Poll pressure, acting to lower the head, is common to all the multi-ring family, although rarely acknowledged by manufacturers or retailers, sections of the industry which display an extraordinary ignorance of bitting principles when it comes to the marketing of these bitting hybrids.

The principal influence is American and it is the American nomenclature which is the source of so much confusion and contradiction. An 'Argentine' snaffle, or an American 'long-shank snaffle', which has a 15–18 cm (6–7 in) cheek, are examples. Both are arrant nonsense and display a disturbing and misleading ignorance.

Nevertheless, two or three rings fitted to a single mouthpiece and offering in consequence variations in the strength of the action, is not an unattractive concept. I am less certain about the 'elevators' fitted with long cheeks, but they, too, offer options in the manner of their use.

A number of these bits are fitted with polyurethane mouthpieces, some of which are very sensibly shaped and, one imagines, comfortable as well as effective.

Fig. 59 A mild version of the multi-ring group with the central spatula mitigating the action across the lower jaw. Poll action is still present and the bit, not being a gag, does not raise the head.

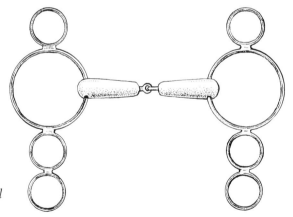

Fig. 60 Multi-ringed but employing a mild, polyurethane mouthpiece. Without a curb bit it is still an example of irrational thought.

However, those committed to the removal or reduction in applied poll pressure should appreciate that the cheeked 'elevators' or 'gags', contrary to what might be expected from a bit marketed under those misnomers, rely upon poll pressure, without the mitigating influence of a curb chain, to give control and impose a head carriage. Perhaps they should all be called the 'poll-pressure snaffles'.

Snaffle Bridles

There remain three snaffle bridles as opposed to bits where the combination is such that their action is a little outside that of their family group. They are the Rockwell, the Norton Perfection (the horse Citation wore a bridle of this type and it is sometimes so named) and a near relative of the Rockwell, the Newmarket. Incidentally I have never seen the latter ever used in Newmarket, though it may have acquired its name by being confused with the Rockwell. In fact, it was also known as the Weedon bridle, which is the more appropriate name.

The first two are almost exclusive to racing but the Rockwell (Fig. 61) is certainly suitable for other purposes, too. It is the milder of the two bridles and consists of an ordinary fairly thick mouthpiece, round which the lower loop of a metal figure of eight link is permanently attached; the top loops then have an adjustable elastic nosepiece attached to them, which in turn is supported by a strap running up the nose through a central slot on the browband and fastening to the head of the bridle. By combining pressure on the nose with the action of the snaffle, the head is lowered, giving greater control on a pulling horse and encouraging a young one to drop his nose. In addition there is the important, and largely unappreciated, psychological restraint imposed by the divided central strap running up the face. Anything of this nature dissuades a horse from poking his nose and getting his head into a high and uncontrollable position. The nosepiece also tends to lift the bit in the mouth, making it a little more difficult for the horse to get his tongue over it (a habit discussed in Chapter 12) should he be addicted to this evasion.

The Norton Perfection (Fig. 61) employs, like the Scorrier, four rings with the reins on the outside ones, but two mouthpieces, the inside one, which has metal loops to which the nosepiece is attached, being particularly thin and sharp. It produces a squeezing action on the jaw similar to the Scorrier and otherwise operates in much the same way, but more severely, than the Rockwell. It should stop practically anything on four legs!

The Newmarket bridle (Fig. 61), now much neglected, is not a racing requisite but rather an extremely good training bridle for a young horse, and that is how it was regarded at the Weedon Cavalry School. Its action can be seen clearly from the illustration and it was recommended for use on a young horse to obtain a lowered position of the head through the

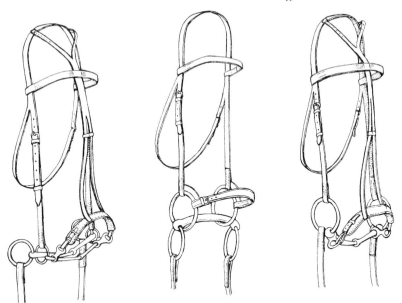

Fig. 61 A trio of unusual bridles. Left: the Norton Perfection with two mouthpieces. Centre: the Weedon or Newmarket bridle – a training bridle and, right: the Rockwell, which like the Norton employs a noseband and a fitting running up the face.

medium of the nose before starting with a double bridle. (*Brigadier Bowden-Smith, an instructor at Weedon and a member of the pre-war British Olympic eventing and jumping teams had this to say about this forgotten bridle:*

> *It is an excellent form of snaffle for training a young horse, for it can be adjusted to take a considerable amount of pressure on the nose, thus saving the sensitive young mouth. By using the rein on the top or noseband ring only, the mouth can be completely rested.*
>
> *The bridle is vastly superior to any combination of cavesson and snaffle with one pair of reins attached to the rings of the cavesson and one pair to the snaffle. This is a cumbersome contrivance and makes horses' noses and lips sore.*

In the second paragraph the Brigadier was referring to the use of a lunge cavesson with a snaffle, a practice dating from the early Renaissance schools which was, at that time, still used at the German cavalry schools and at the

Spanish School in Vienna. The four-ring snaffle, made with either a mullen mouth or a jointed one, is, in fact, a driving bit and is usually known as a Wilson snaffle. Christopher Wilson of Kirkby Lonsdale in Cumbria was largely responsible for the evolution of the Hackney Pony using selected Fell ponies as the base stock.)

The snaffle family is a very large one and, therefore, mention has been restricted to those either in common use or of special interest. There are many that have been omitted, but, generally, they will be found to be variants of the better known ones, or ones accentuating a particular characteristic of the parent.

Snaffle bits are measured between the rings when laid flat. The following measurements are a rough guide (for jointed snaffles) as to the sizes to which they are applicable:

14.5–15 cm (5¾–6 in)	Usual hunter size.
13.3–14 cm (5¼–5½ in)	Medium size (14.2–15 h.h.).
12–12.5 cm (4¾–5 in)	Pony sizes.

A mullen mouthpiece is, again, measured between the rings, the sizes being:

14 cm (5½ in) Full-size hunter.
13.3 cm (5¼ in) Blood horses.
12.5 cm (5 in) Medium size (14.2–15 h.h.).
11.5 and 12 cm (4½ and 4¾ in) Pony sizes.

7 The Double Bridle

*'There are three kinds of fool: the fool, the damn fool
and the fool that hunts in a snaffle.'
(There is one more – the fool that believes this. Author.)*

The double bridle consists of a bradoon or snaffle bit and a curb bit fitted with a curb chain which lies in the chin groove. In former days when the accent on bitting was on the curb bit, there was an impressive array of shapes and types available and even now one can savour the names they bore: 'Harry Highover', 'Melton', 'Thurlow' and so on. Today, much less emphasis is given to the curb bit and few modern horsemen concern themselves with the subtle nuances obtainable by minimal variations in the shaping of the mouthpiece and the port and in the length of the cheek both above and below the mouth. These were all matters of great moment to the horsemen of previous generations, many of whom made the most detailed studies of the bit in relation to the conformation of the mouth.

Indeed, it would be true to say that the general ignorance about bitting nowadays is reflected in the limited variety of curb bits on the market. In a sense, the restricted choice is a good thing since it limits the amount of damage that can be done by uneducated hands, even though there will be individual horses who will be bitted less than satisfactorily as a result. In recent years, curb bits have been lumped together under the generic title of Weymouth, a name unknown a century ago. In fact, Weymouth, previously Ward Union, refers correctly to a curb bit with a slide or turn cheek, i.e. the cheek is made to allow the mouthpiece a limited movement within the cheekpiece.

The etymological considerations apart, the types of curb bit in general use are the slide mouth curb (Weymouth, if you like); the fixed cheek; the lesser-known Banbury and the single-rein curb, used without an companying bradoon, which has an often elegantly curved cheek and used to be associated with very well-schooled show hacks. A similar bit to the hack curb and operated with a single rein is the Globe cheek, occasionally and incorrectly referred to as a Hunloke and still much loved by the producers of show ponies. Whatever the prefix it is always classed as a pelham – which it most certainly is not. It is a plain curb bit and no provision is made for an upper, bradoon rein.

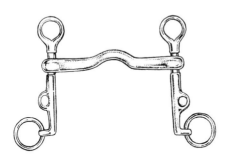

Fig. 62 The slide- or turn-cheek Weymouth curb bit, formerly called the Ward Union.

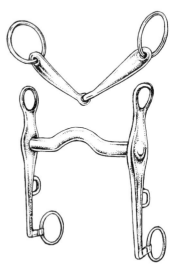

Fig. 63 A fixed-cheek curb, the eyes correctly inclined outwards, and a loose-ring bradoon.

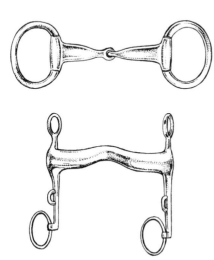

Fig. 64 A dressage curb with the port inclined a little forward and its accompanying eggbutt bradoon.

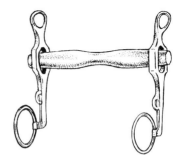

Fig. 65 The Banbury curb bit with revolving mouthpiece and independent cheeks.

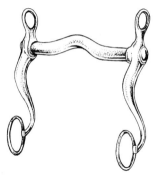

Fig. 66 A curved-cheek, hack curb bit.

*Fig. 67 The Hunloke or Globe pelham.
It is, in fact, a curb bit, not a pelham,
and is still popular among producers
of show ponies.*

There is a further difference between thick (German or dressage) mouths, often made with the port inclined a little forward, and the lighter Cambridge mouth. The length of the cheeks usually, but not always, approximates to the width of the mouthpiece. A very short cheek, not more than 8.75 cm (3½ in) overall in length is still called a Tom Thumb – a not inappropriate description.

The purpose of the slide cheek was to allow the bit to be moved up and down in the mouth, thus encouraging salivation and relaxation. It was suggested, too, that the action was, on that account, made less severe – an assumption that cannot, in fact, be substantiated. If anything the slide cheek is more severe, and certainly less consistent in its effect, than the fixed variety. It allows, for instance, something like an extra 1.25 cm (½ in) of leverage when the bit is brought into play. More significantly it is an arrangement which produces an uneven and imprecise action unless both cheeks slide up and down with equal facility, and that is something that happens only rarely, if at all. If you want the mouthpiece to be movable, the Banbury is a more logical choice and will usually produce a better result.

The bradoon may be either of the loose-ring variety, with usually a light mouthpiece, or the wider eggbutt type tapering smoothly to the central joint. Logically (although I admit to not always thinking so) the former accompanies a slide cheek curb and the latter one a fixed cheek. If you want a compromise, use a loose-ring bradoon with a fixed-cheek Cambridge-mouth curb, but that arrangement calls for what used to be

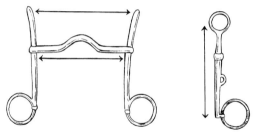

Fig. 68 A correctly constructed curb bit in accordance with nineteenth-century principles. Note that the eyes are bent away from the horse's cheeks.

the aspiration of every horseman, the possession of 'good hands' or, perhaps, 'good *educated* hands', and they are a commodity not much in evidence today.

Whatever the type of bit, it is the length of cheek which governs the extent of leverage obtainable and to some extent its potential severity, for in this regard the shape of the ported mouthpiece and the adjustment of the curb chain are also relevant factors.

To combine effect with a comfortable action – one that is suggestive rather than coercive – it was held that the length of cheek below the mouthpiece should be twice as long as that above it, and I know of no reason why that ruling should not stand. To conform with the principle of levers, the cheek above the mouthpiece (which governs the pressure exerted on the poll) should not exceed 4.4 cm (1¾ in) The cheek below the mouthpiece should be twice as long, i.e. 8.8 cm (3½ in), giving an overall length of 13.2 cm (5¼ in).

A lot more horses than might be imagined are resentful of poll pressure, the use of which was almost universally condemned in days gone by. Poll pressure is reduced by employing the shortest possible cheek above the mouthpiece. (Some patterns of curb bit in use in the last century and, indeed, between the two World Wars, were constructed so that the eye of the cheekpiece, to which the leather bridle cheek is attached, was independent of the cheek below the mouth-piece and produced no poll pressure at all – see also observations on Chifney's bit, p.48.)

Another way to reduce poll pressure is to adjust the curb chain fairly tightly so that the bit comes into action when it assumes an angle of about 30 degrees in relation to the mouth, rather than the usual 45 degrees. So long as no further pressure is applied to the rein to increase that angle the amount of poll pressure exerted is lessened commensurately, but that requires great sensitivity in the hands.

The shape and depth of the port, as we have seen, controls the degree of pressure exerted on the tongue or the bars.

To my mind, the Banbury is a much-neglected bit, for it often proves to be the answer to a 'problem' mouth. The mouthpiece is a round bar, tapered towards its centre, and it allows, therefore, a little room for the tongue, although it is that organ, rather than the bars of the mouth, which bears most of the applied pressure. Additionally, the mouthpiece is fitted into slots in the cheeks, enabling it both to revolve and move up and down in the mouth. The horse can, therefore, 'play' with the mouthpiece but he cannot 'catch hold' of it. This imprecision of action is probably why the bit often proves to be so successful: the very lack of fixed coercion encourages the horse's co-operation.

The cheeks, fitted loose to the mouthpiece, can be operated independently, a facility which can be an advantage if one has acquired the requisite dexterity in the fingers.

I first used a Banbury on an iron-mouthed Indian country-bred who had the ability, and a pronounced inclination, to run away at walk. It proved to be a revelation and in the Banbury I could ride him with one hand on a looping rein and 'turn on a dime…' while he 'tossed back nine cents change'.

(Although the Germans are responsible for introducing an element of rigidity and even regimentation into the double bridle and, perhaps, into the equitational concept itself, their bits are nonetheless well constructed. The flattish, broad mouthpieces, the slight forward inclination of the port, conforming to the tongue's position in the mouth, and the attention given to the depth and width of the port are all commendable.)

8   The Pelham

'Compromises are rarely satisfactory to either side.'

No group of bits seems to have received so much attention from the pundits as this one, and as a result the pelham appears in an almost confusing welter of differing shapes, all purporting to improve its basic action. None of them, of course, surmount the obvious difficulty that it is still trying to do two jobs with one mouthpiece. Nevertheless its continued popularity shows that it does, in one or other of its shapes, fulfil a need.

(In Britain, a pelham bit is a permissible piece of equipment in the Pony Club Horse Trials Junior Dressage Test 1976 but it is otherwise forbidden in dressage tests.)

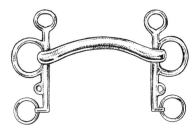

Fig. 69 The arch-mouth Pelham, more mechanically efficient than the conventional shape.

Fig. 70 The conventional mullen-mouth pelham. The mouthpiece may be metal, vulcanite, rubber or nylon.

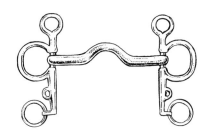

Fig. 71 The Hartwell ported-mouth pelham.

Apart from the normal mullen mouthpiece made either in metal, vulcanite or flexible rubber, the shape of the mouthpiece can vary considerably.

One of the most efficient shapes to be found in the pelham group is the arch mouth (Fig. 69) where the mouthpiece has an upward curve allowing ample room for the tongue and permitting the bit to lie more across the bars of the mouth as opposed to resting on the tongue as it does with the mullen mouthpiece (Fig. 70). The Hartwell pelham (Fig. 71) is also constructed with this object in view, but has a normal ported mouthpiece, which is almost as good.

The jointed Pelham (Fig. 72), by its construction, adds the familiar nutcracker action to its repertoire and, by so doing, seems to me to be trying to do too much and failing to achieve one definite action. In the use of this bit the curb chain must be passed through the top rein loop if it is going to produce any form of pressure and, indeed, this is the case with most pelhams, the notable exceptions being the S.M. (Sam Marsh) pattern and the Rugby. Without this adjustment the curb chain of a jointed-mouth pelham will fall away from the groove when the mouthpiece assumes a V shape in the mouth in response to pressure on the snaffle rein. This is also true, to a lesser degree, with a flexible rubber mouthpiece. *(The pelham bit group has always been a source of irritation to me because in theory it should not work, whilst in practice it is often quite effective. What the horses think of a jointed pelham I do not know, but I cannot come to terms with it.)*

The Hanoverian mouthpiece (Fig. 73), while being fairly 'strong', has a certain amount of logic behind it and is still in demand for children's show ponies, and, until the almost universal adoption of the gag and the kitchen sink in polo, was a bit used quite frequently in that sport. The

Fig. 72 The jointed-mouth pelham is one of the most unintelligent bits in a group noted for illogicality of design.

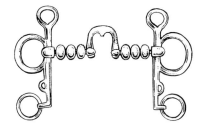

Fig. 73 The Hanoverian pelham is jointed at each side of the port.

Fig. 74 The late Sam Marsh's Scamperdale pelham which, by its construction, sought to eliminate chafing at the lips.

mouthpiece is a jointed one but the joints occur on either side of the central port, which reduces the nutcracker element and increases the effectiveness of the bit. The rollers on the mouthpiece act in exactly the same way as rollers on a snaffle, but because of the port there is rather more bearing over the bars. I would still put the curb chain through the top ring of this bit in the interest of a more direct action. Occasionally, particularly in older bits of this type, the port was so high as to bear upon the roof of the mouth and this strong bit then became an unacceptably severe one.

One of the disadvantages of the pelham is that it does tend to chafe the lips and just above the corners of the mouth. The Scamperdale (Fig. 74), popularised by Mr Sam Marsh, a noted British horseman and trainer in the years both prior to and after World War II, attempts to overcome this by having the mouthpiece turned back at each end to bring the cheekpiece a few centimetres farther back and away from the area where chafing occurs. Otherwise it does not alter the action in any definite sense.

A more logical construction and an altogether more effective bit is the so-called S.M. pelham (Fig. 75) which can still be obtained here and there. It also appears in pre-war catalogues as the Faudel-Phillips pelham; Faudel-Phillips being a contemporary of Sam Marsh and a prominent figure in the British horse world of his time. Both these gentlemen certainly made use of this bit, but in fact it originated in the United States and was introduced to the British market in the 1930s (the heyday of the pelham) by the Distas Saddlery Co. The bit is distinctive on a number

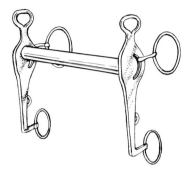

Fig. 75 A far more intelligent bit is that adopted by both the late Sam Marsh and Major Faudel-Phillips. In fact, this very good example originated in America and was imported to Britain in the 1930s by the enterprising firm of Distas.

Fig. 76 The Rugby pelham, fitted in this instance with a straight bar mouthpiece but often employing a Hartwell mouth.

of counts. The cheeks, which move independently in a restricted arc (restricted because of the small stud set on the mouthpiece, which also has an arc of movement of the same degree), are combined with a broad, flat mouthpiece, ported to allow room for the tongue and, again, giving the desirable wide coverage over the bars. I am not a devotee of pelhams, but this particular one, in spite of having the defects common to its family, does have several points in its favour.

The Rugby Pelham (Fig. 76), made either with a plain mouth or with the addition of a port and, sometimes, rollers is something different altogether and has even more to commend it. The bit has an independent link for the bradoon rein. It allows a stronger and more clearly defined curb pressure and also some action on the poll. Its character is, therefore, closer to the curb bit than otherwise.

The difficulty with pelhams is that, to accommodate the addition of a top bradoon ring, the cheek above the mouthpiece has to be made longer – very often, it is too long. It is this top bradoon ring which interferes, in part, with the curb chain, which to some degree is why the chain is better fitted through the rings. The link on the Rugby is the solution to these problems. The Rugby takes its name from the Warwickshire town which was once an important centre for British polo, and it was one of the most popular bits with polo players until relatively recent times.

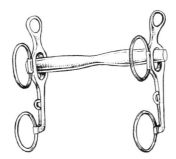

Fig. 77 Another good polo bit, the Banbury
mouthpiece made up with pelham cheeks.

*(The Rugby is probably neither appreciated nor fully understood in the current
equestrian climate, which is a pity for it is a most useful piece of equipment and
suits many horses. Much of the fault, I believe, lies with the compilers of the
glossy catalogues, at least one of which refers to the Rugby as 'the Weymouth
Look-Alike', a description also used by some of our latter-day bitting gurus.)*

The Banbury mouthpiece (Fig. 77) incorporated in a pelham has the
same objective as when used in the form of a curb bit and was discussed
in the previous chapter

Fig. 78 The Kimblewick (its correct name)
was an adaptation of a Spanish jumping bit.

One of the most important members of the pelham group is the
Kimblewick (Fig. 78), although, since it employs a single rein, it could be
argued that it is really an attenuated curb. It was, in fact, an adaptation
of a Spanish jumping bit produced by Lt. Col. F. E. Gibson for Phil Oliver
– the father of the late Alan Oliver, a leading showjumper and course
builder – and it was called the Kimblewick after the village in which
Mr Oliver lived. Since then the name has been corrupted in a variety
of ways; the most common being Kimberwicke, but there are many

more variations on the original name. Its action, the combination of snaffle and curb bit, is purely pelham, but the squared eye as opposed to the usual rounded one allows considerably more downward pressure on the poll. *(The squared eye was fundamental to the concept, since it was crucial to the application of poll pressure, a factor that was itself integral to the action. Many, if not most, of the modern Kimblewicks use a rounded eye which reduces the element of poll action. The ported mouthpiece is equally important if the bit is to act over the bars as it was intended to do. A mullen mouthpiece is less satisfactory and a jointed one an absolute nonsense. Slots in the cheek either increase the severity of the action if the rein is attached to the lower one, or remove it altogether if the rein is fastened in the top slot.)*

The bit achieves its object of lowering the head to the position best calculated to give control, by allowing the rein to slip slightly down the cheek when the hand is lowered, thus causing immediate and direct poll and curb pressure combined with a downward action of the mouthpiece on the bars. It is important to remember that a low position of the hands is essential if the full effect is to be achieved. Over-employed, the Kimblewick tends to make a horse hang on the bit and the hands, and I would reserve it as an extremely effective 'change' bit. In the case of a particularly exuberant Thoroughbred horse of my own, I found it very successful for hunting and jumping, but otherwise always rode him in a plain snaffle.

(This bears out the wisdom of not allowing a horse to become too familiar with a 'change' bit which works very well under certain circumstances. Most animals respond to a new type of bit, the secret is in using it sparingly.)

This bit too has its critics and I know of good horsemen and horsemasters who condemn it as being unduly severe. It can, indeed, in bad hands cause bruising of the lips and bars but then so will anything else if the rider is that bad. Whether it is a bit suitable for a child is arguable. There is a case for its employment on a strong pony but I would be wary of recommending it for the good reason that very few children have had time to develop a seat which allows for the use of sensitive hands. Most of them, on strong ponies, have no hands at all. It should also be remembered that the action is intensified if the bit is used in conjunction with a running martingale.

Two more of the pelham group are the army pattern angle-cheek pelham and the Swales '3 in 1'. (Figs. 79 and 80) The former can be used

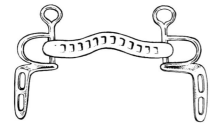

Fig. 79 The army pattern angle-cheek pelham was ingeniously constructed to fit a wide variety of mouths more or less satisfactorily.

Fig. 80 The Swales '3 in 1' pelham is by any standard a severe bit.

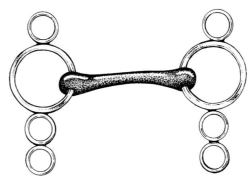

Fig. 81 A somewhat fanciful American variation on the pelham theme but without a curb chain. If the lower rein ring was employed there would be powerful poll pressure.

with either the serrated side of the mouthpiece against the mouth, or the reverse side, which is smooth. It was designed to suit as wide a variety of mouths as might be found in a cavalry troop, or even a regiment, by changing the mouthpiece and the position of the reins in the cheek slots. As such I suppose it was a clever and workable compromise epitomising the pelham tradition. Otherwise it has nothing to recommend it over and above the usual run of pelhams.

The Swales bit is a severe one with the squeezing action of the inside rings on the fixed mouthpiece making it uncomfortable. I do not believe that any horse is better controlled by imposing discomfort on him and, even though some horses may go in it, I still regard it as one of those bits without which we and the horse would be better off.

(a)

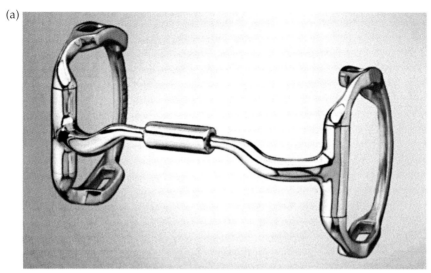

(b)

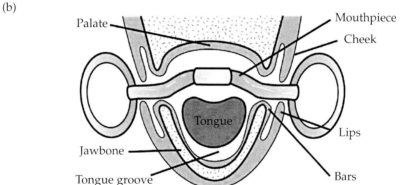

Figs. 82(a) the Myler Comfort Snaffle, (b) cross-section to show fitting. The Myler system devised in America but now used increasingly in Europe is naturally enough based on American practice and in many instances involves the use of curb cheeks (shanks) which do not feature in the accepted disciplines. The snaffle bits, more relevant to Europe, are well made with a variety of mouthpieces but still rely on a mechanical action that calls for a competent horseman if they are to be used to their full potential. They are divided into three categories according to the horse's level of training (and perhaps that of the rider, too). Much attention has also been given to the construction of the horse's mouth and the comfort zone afforded by the bit. There is, indeed, something to commend in the system. Where it fails, in some instances, is in the instigator's lack of accepted equestrian theory. (Photo and diagram courtesy Belstane Marketing)

(In recent years a wide range of American bits has become available in Europe to stand alongside the traditional patterns and the excellent German product. The American bits, replete with ports, copper rollers and the like, are of high quality and, as might be expected, vigorously promoted. Without doubt much thought has been given to the creation of a system of bitting and the construction of the bits is often ingenious. There is, nonetheless, considerable emphasis upon the mechanical action, to the extent that the less experienced may come to rely too much on the hand to compensate for their equestrian inadequacies.

The American Combination bridles are something else. One or two are acceptable when used by experienced riders on hard-pulling, impetuous animals, otherwise they are not.

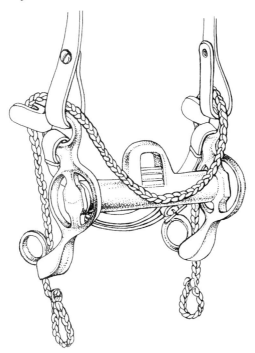

Fig. 83 An American Combination bit which might qualify for the title 'ultimate blunt instrument'.

9 The Gag

'And be ye lifted up…'

The group of gag bits can be divided into two sections, those that are used on their own and those used in a double bridle, where they give a greater upward action than a normal bradoon.

In the former category the mouthpiece is usually jointed and smooth, or it can be fitted with rollers round the mouth (Fig. 84). This latter, while being an old pattern, became known as Colonel Rodzianko's gag; the object of the rollers has already been explained. (Paul Rodzianko was a member of the crack Russian jumping team of pre-World War I days which won the 1913 Nations Cup at London's International Horse Show. After the Revolution Rodzianko came to Britain where he ran a training centre. He was also the trainer of the Irish Army team which won no less than 23 Nations Cups between 1928 and 1939.)

Whether there is an advantage in having an eggbutt cheek on a gag as in the Cheltenham (Fig. 85) is problematical, but some people claim that the bit slides down more easily when the gag rein is released.

Where a gag is used as a bradoon in the double bridle, the ring must obviously be smaller or can disappear altogether and be replaced with a Duncan cheek (Fig. 86). There is also a very sharp twisted gag with rings so small that only a cord can pass through the holes in the ring. It is termed a 'hack overcheck' (Fig. 87) and is a salutary method of raising

Fig. 84 A gag employing rollers round the mouthpiece.

Fig. 85 The Cheltenham; an eggbutt gag which is said to slide down more easily on the cheekpieces because of its greater weight.

Fig. 86 The Duncan gag is suitable for use with a curb bit in a double bridle.

Fig. 87 For experts only. The light 'hack overcheck' with twisted wire mouth is used in conjunction with a curb bit but requires a pair of very sensitive hands.

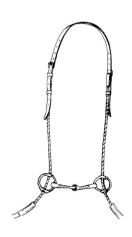

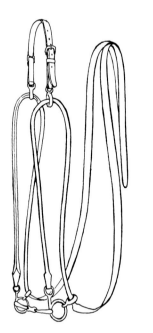

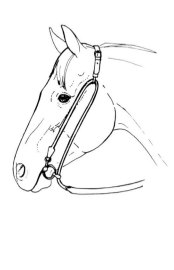

Fig. 88 The Hitchcock polo gag can operate with extraordinary speed.

the head to the correct position. While it might be of assistance to an experienced nagsman, it could be very dangerous in other hands.

In days now long past, gag rings were fixed to pelhams to incorporate a gag action in that bit. I remember seeing them on polo ponies and presumably they worked even though such a combination would seem to be illogical. A gag used in polo and possessed of a considerable 'winding up' action is that produced by Hitchcock, the American expert after whom it was named. The illustration (Fig. 88) shows the extent of its elevatory power and gives some idea of the speed with which this can be obtained.

The basic function of the gag is to raise the head, but it is often used with a standing martingale as a method of control on very strong, impetuous animals and is used in that way on polo ponies and event horses.

10 The Bitless Bridle

'Simplicity is the keynote.'

This is a group of bridles used only infrequently, but which do have advantages in certain instances. A bitless bridle need not necessarily be an elaborate affair and quite an effective one can be made with a stout noseband and judiciously placed rings. In fact, with a little thought it is quite easy to produce a very workable one which can be used with or without a bit.

Fig. 89 A simple pattern of bitless bridle that is relatively mild in its action.

A product of such thought, and a refinement on the basic noseband, is the Scawbrig bridle (Fig. 90). It is not original in design and many other forms of 'control nosebands', as they are sometimes called, preceded it, but it does illustrate the simpler type of bitless bridle and also reveals the potential of such bridles.

Briefly, it consists of a bridle head and cheeks with a broad nosepiece, a backstrap to hold the nosepiece in place, and a rein which is passed through the two rings at either side of the nosepiece, being joined in the centre by a padded curbpiece. In this, the simplest form – Fig. 90(a) – control is obtained by pressure on the nose and curb groove and by slight poll pressure. If, however, a broader view is taken, the addition of a sliphead can make the bridle into a very useful training device, particularly for jumping. In the first stages the horse learns to jump when guided entirely by pressure on the nose, etc., and as there is no bit, his confidence is not damaged by his receiving a jab in the mouth, and so with the absence of pain his training proceeds calmly.

Later on the sliphead is added and a bit suspended in his mouth without the attachment of a rein – Fig. 90(b). During this period, while still ensuring that his mouth is not touched, he is becoming accustomed to the feel of the bit without it being associated with any pain or discomfort.

The final method – Fig. 90(c) entails the addition of a rein to the bit and the increased use of the latter, while still having the restraint of the bridle on nose and curb groove.

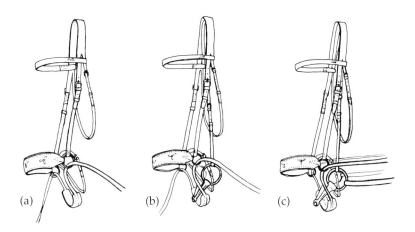

(a)   (b)   (c)

Fig. 90 A useful form of training bridle.
The Scawbrig can be used
(a) without a bit,
(b) with the bit just suspended in the mouth, and then
(c) with the addition of a rein in conjunction with the bit.

As a training bridle it did, in fact, prove to be a most successful device in which to teach a horse to jump, as well as the inexperienced rider. It originated some years ago at the home of the Robinette family in Lincolnshire and may now be experiencing a revival.

'Blair's' pattern (see Fig. 24, p.43) is more restricted in its scope, but is a true bitless bridle. The length of cheek produces sufficient pressure on the nose to restrain any horse who is not mentally afflicted, but it is important to have the nose and curbpieces well padded to avoid chafing. Lateral movement of the head, comparatively easily obtained with the Scawbrig, entails, with Blair's pattern, an exaggerated opening of the hand before a positive result is obtained.

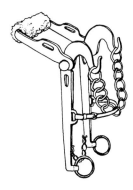

Fig. 91 William Stone's (W.S.) bitless Pelham.

The 'W. S. (William Stone) bitless pelham' (Fig. 91), sometimes known as the Distas bridle, is another true bitless bridle, shorter in the cheeks than Blair's pattern, but the cheeks are movable and not fixed. It is designed for use with two reins, the lower one operating the curb chain so that pressure can be applied to either nose or curb groove with some degree of independence. (William Stone was a well-known character in the Walsall bit-making trade for well over half a century and was instrumental in producing some of the less common bit patterns.)

The Western hackamore *(la jaquima), bosal, latigo, fiador, mecate,* heel knot and all is the apotheosis of the nose bridle used within a system of bitting that 'mouths' the horse from his nose. It has no relevance to European ('Eastern', 'English seat') riding but it is deserving of study by the serious horseman.

The Hackamore

In the seventh and eighth centuries, during the Moorish occupation of the Iberian Peninsula, a system of schooling horses evolved based on *la jaquima*, from which word 'hackamore' is derived. It relied on the use of the nose to introduce, by very gradual stages, a potentially powerful bit, and it was concerned with the making of a highly obedient, superbly balanced horse who could be ridden at speed, on one hand, either in combat or when working the fierce, black fighting bulls which are traditional to the Peninsula.

The 700 years of Moorish occupation ended in 1492 and early in the following century the Spanish *conquistadores* (conquerors), spurred on by tales of fabulous wealth and the rich pickings that were to be had in the New World, were becoming established in Mexico (Cortes landed there in 1519) and in South America.

With them they took their horses, a species which had been extinct on the American continent for 8–10,000 years. They also took their unique horse culture and the equipment supporting their methods of training.

All three survive today. The first in the pervasive influence of the Spanish horse in the varied and colourful equine population; the last two, modified to the needs of the country, in the art and culture of the Western reinsman.

The true hackamore is not a bitless bridle in the manner of the long-cheeked nose bridles, but rather a system of bitting comprised of a number of nosebands of decreasing weight to which is attached a rope rein.

In the first instance it is made up of a heavy, braided rawhide noseband shaped like an old-fashioned tennis racquet, the rein, and a headpiece that may include the Western equivalent of a throatlatch.

The noseband, termed after the Spanish, *bosal* (*bosalillo*) has a substantial 'heel' knot at the rear that lies between the lower jawbones. Its position is secured by a lightweight head stall, *latigo*. This can be made with an appropriately positioned slit that can be slipped over one ear (as in a one-ear bridle) or the fitting can be made more secure by the addition of a browband, *cavesada*.

The heavy rope rein, traditionally made from mane hair and named the *mecate*, is attached to the heel knot by a system of 'wraps', which can be adjusted to produce an extraordinarily delicate balance in the *bosal*, the weight of the rein and the heel knot acting as a counterbalance to the heavy nosepiece that lies some 5 cm (2 in) above the end of the nasal cartilage. The sides of the *bosal* slope downwards to the curb groove, behind and below which lies the heel knot.

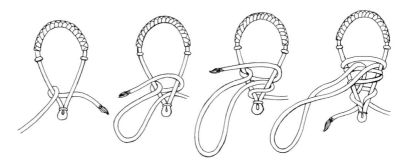

Fig. 92 *The method employed to attach the mecate to the heel-knot of the bosal in a series of wraps. The reins and heel-knot act to counterbalance the substantial nosepiece.*

Also attached to the heel knot is the *fiador*, a carefully designed throat-latch in effect. Its purpose is to maintain the position of the heel knot and to prevent it bumping irritatingly against the lower jawbones when the horse is in motion.

The acceptable position of the head is governed by the number of 'wraps' taken round the heel knot. When the head is carried in the desired position, or when the horse is at rest, neither heel knot nor nose-piece are in contact and the sides of the *bosal* just touch the face lightly.

When the hand is raised, the nosepiece of the *bosal* comes into play to apply a momentary restraint, encouraging the horse to 'tuck in', i.e. retract the nose. Conversely, should the nose be raised upwards beyond the limits imposed by the adjustment of the 'wraps' the noseband acts in the same way to correct the head position. Meanwhile, the heel knot, lying between and against the jawbones, acts in opposition to discourage the horse from overbending in an evasion of the momentarily imposed nose pressure.

There is thus created a precision instrument that is capable of very fine adjustment, for which there is no equivalent in conventional European bridles.

Initially the rein is held in both hands, changes of direction being made by it being carried out one side or the other while on the opposite side it

Fig. 93 The Western hackamore.

is laid on the neck to reinforce the message. As the training progresses, the rein will be held in one hand only and turns made by carrying the rein outwards in the direction of the turn which, at the same time, has the effect of laying the opposite side on the neck (hence neck-rein or neck-reining.)

Very importantly, changes of direction are always accompanied by an appropriate and simultaneous shift of the rider's weight.

The schooled hackamore horse performs for the most part at speed while remaining constantly in balance. The sliding stops; the pivots on the deeply engaged quarters; the sharp turns, as in barrel racing, and the rein-back are all made on a looping rein without the mouth being touched.

Of course, the transition to the bit is the ultimate refinement. The Western bit is fearsome in appearance and potentially very severe but in the hands of a skilful reinsman softer than any European bit. It is fitted with long cheeks and a high-ported mouthpiece (spade) and the transition from *bosal* to bit is made via ever lighter *bosals*, through a two-rein *bosal* (a light noseband fitted with thin rein ropes), until control is wholly through the agency of the bit supported by a pencil-slim *bosal*.

Finally, even that is discarded and the finished horse performs in the bit alone with no noseband and on a 'floating' rein that exerts minimal pressure on the mouth.

Fig. 94 The Western curb bit which is the last stage in the Californian system of bridling.

The rein may be made a little heavier by small decorative pieces of metal being wrapped round it, but the ideal is for the horse to be ridden on the weight of a rawhide rein no more than 6 mm (¼ in) wide – the apotheosis of a tradition now lost to most of Europe.

11 Curb Chains and Other Bit Accessories

'For the sake of a nail the shoe was lost, for the sake of..'

Curb chains or curbs are made either of a series of linked metal rings or of leather or elastic (Fig. 95). In the first case the links may be either single ones or double to form a kind of mesh. In either case there is often a variation in the width and, on the principle of distributing pressure over as large an area as possible, I think a broad-linked chain is preferable to a narrow one, which might be too sharp in its action.

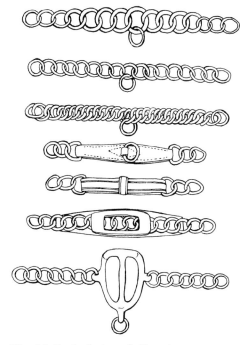

Fig. 95 Curb chains of all sorts.
From the top: flat-link curb; plain single link; double link;
leather curb; elastic curb; curb guard and the Jodhpur polo curb.

A leather curb, often termed 'humane', is a good one and providing it is kept soft and is properly adjusted it will not cause chafing.

Smart and expensive leather curbs can be made of swelled and neatly stitched leather (rather like a show noseband), or they can be made out of a strip of plain, soft, red buffalo hide, which is cheaper and just as good or better.

My own preference is for a curb made of doubled elastic and I expect that most horses would agree with me. It is certainly more comfortable than metal, there is less chance of it chafing and in most instances a better response is produced as a result. Indeed the elastic curb is as effective as any and particularly so on horses who may resent the curb action. *(This is an example of how one's opinions can change over the years. I appreciate that the elastic curb contributes to the rider's 'feel good factor', but it has to be recognised that it may prevent the immediate response that is obtainable (on a schooled horse) when using a properly adjusted metal-link chain which is sharper, or more direct, in its action. There is, too, a likelihood, along with the delayed response, of the horse hanging on the elastic curb, which, of course, 'gives' when pressure is applied. For all that, it has a practical use with some very sensitive animals who find it difficult to accept the metal-link chain.)*

Fig. 96 The flat, circle curb hook which is infinitely preferable to any other.

Should a metal curb cause soreness, a rubber curb guard or one made of leather, through which the chain is slipped, is a simple remedy.

The Jodhpur polo curb is a stronger device, the oval shape fitting between the jawbones and exerting considerable pressure. However, it rarely causes chafing if properly adjusted.

The curb hooks, on the other hand, do sometimes cause discomfort and chafing and if a horse is invariably found to be sore because of them, the circle pattern curb hook (Fig. 96) will be a good antidote. The hook is shaped so as to lie flat and, therefore, cannot chafe. I would certainly never use anything else.

A lipstrap, which passes through the 'fly' link on the chain, is an essential addition to a bit having a curb chain and will prevent the curb rising out of the curb groove; the rounded leather variety looks neater but a flat leather one will last longer. *(The lipstrap also prevents the bit from becoming reversed in the mouth. I have never experienced such a dire extremity but I am assured that it is most unpleasant.)*

It is a mistaken kindness to adjust the curb chain loosely. Such an adjustment involves greater use being made of the curb bit before the chain is brought into action and it may also cause the chain to be pulled up out of the chin groove. To be both efficient and humane the chain should fit snugly without being overtight.

In cases where a snaffle bit or a pelham is pinching or chafing the lips, a pair of thin rubber cheek guards are the ideal preventive. The rubber is sufficiently flexible to be pulled over a 10 cm (4 in) bit ring without tearing. Circles of leather fastened round the mouthpiece with a lace are not nearly so satisfactory, as the lace itself can chafe and the leather becomes hard in use.

All these items are small enough in themselves but, as our object is to make sure that no unnecessary discomfort is caused in the process of bitting the horse, they deserve our attention.

(Rubber or leather curb guards are permitted in F.E.I. and British Dressage and British Eventing competitions. Leather and elastic curbs, however, are omitted from the list of permissible items and one must presume that they are forbidden.)

12 Common Evasions and Some Remedies

'No horse was born a rogue but man made him so.'

The horse can produce an alarming number of evasions to the various indications of the bit, many being caused by incorrect early training. Some of these can be cured by a course of retraining, but some remain obstinately with us and defy our efforts to cure them. I do not suggest that any of the articles dealt with in this chapter are certain cures, but they can work even if they are not always 100 per cent successful.

One of the most common and irritating evasions is that of getting the tongue over the bit. To do so the horse draws the tongue backwards before clamping it down over the bit. To all intents the horse then becomes out of control and in extreme instances the tongue may be drawn so far back as to block the larynx. The condition is described as 'swallowing' the tongue; when this happens the horse comes to an abrupt halt and, unless the obstruction is removed, is in danger of choking.

The habit can be caused by careless bitting, particularly in the early stages of training. Too large a jointed snaffle or a bit adjusted too low in the mouth are invitations to the horse to put his tongue over the top. Otherwise, the tongue may have been pinched or bruised at some point and so it is drawn back to avoid the discomfort. A shallow tongue channel, for instance, may result in the tongue itself being damaged by bit pressure. Whatever the reason, the habit highlights the need for owners to study the conformation of the mouth and then to select a bit in accordance with the peculiarity of the mouth, thereafter fitting it with the greatest care.

However, once the evasion has become habitual it may be necessary for it to be countered with one device or another, although the use of such an item does not remove the necessity for examining the mouth and selecting a bit suitable to the conformation.

The first thing to realise when confronted with this frustrating habit is that it is unlikely to be cured while the horse has a jointed snaffle in his mouth. Replacement by a simple mullen mouthpiece may, indeed, provide an immediate solution. There will be no risk of the tongue being pinched, and, so long as the bit is adjusted sufficiently high in the mouth, it is only by making a very determined effort that the horse will be able to get his tongue over it. If this fails, the addition of a rubber tongue port (Fig. 97), which is easily fastened round a mullen mouthpiece and lies flat on the tongue facing to the rear, will make it even more difficult and may dissuade him altogether.

There is also a jointed bit (Fig. 98), formerly called the Nagbut snaffle, that has a metal grid set in the centre which lies on the tongue and achieves the same purpose. Whichever one of these is used, it is important that the horse has no opportunity to slide the bit through the mouth, removing the port from its central position over the tongue.

A device which does in many cases effect a cure is shown in Fig. 99(a). It consists of two circular pieces of leather placed round a mullen mouthpiece, the connecting strap being adjusted across the nose and secured by the small central strap to the noseband. This has the effect of raising the bit in the mouth, which is essential, and it also, of course, places pressure on the nose, which is no bad thing in cases of this kind.

A tongue grid (Fig. 97) suspended above the bit will also stop the habit in most cases.

In racing circles a tongue strap enclosing the tongue and fastened under the lower jaw is occasionally used, but it is at best pretty barbaric and can cause acute pain, even though it ensures that the tongue cannot be moved. It could not be used for anything but short periods and is therefore impracticable outside flat racing.

Fig. 97 Left: the Juba port, an effective item in countering the problem of 'tongue over the bit'. Right: a tongue grid which can be suspended in the mouth above the bit.

Fig. 98 This tongue bit with the grid lying over the tongue is usually successful in all but most difficult cases.

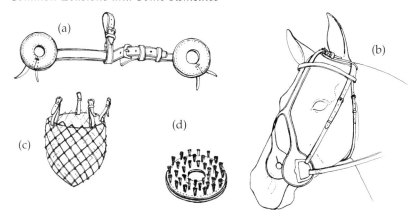

Fig. 99 (a) A simple device for fastening to the noseband and round the ends of the mouthpiece to raise the bit in the mouth (it also acts as an additional noseband);
(b) the Australian cheeker, made of rubber, once more lifts the bit upwards and at the same time applies a psychological restraint by the central portion running up the face;
(c) a nose net fastened tightly up against the muzzle will often deter the tearaway intent upon making off;
(d) a brush pricker pressing into the cheek may come as a surprise to the horse who will not run straight.

Another racing device is the Australian cheeker – Fig. 99(b) – which is made of rubber and lifts the bit in the mouth. The psychological restraint induced by the central portion running up the face is also apparent, as in the Rockwell bridle.

Hard-pulling, runaway horses are also evading the bit and are in fact running away from the pain imposed upon them. A horse who is hard to handle in a plain snaffle may be quite amenable in something a little stronger, but a real tearaway will never be cured of his behaviour by the infliction of more pain on him through increasingly severe bitting. A good rule is to try something very much milder. If, however, you want to race him or play polo with him and still find him too strong, a very simple device which will, nine times out of ten, do the trick is a nose net – Fig. 99(c) – much the same as those fitted to calves to prevent them suckling. It is put over the nose and fastened fairly tightly to the nose-band and will stop the majority of tearaways. It inflicts no pain, but the slight pressure surrounding the tender muzzle, and the very fact that it is there, cause the horse to draw back from it, as it were. The effect is largely psychological but it does work.

Lastly, there are animals who are one-sided in their mouths or stiff in their backs, or who, for one reason or another, favour a particular leg so that when racing they hang to one side or another; and there are also those who have developed a happy knack of running down the length of a fence before screwing over it. In the latter case, the other jockeys will probably effect a cure as far as they are concerned by being so pointed in their remarks that the animal does not appear again until a reformation has been accomplished! Seriously, however, it is important when racing that a horse should run straight and there are a number of articles designed to encourage him to do so. A 'brush pricker' – Fig. 99(d) – on whichever side it is needed, will cause him sufficient surprise and discomfort to change his course. Horses do, however, get used to brush prickers and on that account they should be used sparingly.

The 'anti-lug' bit – Fig. 100(a) – with its odd-shaped mouthpiece, can also be of assistance. The short side, which is curved back, is on the opposite side to that to which the horse hangs.

A circle-cheek bit – Fig. 100(b) – with its slight squeezing action and large cheekpieces, will again help to keep a horse straight. Another

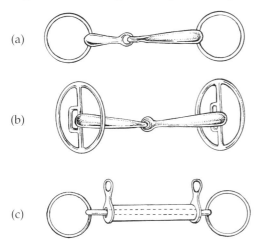

Fig. 100 (a) An anti-lug bit used on horses hanging strongly to one side; (b) another bit, a circle cheek, which is designed to hold a horse straight; (c) an ingenious slide held in a hollow mouthpiece which is used in America to combat the hanging horse.

Fig. 101 Blinkers, or 'visors', are used to keep a horse's mind on his work and often produce results with horses labelled as non-triers.

design is an American pattern bit – Fig. 100(c) – with the rings set on a metal rod passing through the mouthpiece itself. In both these cases the bit cannot slide through the mouth, and this is the first object we should try to attain when a horse shows any desire to hang to one side or the other. The Americans with their sharply turning tracks are far more conscious of steerage than we are, and they have developed a variety of ingenious devices which are rarely seen in Europe.

Then there are blinkers (Fig. 101), now more often called visors by the TV commentators, whose observations on the items of tack to be seen in the paddock are always entertaining but only rarely accurate. Traditionally, blinkers were known as the 'rogue's badge' to be fitted to the non-trier. They are still used on the doggy customer who drops his bit when he hits the front but they are also useful to keep a horse paying attention to his work, or for one who 'peeks' apprehensively at objects just within the range of his lateral vision. There are a number of eye-cup patterns but virtually all modern blinkers can be fitted quickly with clip fastenings or Velcro straps – items which have replaced the less satisfactory straps and buckles.

The action of nosebands in combating evasions has been discussed in Chapter 5.

13 Schooling Martingales and Reins

'They scoff at progress who do not understand it.'

In addition to the more common martingales, there are those which act as schooling aids or corrective apparatus, the aim of which is to develop the muscles of the neck and back in order to produce a correct positioning and engagement of these parts and to improve the balance and the overall way of going. As their scope is beyond that of the martingales previously discussed they justify examination in a separate chapter.

The two principal schooling martingales are the Chambon and the De Gogue. There is also an earlier, less sophisticated pattern which in Britain became known as the Continental (Fig. 102). All three are of French origin and the latter must now be considered to have been superseded

Fig. 102 The old pattern 'Continental' schooling martingale, the prototype for the more sophisticated Chambon and De Gogue.

by the more farreaching Chambon and De Gogue. They provide the basis for a small number of other schooling devices but remain the most effective of the schooling martingales.

In general terms the object of these martingales is to induce a lowering and stretching of the head and neck. The result of this, apart from breaking down the resistance in these parts and suppling the relative muscles, is to raise the *base* of the neck (the balancing agent of the horse) and to exercise the muscles of the back and loins, enabling the back to be rounded, with the consequent engagement of the hocks. They are used frequently in the training of showjumpers, but are equally useful in the schooling or reschooling of any type of riding horse, particularly those who, as a result of bad riding, etc., have developed an incorrect musculature and outline. Horses of this latter category, particularly, respond extraordinarily well to these schooling devices, which counteract the restriction such a conformation tends to impose upon the free movement of the horse.

A ewe-necked horse or one who 'star-gazes' (usually through having his head *pulled* up by the rider's hand rather than being pushed by the legs on to an intermittently resistant hand) is invariably hollow backed with a resultant cramping of the muscles of the quarters. In this state the horse is 'above the bit' and to a lesser or greater degree – dependent upon the extent to which he is above the bit – the following defects will become apparent.

Action will be seriously restricted and the stride shortened. There will be a general stiffness and a lack of engagement of the hind legs which will prevent the stifle and hip joints working to full capacity; additionally the hind toes will probably be dragged.

As the shoulder muscles remain undeveloped and because of the hollowed back, the saddle will have a tendency to move forward, bringing the girth right under the elbows and probably causing girth galls. *(This sort of conformation is the saddler's nightmare. No saddle will overcome the problem. The only solution is in reschooling the horse with the object of developing his muscles in the correct form to encourage a rounded top line. The wise, responsible saddler will not undertake the task of remedial saddle fitting, knowing it to be impossible, and risks being labelled 'useless' for his honesty. The man who tries to supply a saddle and fails, inevitably, will be called 'incompetent'. Both adjectives would be better applied to the owner.)*

Similarly, the muscles of the back and loin will remain stiff and undeveloped, becoming painful when subjected to the rider's weight and causing the horse to flinch or even to crouch when mounted, and an animal so cramped and stiff will be quite unable to round his back and jump correctly, if indeed he will jump at all.

When the condition becomes as advanced as the one I have described, it does not cure itself and in fact gets worse unless corrective treatment is given.

No horse is born supple, with his muscles developed correctly, and to achieve this development must, therefore, be the principal object of schooling. When we have appreciated this fact and are sufficiently expert to produce a horse so developed, we shall find that many of our bitting problems disappear and then the bit itself will be seen in proper perspective as an extension of the seat and legs instead of being regarded only as a fundamental means of obtaining head carriage conducive to control. It would be a mistake to regard these training aids as 'gadgets' used to obtain quick results. They are, indeed, a part of the horseman's armoury and as legitimate as any other piece of equipment and considerably less dangerous than some.

Both the Continental and the Chambon employ pressure on the poll to induce a lowered head carriage. They differ in that the Continental applies pressure between the nose and the poll by means of the strap connecting these two points sliding through a ring on the body of the martingale, while the Chambon is directly connected to the poll from the girth; extending by means of a clip attachment to the rings of the bit. In either case, however, the best results will be gained by working the animal loose in a closed school or some other confined space. A little gentle diplomacy, combined with a reward in the form of some titbit, will make

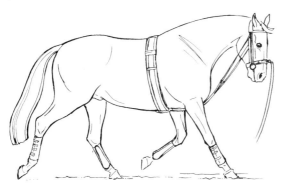

Fig. 103 The outline produced by the Chambon which also encourages a regular, rhythmic gait.

the horse realise that comfort is in a lowered head carriage. To begin, no gait other than a walk should be attempted then, when the horse lowers his head without resistance at this gait, a trot can be asked for and work begun to free and develop the muscles of shoulder, back and neck. Gradually the joints of hip, stifle and hock will begin to flex and bend, causing the hocks to be brought well under the body with a consequent improvement in the balance and action of the horse. In neither case should the apparatus be used for more than twenty minutes at a time during the early stages; nor should it be adjusted too tightly. The tension should be increased gradually as the daily schooling proceeds until the head is carried just a little above the level of the knees.

Very occasionally a horse will be met who persists in evading the action by arching the neck, although he may still lower his head well enough. In these cases Benoist-Gironière (one of the most skilled of the French post-war horsemen and author of *The Conquest of the Horse*) recommends that, in the case of the Chambon, the cord attached to the offside of the bit (which should be a plain mullen-mouth rubber snaffle) should be crossed over the face and attached to the nearside bit ring, the nearside attachment being treated in the same way and fastened to the offside ring. Whilst, in my experience, the Chambon is most effective when working the horse loose, at least in the initial stages of training, it is also used extensively in the lunge exercises. Indeed, in many European countries the Chambon is regarded as being as integral to the work on the lunge as the cavesson or the lunge whip (Fig. 104). Other than the fitting of a soft bit, a light, close-fitting cavesson is an obvious essential.

Fig. 104 The Chambon is often an integral part of lungeing equipment in mainland Europe.

In the case of both the Continental and the Chambon, their use is restricted to unmounted work alone (I believe there are one or two people who have attempted ridden work in the Continental, but this is really outside its scope) and it may be that there will be times during the training under saddle when the horse will not react as satisfactorily without the restraint of the apparatus to assist him. To overcome this admitted defect, the De Gogue system was produced as an expansion and extension of the Chambon, having far greater possibilities than the latter. The object remains the same, but the means to attain it reveal more advanced thought and allow the horseman to use the device in both unmounted and mounted work.

In its 'independent' position (Fig. 105a), the De Gogue is fitted with an additional strap at point A which fastens into the same buckle as the bifurcated strap B, and the fastening at point C is attached to this. In this position, unmounted work can be carried out in the same way as with the Chambon, although with this system there is a change in the way in which the head position is controlled. A triangle is formed of the three major resistance points – the poll, mouth and base of the neck. Within the confines of the triangle, the horse can carry his head lowered and with comfort and, after the initial training period required to obtain the lowering of the head, and when sufficient suppleness has been achieved throughout the body, adjustments can be made to bring the nose in and to flex the poll even more. It is not possible to overbend the horse because of a stop (D) placed on the running part of the rein below the small pulley on the poll strap. With the device in this position, No. 2 (Fig. 105b), an ordinary rein (indicated by the dotted line E) can then be added for the first stages of mounted work.

The last stage in the system is that shown in position No. 2, where the rein from the hand is directly attached to the roundings at point F. In this position, the horse can be schooled either on the ground or over fences, when the neck will be found to have attained a remarkable degree of elasticity enabling the horse to respond smoothly to the indications of the hand.

It is possible to add a further rein in this position, if it is required, but it is hardly necessary. There is no reason why the De Gogue in this advanced position should not be used for showjumping and cross-country work, and in the past I have seen it used, in fact, in the cross-country phase of full-blown three-day horse trials both in Britain and elsewhere in Europe.

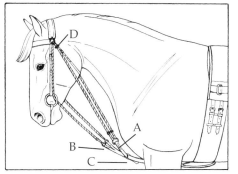

Fig. 105a The more advanced De Gogue adjusted in the lunge position.

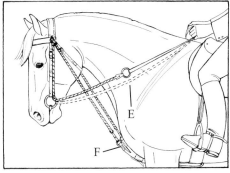

Fig. 105b The De Gogue in the riding position.

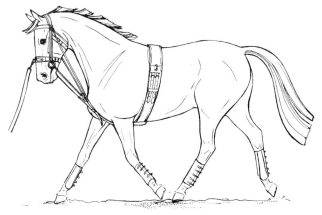

Fig. 105c Working the horse on the lunge with the De Gogue, which allows for a greater flexibility than the Chambon.

Used as a 'system' of training – and in my opinion the De Gogue justifies this title – the device is logical throughout its sequence, always demanding from the horse the same response by means of similar indications, to which he has become accustomed from the beginning of his training.

If the object of training is to produce a horse so supple throughout his body that he is able to obey the directions of the rider without opposition, then certainly the system goes a long way to achieving this end without the danger of encouraging resistances which can arise with other methods.

Obviously the De Gogue must remain within the province of the more accomplished horseman who can appreciate its value and is therefore capable of obtaining the maximum benefit from it but, on the other hand, it would be foolish of others to condemn out of hand what is a very useful and successful system without carefully studying either its principles or its potential.

(Unfortunately, particular care needs to be taken when purchasing a De Gogue or, to a lesser degree, the Chambon. Too many British manufacturers, out of ignorance, one imagines, have strayed from the original patterns and produced some very strange and quite unworkable pieces of equipment. I bought a De Gogue from a well-known company, only to find that it had been made the wrong way round, without the stops, and with a most peculiar and quite impractical fastening to the poll pad. I returned it, to be told by a young assistant that 'We always make them that way'. I pointed out the error of their ways but it took another two months before I obtained a De Gogue made according to the directions of its inventor. In the meantime I had found two other 'patterns', both of which for all sorts of reasons were useless. A case of caveat emptor *[let the buyer beware], indeed!)*

The Balancing Rein

A far more controversial item and one that is, perhaps, even less perfectly understood, is the balancing rein which was the invention of the late Major Peter Abbot-Davies. When it appeared over a twenty years ago it was condemned, predictably, by the 'establishment', but for all that, it has survived the test of time. Today, it is marketed successfully from a riding centre in Northampton and is used by a number of notable riders with apparent success. Since the rein clearly achieves results, and is likely to be with us for the foreseeable future and probably beyond, it deserves consideration rather than outright and unthinking condemnation.

The rein in its initial stages makes use of the tail, which is connected to the mouth under the belly and through the legs. It is in effect an extension of the running rein principle, which, along with tail-reining, has been practised for over 3,000 years.

Abbot-Davies combined the two principles, mitigating the inhibiting action of the draw/running rein by the use of a shock-absorbing system based on an ingenious pulley and spring arrangement.

It is claimed that the system 'has a calming influence on even the most wayward of characters, never fails to position the horse correctly and it prevents all resistance'. The object of the rein is to build up the muscles of the back and upper neck in a relatively short time or, of course, it is used to correct a faulty development.

Its use causes the back to be rounded, the shoulders lifted and the quarters to be actively engaged under the body. The head is held in a strongly flexed position and both it and the neck are lowered. In fact, the two ends are brought together to produce a rounded top line with a raised shoulder. The usual running or draw rein only operates on the front end of the horse, which is the weakness of these reins, leaving the rider's legs to encourage the engagement of the quarters. Clearly, there is a great improvement in the balance, and after a course of short lessons in the balancing rein it is claimed that the improved outline can be maintained when the horse is ridden in an ordinary snaffle, the muscles having been built up to produce the rounded form. The pulleys are held to counteract any tendency towards being one-sided and the spring action softens the effect of the hands.

The rein is used in three positions:

   a. Attached from the mouth to the girth.
   b. From mouth to tail with a rope passed through a soft, sheep skin sleeve.
   c. From mouth to behind the ears by means of a rubber connection.

This last position is the one usually employed for lungeing and long-reining but it can also be used under saddle. It produces an exaggerated lowering of the head and neck, which works and develops the muscles of the neck and back and produces an accompanying engagement of the hind legs.

The second, mouth to tail, position, is crucial and acts to introduce the horse to the system, accustoming the animal to the pressures of the rein – pressures that will not have been experienced before – and producing the initial rounded outline.

If the position is crucial within the system, its sparing and sympathetic use is of equal importance. Used for too long a period in unthinking hands it can become an abuse of the horse, causing pain and resentment. Two short lessons at the outset of no more than possibly fifteen minutes are sufficient to place the horse in the rounded outline. Thereafter the

Fig. 106 The Abbot-Davies balancing rein in the initial nose to tail position.

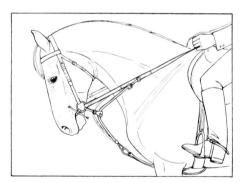

*Fig. 106a The rein in the subsequent position
fastened to the girth by a strong rubber connection.*

rein in this position takes on a 'booster' role and need not be used in this
way for more than one short period each month.

The everyday use of the rein is made in the first position, when the
attachment is made from the mouth to the girth through a strong rubber
rod. With the rein in this position the horse can be jumped over fences up
to 1 m (3 ft 3 in) in height.

Abbot-Davies summed up the advantages of his rein in these words: 'This patent rein will act as an accelerator, doing in one week what would normally take months of work.'

In that sentence, perhaps, are encapsulated the disadvantages of the system. There is, without doubt, a danger that the inexperienced will be attracted by the prospect of producing a schooled horse in double-quick time. In fact, any benefits obtainable depend upon the user having above average riding ability. Without that advantage, work with the rein needs to be carried out under the supervision of a skilful trainer.

The success of the balancing rein has undoubtedly produced a rash of imitations. They may represent the sincerest form of flattery but they remain imitations and should not be preferred to the real thing.

14 Draw and Running Reins

'The razor in the monkey's paw.'

(In the first editions of Saddlery only passing reference was made to these reins, probably because their construction is hardly noteworthy. Of course, they were used forty years ago, and for years before that the reins were accepted as being part of the normal training equipment of the European military schools.

Today, largely, I suspect because of an overriding German influence – the German National Equestrian Federation acknowledges the draw rein's limited value in its instructional manual – I discern a more general use of draw/running reins but not much more appreciation of how they should be used. That is sufficient reason for their inclusion in this revised edition.)

Draw and running reins are not one and the same thing, but they are closely related. There is a handful of patterns, all operating on the same principle but differing in points of detail.

A *draw* rein (Fig. 107) originates at the girth, passes through the forelegs and thence through the bit rings to the hand, or, in some instances, it may be secured to the girth straps of the saddle, when it acts

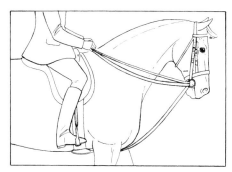

Fig. 107 The draw rein used properly in conjunction with the usual bit rein.

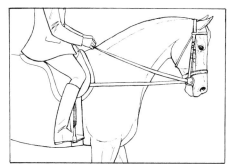

Fig. 108 The running rein claimed as the invention of the English Master, William Cavendish, Duke of Newcastle (1592–1676).

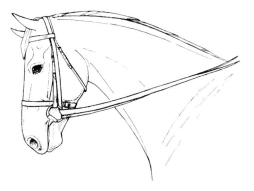

Fig. 109 A variation on the running rein
which puts downward pressure on the poll.

as a kind of 'improved' side rein.

The *running* rein (Fig. 108), claimed as the invention of the English Master, William Cavendish, Duke of Newcastle (1592–1676), fastens round the girth under the saddle flaps and then returns to the hands through the bit rings or, when it was used by Newcastle and his contemporaries, it came to the hand via the side rings of a schooling cavesson (i.e. what we would now recognise as a lunge cavesson).

In both instances the rein is passed from the *inside* to the *outside* of the bit ring, so that an inward squeezing action is avoided to some degree. It is usually recommended that both reins should be operated in conjunction with a drop noseband to prevent the horse evading the restraint by opening the mouth.

There is a small difference in the action of the reins. The draw rein is, by a little, the stronger of the two. It 'draws' the head down as well as causing a retraction of the nose and is on that score more direct in its action.

The running rein brings the nose in, but it does not act so directly to lower the head. A variation of the running rein (Fig. 109), shown in Italian illustrations of the Renaissance period, has the rein passing over the poll, down the side of the face and then through the bit rings. The powerful pressure exerted on the poll obviously induces a lowering of the head. It was this early type of running rein from which the gag bridle derived.

There are arguments in favour of the occasional use of the draw/running rein, but there are some obvious dangers in its employment in the hands of any but the most competent. When novice riders make use of the rein, other than under strict supervision, then, certainly, it becomes a case of 'the razor in the monkey's paw'. The horse is compelled to shorten in front without a corresponding engagement of the hind legs and the consequent rounding of the back, all because the rider is incapable of using the legs to drive the horse's hind legs under the body. If such a rider persists with the rein the result is likely to be a very spoilt horse, indeed. He will evade by becoming behind the bit, i.e. he will tuck his nose into the chest. He then ceases to go forward with any freedom at all and will exhibit stiffness throughout his frame, and, of course, a hollowed back.

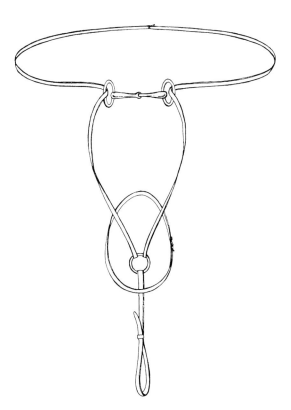

Fig. 110 A good pattern of draw rein fastened at the chest.

The proper and productive way to use the rein is for it to be used in conjunction with a direct rein fastened to the bit ring and placed above the draw/running rein. The draw rein is held some 5 cm (2 in) shorter than the direct rein and comes into play by bringing the bit across the bars of the lower jaw when the rider's legs push the horse forward into contact with the bridle. In response, the horse drops the nose and comes back onto the direct rein. The draw rein then becomes inactive and is held in reserve until the horse raises the mouth to come above the action of the direct rein, when once more it exerts downward pressure across the lower jaw. Horses are not stupid and they soon understand that the stronger pressure of the draw rein will be eased when the nose is dropped and the direct rein accepted.

When the rein is used in this way the horse quickly learns to lower the nose, relax the jaw and flex *at the poll* (not at a point two-thirds up the neck) when the rider's legs push him forward into contact with the hand.

A simple form of running rein, less compelling in its action, is a running martingale, adjusted tight enough to create an angle in the rein between mouth and hand, and used beneath a direct rein fastened to the bit.

Draw and running reins are usually made from web because of the length required. Probably the best pattern is that in which the rein is fastened at the chest to a ring on the end of a martingale body which is connected in the usual way to the girth after passing between the forelegs. (Fig. 110).

15 Development of the Modern Saddle

'Hang your old saddles on the wall of your home as antiques.
They might serve as a substitute for etchings.' Count Ilias Toptani.

The distinctive modern saddle, whatever its country of origin, was developed in the first half of the twentieth century, largely as a result of the teachings of the Italian cavalry officer, Federico Caprilli (1868–1907) who, after instructing at Tor di Quinto, an adjunct of the principal cavalry school at Pinerolo, became Pinerolo's chief instructor.

Caprilli, along with the system of riding he taught and practised, represents a watershed in equestrian history and in the development of the principles of modern riding.

Outside the hunting fields of Britain and Ireland, nineteenth-century equestrian thinking and practice was dominated by the great cavalry schools of Europe, which based their teaching on the *manège* riding of the seventeenth and eighteenth centuries. The accent was on the collected horse, ridden on the curb bit at relatively slow gaits. It was a system that suited the parade ground spectacle and made it possible to manoeuvre very large bodies of horsemen in open country unenclosed with fences, ditches, banks and so on. However, the very principles of classicism, so far as sporting pursuits and the overriding military requirement were concerned, had become largely debased as early as the end of the sixteenth century and 300 years later were hardly relevant at all. Jumping, for instance, played little or no part in basic cavalry instruction at most schools, and where it was included it was very imperfectly understood.

Caprilli, although he personified the dashing, party-loving cavalry officer of the period and indulged in the usual and traditional escapades of the privileged upper class, was nonetheless a serious and intelligent professional soldier absorbed in his study of cavalry tactics and an innovative, far-sighted thinker.

Unlike the generals, who at one time sought to suppress his rational methods as dangerous heresies, Caprilli was able to put the cavalry arm in perspective against the background of increasingly lethal and inhibiting fire power.

Accepting the futility of the death or glory charge against machine guns and the rapid-fire small-arms capability of well-trained infantry, Caprilli argued that the new role of cavalry was as a swiftly moving screen, reconnoitring the front of the main force and guarding its flanks. It was to be the eyes of the army and then, finally, the means by which a breakthrough in the enemy line could be exploited.

If it was to be effective, the mounted arm had to be able to operate cross-country, at speed, while negotiating whatever natural obstacles might be in its path. The incidence of such barriers was, indeed, increasingly significant as land enclosures became more commonplace throughout Europe.

The bulk of European cavalry, its men and horses schooled in the collected gaits of the *manège*, was painfully inadequate for what was essentially a light cavalry role exemplified in Europe only by the Hungarian hussars, the natural inheritors of the traditions of steppe horsemen culminating in the irregular Hun and Magyar formations.

Under Caprilli's *il sistema* the established 'school' methods were abolished at both Tor di Quinto and then at Pinerolo and with them went the curb bits on which they so largely depended. *Manège* riding was replaced by a 'natural' system in which both horses and riders were trained in the open country on the sort of terrain over which cavalry might be expected to operate on active service. Jumping was, of course, a central element in cross-country riding, and horses and riders acquired the necessary skills by practising over artificial fences as well as natural obstacles. Such training, however, was never more than a means to an end. All the training exercises contained in the system were regarded 'as a means of getting cavalry across a country with the least possible strain on both men and horses'.

Caprilli's horses, unlike those dominated in the conventional *manège* exercises, and always ridden in snaffles, were encouraged to move in what amounted to an almost unfettered extension. They carried the head and neck naturally and without restriction so that they were able to adapt their balance according to the irregularities of the ground on which they were operating.

The old system of cavalry training, like that practised at the early classical schools, compelled the horse to conform to an outline dictated by the rider's hand through the system of levers inherent within the curb bit and supported by spurs at the other end. Caprilli's natural system was based on the opposite approach. It called for the *rider* to conform to the horse's movement and outline, not the other way about.

Horses trained in this way, with the bulk of their work being performed in open country, quickly found their own balance and developed powers of initiative that would have been impossible for the *manège*-trained animal.

The system, however, demanded that the rider, too, should reject the principles of the *manège*, which encouraged the weight to be held to the rear and, perhaps, caused the rider to think in the same direction.

To conform to the horse, the rider had both to think and sit *forward*, positioning his weight in line with the horse's advancing centre of balance, with his hands going forward and never being drawn to the rear. As a result the horse's loins were freed and, unencumbered by inhibiting weight, he was able to jump naturally with a rounded back, and head and neck lowered and extended.

The principle was certainly one of minimal intervention by the rider but whilst non-interference with the horse's balance was of paramount concern there was no suggestion of passivity on the rider's part. The horse was required to maintain an even gait and, even when riding in file over the awesome obstacles on the Tor di Quinto training grounds, riders were expected to maintain a constant distance of two lengths between the horses.

The seat employed became known as the 'forward seat', an over-simplified description of the outward manifestation of a ruling principle. It called, of course, for a shorter leather if the weight was to be adjusted forward to accord with the horse's centre of balance and it required a change in the design of the saddle, too, if that was to accommodate the shortened leg position and help the rider to maintain his position without excessive physical effort.

The firm of Pariani, in Milan, was probably the first to make a saddle cut forward to conform, at least in part, with the new theory of the forward position and it was Pariani that was responsible for the early use of the spring tree. (This is disputed by the Walsall manufacturers who claim the spring tree was the result of their own inventive talent. There is, however, insufficient evidence to substantiate the claim and Pariani is generally credited with its introduction in the years following World War I.)

It was not until almost fifty years after the death of Caprilli, when his teaching had become generally accepted, at least in respect of the principles involved in cross-country riding and jumping, that a saddle was produced that fulfilled in almost every respect the requirement of his forward system of riding. It was made in Walsall, at that time still the epicentre of the world's saddlery industry, on the initiative of an Albanian nobleman, Count Ilias Toptani, a relative of the Albanian King Zog.

Although all credit must be given to this unlikely innovator and his collaborators for the saddle which became the principal influence on saddle design and construction in the last half of the twentieth century, there were other saddles made between the Wars which acted, if not as prototypes, then at least as stepping stones for Toptani's more complete model.

One of the most notable patterns was that designed by Caprilli's pupil and disciple, Major Piero Santini, who interpreted and expanded his mentor's teaching in a number of books and scores of magazine articles. (Caprilli left no more than the scrappiest of written notes and never attempted to present his theories in the written word. Santini, a most literate author both in his own language and in English, expounded the system most lucidly in his books *Riding Reflections* and *The Forward Impulse*, published in Britain and America in the 1930s.)

Santini, acknowledging the supremacy of Walsall craftsmanship and materials, had his saddle made in the town as Toptani was to do twenty years later in the immediate post-war years (Fig. 111). It was built on what was termed a 'parchment' tree, which had considerable resilience,

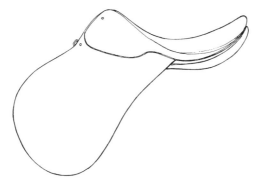

*Fig. 111 Outline of the saddle designed by Piero Santini
and made between the two World Wars in Walsall, England.*

and it bore a noticeable resemblance to the later Toptani model. Its impact was not as great as might have been expected however, the more conservative Weedon-trained horsemen, who had developed their own very effective 'balanced seat', being content to use a modified form of the conventional hunting saddle with the flap and panel cut more forward.

A saddle that had a more significant effect upon the Toptani was the Distas Central Position saddle, made to a design of Lieutenant Colonel F. E. Gibson, the founder of the Distas Saddlery Co. and, later, of the Newmarket firm which still bears his name, following, it is said, a conversation between him and Lieutenant Colonel Jack Hance, one of the most prominent of British riding instructors before and immediately after World War II. The Distas saddle was less extreme in its line than the Santini and probably on that account was more acceptable to the British public. It did, however, like the Santini, feature a seat more dipped than the usual hunting patterns.

(Gibson recalled that initially his Distas saddle met with resistance and even ridicule, usually from ex-military men and some of the hunting fraternity. His riposte was to refer the detractors to the British Army Universal Pattern saddle, used by cavalry and police forces throughout the world, and to the American McClellan which was based on the early nineteenth- century Hungarian light cavalry saddle and remained in service with the US Army up to 1940.

Interestingly, in de la Guérinière's classic Ecole de Cavalerie, *published in 1733, the saddles illustrated by the Master include the 'English Saddle', which is notably more dipped in the seat than the school saddles. The English saddle is recommended for 'the hunt' and cross-country riding.)*

Ilias Toptani visited Britain in the early 1950s, after the 1948 Olympics which were staged in London. He was himself a brilliant horseman of international calibre in the pure Caprilli tradition, and had been very successful as the trainer of some exceptional South American and Mexican teams, none of which had the advantage of riding the big, classy horses to which the Americans and Europeans were accustomed. He was in addition, intelligent, highly articulate and possessed of great personal charm.

In South America he had appreciated, as Hance had done previously in England, how crucial was the saddle in positioning the rider to increase his effective performance and that of his horse. In South America, however, at that time, there was no leather and saddlery industry comparable to that of Walsall and so his attempts at producing a saddle

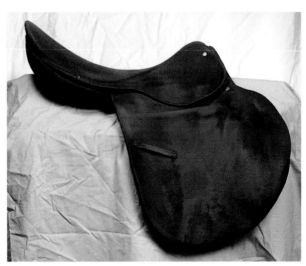

Fig. 112 A Mk1 Toptani covered in doeskin from the Creaton collection. This saddle was owned by John Shedden, winner of the Badminton Horse Trials in 1949 and taken by him to Australia for·use in instructional clinics. (Photo: Mary Herbert)

that would encourage precision riding were not wholly successful, although they were vastly better than what had been built before.

Toptani, impressed by the Distas saddle, sought the help of its designer, Gibson, at a time that was entirely fortuitous for their joint purpose because of the work being done on tree construction by Len Holmes, proprietor of the Walsall Riding Saddle Co. and arguably one of the greatest innovatory influences in Walsall during the past century. Holmes pioneered the Pli-bond tree (developed initially in his garden shed). This was the first laminated, moulded tree and very much lighter than its predecessors. It provided a pattern for subsequent tree construction and it was this spring tree, in a specially adapted form, which formed the basis of Toptani's saddle.

The principle features of the saddle were those which are described in Chapter 17 under the heading Rider Considerations, but Toptani made absolutely sure of positioning the rider in balance for the purposes of jumping by the forward placement of the stirrup bars, a vital feature which had never before been appreciated by either saddle-maker or rider. The conventional hunting saddle was built on a straight-headed

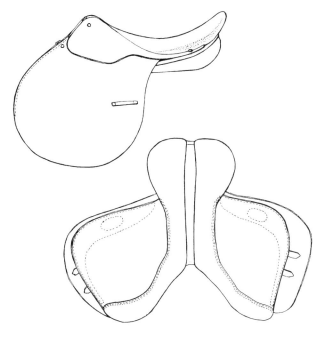

Fig. 113 Outline and panel of Toptani's saddle which was built on a sloped head Pli-bond tree.

tree, that is, the head was vertical. Toptani had the bars positioned further forward by sloping the head at an angle of nearly 45 degrees. By this expedient the points were brought forward and, in consequence, the setting of the bars which were attached to them (see Fig. 139, p.172).

Toptani's saddles fitted snugly to the back allowing the rider to sit in very close contact. In conjunction with the shape of the tree (the long, dipped seat and narrowed waist) it was this important feature that caused the rider's centre of gravity to be lowered, thus increasing the strength of the base. It follows that a heavily stuffed panel, broad in the waist, will act in opposite fashion to raise the rider away from the back, reducing the closeness of contact and the strength of the base.

In furtherance of the principle of close contact, Toptani had his saddle made from leathers of very light substance, a practice at variance with the English tradition of heavy flap leathers of the best quality which were designed to give service over many years and a number of generations. They gave just such a service but only became supple after a correspondingly long period of use. The light flaps of the Toptani saddles were not, of course, so durable but they did allow the leg to lie close to the horse. Sometimes in the normal course of wear and tear they wore so thin that they rumpled, but that was a failing that could be easily remedied by fitting new ones. There were, of course, other saddles made between the Wars that attempted to fulfil the competitive requirement more effectively than did the often flatseated, rigidtree English hunting saddle, which gave little or no support to the rider, and because of its shape and the position of the bars ensured that the weight was more frequently carried behind the movement and the centre of balance than otherwise.

Nonetheless the 'English' saddle, esteemed for its quality, acted as a pattern for a number of European makers and they used it as a base for the development of their own jumping saddles. Pariani, in Milan, produced a jumping saddle early in the century and so did the French and Germans. On the whole, however, the quality of the materials used was poor, particularly in respect of the tree and, of course, the bars were positioned insufficiently forward for jumping.

The first Toptanis had their teething troubles, of course. The girth straps, for instance, largely because of the position dictated by the tree, had a tendency to slide backwards off the sweat flap. This was solved initially by the addition of a 'thigh' roll on the rear edge of the flap. It was a feature copied by other manufacturers and it has persisted to this day, when its presence is no longer relevant either to prevent a backward slipping girth or as a supportive 'thigh' roll, for which purpose it never was of any use at all.

The problem was overcome in the Toptani fairly quickly but the roll was never discarded. There was, too, another difficulty caused not by the design or the saddle's construction but by riders not sufficiently knowledgeable to understand the real purpose of the saddle and its design features. The original Toptani was intended by its designer to be a *showjumping* saddle. This was Toptani's overriding interest, he was not a cross-country rider, much less a hunting man prepared to spend up to five hours or so in the saddle, nor was he much concerned with the niceties of horse management, an omission he shared with more than one otherwise gifted rider. As a jumping saddle the early Toptani pattern was excellent but it was probably in advance of the riding public's limited knowledge of equestrian theory and its even greater ignorance of the latter's relationship to saddle fitting and design. Used as a hunting saddle, as it sometimes was, it was not nearly so good, but then it was neither intended nor designed for that purpose. The narrowed twist (initially very narrow) obviously reduced the bearing surface on the back, a matter that was of little consequence when schooling over fences or competing in the ring, but one that assumed an altogether different complexion when the saddle was in use for protracted periods of time. Additionally, the jumping rider spent little time actually sitting in the saddle, which was not the case with the man out for a day's hunting. When used for the latter purpose, it was possible for the saddle to develop a rock, and move a little forward on the back. This movement combined with the narrow bearing surface at the waist could cause soreness. In later models the failing was largely corrected and, with the less extreme 'general-purpose', or 'all-purpose', saddles based on the original Toptani jumping pattern the problem hardly arose at all. What is undeniable is that Toptani's saddle, copied extensively if not always successfully, altered forever the concept of saddle design and construction and established principles relative to riding theory which, though even now less than completely understood by manufacturers or riders, were to have a profound influence on the development of riding techniques.

In the revised, 1972, edition of the book *Modern Showjumping,* which expounded so well the principles and training methods involved, Toptani wrote '…I do now believe that the modern saddle I introduced to England, and which served as a pattern for many others, was partly instrumental in the great post-war equestrian successes of the British teams in international jumping events, and so were the modern methods expounded in this book'. With the advantage of hindsight that judgement is not far from the mark.

The Toptani is still made in England and, in my view and that of many others, remains pre-eminent as a jumping saddle.

The increasing influence of the German manufacturers, whose saddles are now copied almost slavishly (but not always well) by the Walsall makers has resulted in the loss of some of the prime features of Toptani's design. There is an almost universal use of the cut-back head, a practice that has resulted in the bar being misplaced, at least in respect of the pure jumping saddle. The leathers employed are certainly soft and relatively supple but they are otherwise heavy, whilst the often over-stuffed panels are yet another indication of the trend towards a bulkier article, and away from Toptani's streamlined concept.

On the other hand, the French saddles, although less evident in the market, are excellent in terms of design, construction and materials and the best are, in my view, more attractive and effective pieces of equipment than the general German or Walsall product.

Decline of Walsall and the Consequences

By the early 1960s the Walsall trade was in decline. Changes in social and trading patterns were to blame in part, but its fragmented structure, its inability, or unwillingness, to recognise and respond to change were also factors; while the corroding effect of a general malaise resulted in a deplorable drop in acceptable standards.

Indeed, some twenty years later, *Equestrian Trade News*, the journal of the British equestrian industry was prompted, in an editorial entitled 'Clean Up Walsall', to write of 'disreputable practices and inferior merchandise', a condemnation supported by the 1974 report on saddlery and harness markets compiled by the International Trade Centre.

Inevitably, the loss of Walsall's reputation as a world leader opened the way for outside competition, including a flood of low-quality products from India and Pakistan. In compensation there was, at the other end of the scale, the superbly finished German saddles which were marketed and promoted with skill and vigour. Their influence still remains in the modern British product, which in the twenty-first century has happily regained its standing in the global scenario.

Initially, however, the German saddles were copied, often very badly, in every back-street workshop in Walsall. As a result, some of the prime features of Toptani's saddle were lost.

The cut-back tree is still with us but the wheel has turned and German saddles no longer enjoy their former pre-eminence in Europe and America. They are still well finished and of excellent quality but there have been shortcomings in the trees on which they are built and the design has not kept up with the new developments.

Suffragettes in the Saddle

Much of the incentive for development and for a growing 'awareness' of the importance of the saddle to the performance of horse and rider derives from a unique phenomenon that has to be accounted as a watershed in the long history of saddle construction and usage. In brief, the technical innovations made in the first years of this century that, in essence, acknowledge the indivisible relationship between equestrian theory; equine locomotion, structure and musculature and the design, construction and fitting of the saddle, are largely due to the pragmatic feminist movement of the latter part of the twentieth century.

It is a fact that the majority of the riding public nowadays is female, a situation that has pertained since the end of World War II and perhaps a bit before that. Appreciating the preponderance of female participation in equestrianism it is surprising that so few concessions, if indeed any, had been made in building a female-friendly saddle suited to the conformation of the rider. But then, while lip service was certainly paid to the needs and comfort of the horse, there was very little study by tree- and saddle-makers of equine conformation, locomotion, etc. It would, indeed, be true to say that until recently the nearest the average saddle- and tree-maker came to a horse was when he paid the odd visit to the bookmakers on the corner of the road.

In fairness the suffragettes did not direct their efforts specifically towards the advancement of greater comfort in the saddle for their sex; that came later and to all intents unintentionally. Their concern was with the well-being of the horse and the relief from saddles which inhibited movement and performance and might be the source of dangerous behavioural problems as well.

In pursuit of that end these earnest ladies marketed their theories (*and* products, for most of them had a commercial interest in the saddle's improvement) aggressively, skilfully and with a degree of spin worthy of that practised by New Labour at 10 Downing Street.

A particularly vocal group were the 'Balance group', along with a succession of saddle doctors, flying and otherwise, and even a 'Mother Teresa of the Horse-World', a title bestowed by the author of a particularly uninformed article appearing in a leading Sunday newspaper.

With scant respect for the less articulate dinosaurs of Walsall and the industry in general they were often notably intemperate in their criticism, and sometimes given to exaggeration in support of their argument (it is very unlikely that 75 per cent of all horses, later upped to 95 per cent, suffered from back problems, behavioural traumas, etc. as a result of ill-fitting saddles).

But, they were more often right than otherwise. There were far too many asymmetrical trees and, inevitably, the saddles built on them were unbalanced at the outset. Possibly, the ladies said nothing that had not been known before, but they said it so forcefully that neither trade nor a riding public increasingly aware of the saddle's importance as the 'command centre' underpinning successful riding, had any option but to take notice.

Such saddles did and do restrict the movement, causing compensatory resistances in the horse and, one imagines, a degree of justifiable resentment. Moreover, design to suit the purpose, for both horse and rider was, with notable exceptions, not much in evidence and hardly a concern in the backstreet workshop. (Edward Hopper, a respected luminary of the Walsall trade, was quoted in *Equestrian Trade News* July 2001 as saying, 'If the tree is out of line you haven't a hope of going round corners properly! People will say that horses are not symmetrical, and nor are riders, but placing an asymmetrical tree between them will only compound this.' He was right, of course, but was only repeating a basic precept of saddle fitting that had been appreciated and continually reiterated for over 200 years.)

There is no doubt, too, that the ladies' activities focused attention in unprecedented measure on the design and construction of the saddle, the tree and its essential symmetry and the subsequent fitting to the horse. It encouraged, also, the regular seminars and fitting courses staged by both Britain's Society of Master Saddlers and the increasingly influential British Equestrian Trades' Association.

These initiatives led to recognised examinations for qualified saddle fitters. Serious studies were made of the horse's back structure and movement and the effect of both on the rider's position, weight distribution and so on. Indeed, computer technology, pioneered by a Welsh company, Llwynon Saddlers, developed to reveal accurately the degree of imbalance in any one saddle/rider combination. (A far lesser degree of imbalance is very noticeable in the more effective, educated rider and vice-versa.)

One seat of learning went so far as to promote a study of the female conformation relative to the saddle's construction, but the trade was far ahead of the academics on that one and both trees and saddles had already become female-friendly, a broader tree at the waist being conducive to greater comfort. That such a tree also recognised the preponderance of female riders was, alas, incidental, though, one imagines, nonetheless welcome.

Despite one or two compulsive twitches accompanying the twilight years leading to the demise of the Walsall dinosaurs, Britain now has an official standard governing tree manufacture and, indeed, the craft in the twenty-first century has advanced well into the state of the art parameter.

Between the Wars and for some years after the Second World War the aristocrats of the world saddle-makers were the London houses founded in the late eighteenth and early nineteenth centuries. Firms like Champion and Wilton, Sowter, Whippy and Steigall, Owen and Mayhew had the stature of household names throughout the equestrian world and justifiably so. They had all gone by the late nineteen-sixties and for a while, in the twilight of the old Walsall, names like Kieffer, Passier, Stubben, and to a lesser degree Hèrmes, dominated the market.

With the resurgence of the new, vital Walsall of the twenty-first century there emerged a new aristocracy. Albion was certainly in the forefront, along with Frank Baines, Harry Dabbs, Jeffries, Barnsby, the remarkable Wow product and a handful more, while the synthetic market is led indisputably by the formidable Thorowgood team and the Australian based Wintec Company.

Indeed, while the saddle is still dependant on fine workmanship, it is probable that the modern saddle is a distance ahead of the riders in terms of its advanced technology. That is just as well since the new 'saddle awareness' has its downside. In an increasingly litigious society, spawned of the compensation culture, the saddle and its fitting provides every sort of target for the ignorant, the incompetent, and frequently the unscrupulous, to have recourse to the courts for injuries real or imagined. The new breed of technically advanced saddles, backed by a qualified fitting service and a craftsmanship not exceeded elsewhere in the world, are the best means of refuting the unfounded complaint.

16 Saddle Trees, Construction and Panels

'In the beginning…'

The foundation on which the saddle is built is the *tree*, which will be made of either wood or plastic.

The modem wooden trees are produced from strips of beech laminated in moulds with a urea-formaldehyde resin. The tree is reinforced with either steel or the lighter Duralumin. On the underside of the forearch (also called the head or pommel) a strong *gullet plate* is fitted. This is supported by another strip of metal, the *head plate*, laid on the top of the arch. The two are riveted together to form a structure of great strength which prevents the forearch from spreading in use. The cantle is strengthened with a further metal strip fixed to the underside, whilst the stirrup bars are fastened to the tree with two rivets for each bar.

The majority of modern laminated trees are of the 'spring' type (Fig. 114). A spring tree is so called because of the two sections of spring steel which are laid along the frame from head to cantle. A tree not fitted with these 'springs' is termed a 'rigid' tree, since it lacks the resilience given by the springs (Fig. 114a). Resilience in the seat is, of course, the keynote. The 'give' in the seat certainly increases the rider's comfort, allows a closer and more direct contact through the seat bones and, it could be argued, is more comfortable for the horse, since it gives to the movement of the back in a way that is not possible with a rigid tree.

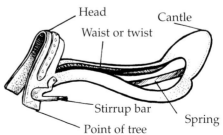

Fig. 114 Parts of the spring tree.

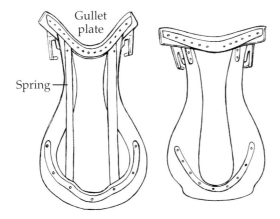

Fig. 114a Left: the spring tree. Right: the older type of rigid tree.

Clearly, a 'spring' seat cannot be incorporated into the moulded polymer trees but the material does have an acceptable degree of resilience and could not be described as 'rigid'.

Crucial to the spring tree is the strength of the spring steel employed. If it is weak it will bend too easily, producing an accentuated dip, and it may become further distorted as the saddle seat is fitted. However, it is rare to find modern spring trees, with the possible exception of the occasional import, that are unsatisfactory in this respect.

Stirrup Bars

Bars are made from either forged or cast steel, the former being considered to have greater strength. In fact, it is very rare indeed that a bar will break, although at one time, with saddles of Asian manufacture, there was a regrettable tendency for the rivets attaching the bar to the tree to shear off under pressure. Bars are usually stamped either 'forged' or 'cast' according to the method of manufacture.

The most common pattern is that fitted with a 'thumbpiece' or 'safety catch' and it has been with us for a very long time (Fig. 115). It was intended that the catch should be in the 'up' position so that the stirrup leather would not slide off the bar during movement. In the event of the rider falling the catch would be snapped open to release the leather, thus preventing the unfortunate horseman from being dragged.

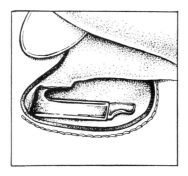

Fig. 115 The conventional and now controversial 'safety' stirrup bar with the catch, or 'thumbpiece', in the open position. The bar is 'inset' to eliminate bulk under the thigh.

A century ago the design of saddles was such that there probably was a need for a bar of this sort. The saddles of that day had the bars set very well clear of the tree. Furthermore, they were attached horizontally to the tree and not at the slight angle which is usual in modern saddles. As a result, it was possible for the leather to slip off unless it was prevented from doing so by a catch of this sort. It was, of course, necessary for the catch mechanism to be oiled frequently if it was to open easily in an emergency, but labour was plentiful and one suspects that the catches were far better made than those on our modern bars.

Today, however, the so-called safety catch is an anachronism and even a potential danger, since its very presence might encourage its use by novice riders. The angle of the bar on modern saddles is sufficient to prevent the inadvertent loss of a stirrup leather and indeed most, if not all, catches can only be operated with some difficulty. Once the mechanism has become corroded this becomes nearly impossible.

Furthermore, for as long as I can remember, the manuals and the equestrian organisations have urged that the catch should never be used in the closed position and that is the recognised practice throughout Britain.

The consumer is surely entitled to ask why on earth this type of bar is employed so generally, particularly since its construction adds unnecessarily to the cost of the saddle. It could be, of course, that the barmaker continues to be resistant to change because he finds this pattern to be more profitable than a simpler, more practical and cheaper one. A bar which *is* simple, practical and cheap is Christie's pattern, a hook-shaped bar with the end of the hook turned slightly outwards. It has been about for almost as long as the safety-catch type but has never become popular, even though it is fitted to that most practical of saddles, the Australian stock pattern, used by the world's most down-to-earth horsemen. Interestingly, it is employed almost exclusively on fabric or synthetic saddles, but they, of course, originated in Australia and the synthetic manufacturers in Britain are among the most forward-looking in Europe.

Adjustable Bars

The position of the stirrup bar has a lot to do with the position adopted by the rider, and since the human being, like the horse, comes in all shapes and sizes, a fixed bar, particularly one which is badly positioned in relation to the head and the line of the flap, is a drawback of considerable proportions. The increase in the popularity of dressage, when the leg position can be crucial to the rider's performance, drew attention to the inadequacies of the fixed bar (largely, I think, because a great many dressage saddles were fitted with general-purpose bars instead of the extended bar which is an obligatory fitting on the normal dressage saddle; even some of the best German patterns had this design fault).

As a result, tentative efforts were made to introduce an adjustable bar that would allow the rider to determine the position of the stirrup leather precisely to accord to his individual requirement. On the whole these early bars were heavy and clumsy, but in very recent years great

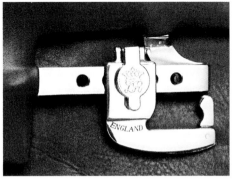

Fig. 116 The adjustable bars patented by Lovatt and Rickets and used extensively by their Arabian Saddle Co. (a) three-hole bar; (b) five-hole bar. (Photo courtesy Arabian Saddle Co.)

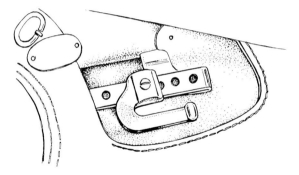

Fig. 117 The neat Wellep adjustable bar which not only meets the needs of safety but allows the stirrup to be placed precisely according to the rider's requirement.

improvements have been made. The Wellep bar (Fig. 117), a simple device allowing for five positions, is probably the best available and it is fitted in increasing numbers not only to dressage saddles but to general-purpose ones also.

The Adjustable Tree

A tree, or saddle, that is capable of adjustment to suit a variety of back shapes has been the concern of the corporate equestrian mind for a very long time. There have, it is true, been periods when tree- and saddle-makers have found it convenient to ignore the basic requirements of saddle fitting and when a variety of pads, numnahs and so on, were used to support the regulation (flocking) of the panel to get the saddle to conform, if only to a degree, to the constantly changing outline of the equine back. Those days are gone and there is general recognition of the fact that the outline of the back and the covering muscle structure alter according to the pertaining circumstance. Clearly, the back of a fat animal brought up from grass early in the year will bear little resemblance to that of the same animal after a hard season's hunting or a period of intensive schooling. (Using a modern, adjustable tree on my three-quarter bred hunter mare, I narrowed the fitting by 2.2 cm (⅞ in) in a six-week conditioning period between mid-August and October.)

At the end of the nineteenth century the British Army was much concerned in the design of a saddle that would meet the democratic ideal of the greatest good for the greatest number, and it was not unsuccessful. The Austrian army, with its background of Hungarian light cavalryman, was in the forefront with an officer's pattern jointed saddle tree adjustable to either a broad or narrow back. Nolan's first saddle (Louis Nolan of Crimea fame) used a stripped tree and a thick felt saddle-cloth or numnah. It led, via the 1890 pattern British Universal saddle, to the simplified 1902 pattern and then to the 1912 pattern which had, for a time, pivoting side-bars to permit universal fitting to any size of horse. In its essentials the Army Universal 1912 is the saddle used today throughout the world by military and police forces. (So why is it not in general civilian use also? In a word, it is not a saddle suitable to the modern requirement since, among other things, it does not allow any degree of contact between the rider and his horse, perching the former some inches above the back.)

The American cavalry produced its own version of the Hungarian saddle, the McClellan. It was introduced to the American mounted arm by the future General George B. McClellan, a brilliant administrator although an indecisive soldier, who had been sent to the Crimea as an observer and had been influenced by Nolan's work.

McClellan's saddle differed from the basic Hungarian pattern only in respect of detail and the addition of Western style stirrups and cinches. It consisted of two arches joined by padded side-bars, the seat being a piece of rawhide stretched between the former, and it was worn over a blanket. It was light, very uncomfortable and not suited to novice riders, but then the American troopers were far better practical horsemen than their European counterparts, other than the Hungarians. It does not seem to have been particularly adjustable other than through the flocking of the pads and the folding of the blanket but it remained in service up to 1940.

A popular saddle, between the Wars, was one employing what was termed a Wykeham panel and, within its limitations, it was a practical solution to the changing back outlines. The panel was composed of felt, so shaped and fitted that pieces could be removed or added in order to meet the altered back conformation.

Today, an inflatable panel has been devised to fulfil the same purpose (see p.160) and in the late 1980s the Wellep company introduced a head plate that could be easily adjusted to fit a whole variety of back structures. This precision-engineered plate was described as being 'infinitely variable'. For the present it does not seem to be generally available but it

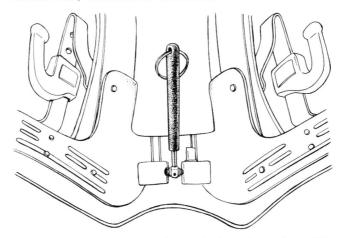

Fig. 118 The Wellep adjustable head plate allows the saddle to be fitted with considerable accuracy to a variety of back structures.

acted as a catalyst for the production of a range of adjustable head plates – the industry, one might say, had got the message, if only in part, for there remained the problem, often unrecognised, of the asymmetrical tree, discussed later in this chapter. (One might be forgiven for thinking that it took an unconscionable time for the message to get through. In the last half of the nineteenth century a number of 'adjustable' patents were registered and at least one inflatable panel.)

In 2004 Albion Saddlemakers of Walsall introduced the space-age concept of the saddle tree, a product involving saddle-makers, computer programmers, aeronautical engineers and one or two riders who, in modern parlance, could get their heads around so complex a construction. In essence this was a tri-form tree with interchangeable heads in five fittings, three seat sizes and three styles of cantle. Central to its success was the precision engineering which allowed for *the assembly of any combination in a matter of minutes and at any time in the life of the completed saddle.*

Once more, this was a catalyst for the further development of adjustable trees. It encouraged a new awareness' among manufacturers of the importance of saddles that could be tailored to the horse's physical condition at any one time and amounted to an acknowledgement of the saddle's role in the performance of horse and rider and, perhaps, a vindication of the Balance Girls, Mother Teresa and the saddle doctors, whose zeal was described in the previous chapter.

In the field of moulded polymer trees, the Thorowgood company, leaders in the production of synthetic saddles, expanded their range of fittings to cover five back formations between narrow and XX wide with longitudinal profiles of withers to match. As an additional means of fine-tuning the fitting they also produce 'Fish' inserts that could be slipped easily into the panel to accommodate weight fluctuations. All a far cry from the traditional front arch fittings of narrow, medium and broad.

More recently, a mechanical device has come on the market with which a polymer tree can be both broadened and made narrower to suit changing back conformations or, indeed, to accommodate a new equine purchase with a different back structure from his predecessor. Apart from driving a coach and horses through the B.S.I. standard, which stipulates that the tree size has to be clearly displayed for the express purpose of preventing the fitting of the headpiece being altered, this device has its drawbacks. It can only be used effectively on polymer trees and then, one would imagine, by a skilled operator. Additionally, there is a real possibility of the tree becoming asymmetrical and, when made broader, of the side-bars moving closer together at the waist of the tree, and thus being more disposed to pinch in that area.

Shapes and Sizes

The principal difference in tree patterns is concerned with the head, or forearch. The head may be *straight* (i.e. vertical in relation to the side-bars); *sloped* as in the Toptani and others or as in the present fashion, *cut-back*. In this last instance, the head is either quarter, half or full cut-back. American show saddles are fully cut-back, being called Lane-Fox or by the less patrician but more descriptive term, 'cow-mouth'.

The cut-back head, an endemic condition to the German saddle, is considered to fit a greater range of back structures and is supposed to be the more suitable construction for the accommodation of high, knifey withers. There are advantages, but the cut-back head can cause difficulty with jumping saddles by not allowing the bar to be positioned sufficiently far forward. It is certainly not a suitable design for horses with a rounder formation of the withers, like the Arab and most cob types, who are better off with a straight head or with one slightly sloped. (The Arabian Saddle Co., part of the Lovatt and Rickets organisation, initially used a straight head tree, which had its origins in the conventional polo tree used between the two World Wars. However, it now employs a specially built quarter cut-back in its saddles.)

Size is important for reasons discussed in Chapter 17 Saddle Fitting. Trees range in length between 38–46 cm (15–18 ins) in 1.25 cm (½ in) steps with seat widths to correspond. The measurement is taken from the centre of the head to the cantle or in the case of a cut-back from the saddle-nail on the pommel to the cantle.

Standards and Symmetry

In Britain standards and specifications are those formulated by the British Standards Institution. They cover all aspects of manufacture including materials and give much emphasis to symmetry, a matter that was inexplicably neglected by some tree-makers and saddle-makers for a period before the implementation of the B.S.I. standards.

It is not difficult to understand that a tree made out of true, that rocks when placed on a level surface, ensures that the saddle subsequently made on so faulty a foundation will reflect the manufacturing error and be out of balance on the back. Saddle-makers, some of whom should have known better, held that the saddler could compensate for the imbalance by adding additional flocking to one side of the panel, rather like putting a wad of paper under the leg of a wobbling table. (Twenty-five years ago when judging exhibits at an early equestrian trade fair I found a number of asymmetrical saddles and said so. I was accused of being hyper-critical. At today's B.E.T.A. (British Equestrian Trades' Association) International Fair it would be very difficult to find even one such saddle.)

Preparing the Tree

The manufacture of the conventional saddle built on a laminated tree begins when the saddle-maker takes delivery of the finished tree, i.e. one covered with the protective, waterproof scrim. He has then to *prepare* the tree before the seat can be set on it. There are two stages to the process: first, the *points*, the projections of the forearch below the stirrup bars, must be enclosed in an oval leather pocket to create a 'flexible' pointending that allows for minor differences in the shape of the back and so adds a little to the available range of fitting. Secondly, the springs have to be covered in light leather to prevent their sharp edges cutting into the finished

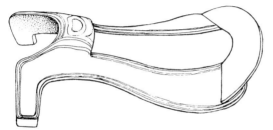

Fig. 119 A laminated cut-back tree in the early process of manufacture.

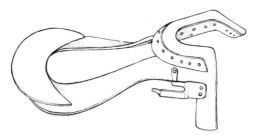

Fig. 120 The tree with the bars, gullet and head plate fitted. At least one company uses separate moulds for the head, side bars and cantle.

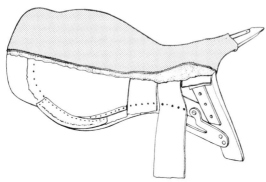

Fig. 121 A seat built in the traditional manner – a painstaking, labour-intensive operation demanding great skill and experience. Very few modern saddles are constructed in this way because of the prohibitive cost involved.

panel and to prevent any corrosion occurring as the result of moisture.

To provide a base on which the seat can be built, pre-stretched canvas webs are laid on the tree from head to cantle. They are fixed with *tingles*, small tacks driven through a strip of leather which will act as a washer.

The girth strap webs are then put on over the waist or twist of the tree and over the seat webs, being secured to the tree bars in similar fashion. The third, forward girth strap, where one is included, is stitched to a separate web passed over the tree or doubled round each bar. *(Nylon web is used increasingly because of its great strength, and some saddles also use nylon girth straps rather than the rawhide or helvetia-type leather straps. The reason for fitting three girth straps to a saddle when a two-buckle girth is employed is discussed in the following chapter and so is the more up-to-date self-adjusting girthing system relying on two straps attached to an independent metal slide.)*

Traditionally the seat webs were covered with a tightly stretched piece of canvas on the edges of which were fixed small crescent-shaped pieces of leather called the *bellies*. Their purpose was to produce a level surface so that the seat did not fall away at the edges and allow the rider to sit on the hard edges of the tree bars.

Thereafter, the seat was built up painstakingly by covering the canvas with a stretched serge cloth stitched down to form the seat shape. Through a small slit in the centre of the serge a wool padding could be inserted, the wool being pushed in with a 'seat steel', a thin, shaped metal rod, and then levelled out with a twinpronged 'awl' that could be pushed through the serge itself.

It was a highly skilled, time-consuming task which would now be cost-prohibitive. Today's saddles have moulded seats of latex or some other form of resilient plastic and they are satisfactory enough – at least in the short-term.

The seat is finished by the leather, of whatever sort, being blocked on and secured to the tree; the skirts, which lie over the bars, being welted to the seat leather.

The skirts, like the flaps, are cut in a press, and the latter are attached once the seat, skirts, etc. are finished. The edges of the leather are chamfered smooth and stained to match or contrast with the overall colour. A cosmetic touch can be added by stitching round the edges of both flaps and skirts but, of course, it is irrelevant to the saddle's purpose and adds to the cost.

The final stage of assembly is the fitting of the panel and the under- or sweat-flap. Pockets are stitched to the underside of the panel to accommodate the points of the tree (they are known as 'point pockets') and then the panel is secured to the tree at the forearch and round the seat. The panel used to be stitched by hand to the tree but modern production methods use a staple gun for that purpose. It is quicker and more efficient in terms of cost-effectiveness.

Panels

In essence, the panel forms a resilient cushion between the tree and the horse's back and with the wool-stuffed panel, for instance, offers a way of adjusting the fit to an individual idiosyncrasy. A stuffed panel is, indeed, a cushion, being a leather cover filled with wool, the two parts being divided by a channel to give clearance to the horse's backbone. In fact, up to thirty years ago the panels were not necessarily, or always, covered with leather ('panel' hide) as they generally are today. Many panels were faced with the usual thin leather on the underside, i.e. that next to the tree, whilst the outer covering was of a thick wool serge.

A serge-lined saddle had its drawbacks. It would absorb sweat, which in time permeated through the wool stuffing and formed hard balls, and it could become impossibly dirty. To keep a serge panel in working order it was necessary to brush it with a stiff brush when dry (it was impossible to wash because the water would pass through into the wool so easily). It was then necessary to beat it with a stick to prevent the formation of lumps. The advantage of the serge-lined panel was the ease with which the wool could be adjusted to ensure an accurate fitting, but that, of course, was when most saddlery establishments had competent working saddlers on the premises. To save the serge from the ravages of sweat and grease the panels were often overcovered with a strong linen. It could then be scrubbed clean but the facility to adjust the wool flocking without taking the whole panel out was lost. *(Recently a leading Walsall manufacturer of dressage saddles has returned to using a heavy serge cloth for his panel linings and seems to feel that the specific advantages to be obtained in terms of fitting, resilience and so on outweigh the drawbacks.)*

The wool used was once merino wool, which was springy and not too easily compressed. Modern flocking, one suspects, is not always merino and the stuff used in many of the Asian-made saddles, as well as some others, is not really of the quality needed to produce a good panel.

A panel has to be stuffed with great accuracy if it is to be level on both sides of the channel and evenly flocked throughout the bearing surface. It has also to be firm whilst retaining a degree of resilience. *(Given that the panel meets these criteria and that one has access to a skilled saddler able to make whatever adjustments are required, the stuffed panel is entirely satisfactory. However, it should be remembered that the panel of a new saddle will bed down, as it were, within a couple of months of purchase. It should then be returned to the saddler to make the regulation that is necessary.)*

A very successful type of panel, particularly when used with a tree employing an adjustable head plate, is one made from felt covered with leather or, preferably, from alternate layers of felt and shock-absorbent latex which will increase the resilience. Such a panel ensures a close fit and close contact for the rider. It cannot flatten or lose resilience like a stuffed panel but, of course, the ability to adjust to a particular back formation is more limited, though not entirely precluded.

We are beginning now to see the introduction of a moulded foam panel which, once the cost of the moulds has been covered, is more economical and saves time and labour. This sort of panel construction retains its shape and resilience, never becomes uneven and is thought to absorb pressure from the rider's weight more effectively – and that is probably true. *(Although I write of the introduction of a moulded panel, it is, in fact, a reintroduction. I have a lightweight 3.18 kg [7 lb] jumping saddle made with a polystyrene panel which has occupied a place in my tack room since 1965. Whilst prophesy is a dangerous practice with a habit of rebounding uncomfortably upon the prophet, I would foresee a greatly increased use of the moulded panel within the next decade.)*

Panel Types

(The following passage is reproduced almost exactly as it appeared in the 1963 edition of Saddlery.)

There are four distinct shapes which the panel can take: full panel, short panel, Saumur panel and continental panel (Fig. 122). Individual saddlers may vary slightly in the way they make the last two, and may even call them by different names from those I have given, but this is not important; basically all shapes will be found to correspond with these four.

These panel shapes evolved in the order I have placed them. The full panel is the oldest and is still in use in a somewhat slimmer form in some patterns of European and South American saddles; properly made with the quilted part kept thin, and with a slight roll for the knee, it is quite good and the large area of bearing surface it affords to the back is excellent from the horse's viewpoint.

Its disadvantage lies in the fact that, should the quilted part be thick, the rider has little contact with the horse and the wide bearing surface at the waist of the saddle will open his thighs. Early saddles (early and mid-nineteenth century) were certainly enormous affairs in which a modern horseman would feel very far away from the horse, and undoubtedly the advent of polo was instrumental in cutting away the bottom of the full panel to make a short one (sometimes known as a Rugby panel or even Whippy panel, after the firm who used it so frequently). With this it was possible for the legs to be in close contact, although there was, of course, no support by way of a roll.

As the tree's shape was gradually altered, becoming a little deeper in the seat to comply with changing trends in equitation which involved the shifting of the rider's weight away from the rear and forward so that he was as nearly as possible over the centre of the horse's centre of balance, so the Saumur and Continental type of panel came into being.

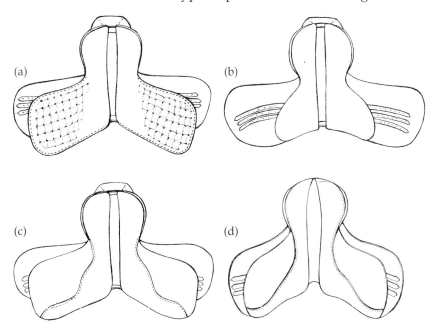

Fig. 122 The four panel types: (a) full panel; (b) short or Rugby panel; (c) Saumur-type; (d) 'Continental'.

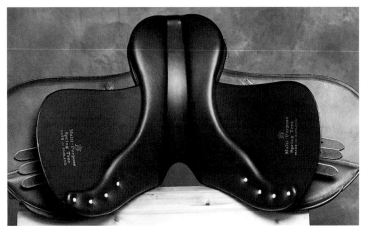

Fig.123 The attractive Saumur-type panel built of felt with a latex overlay. (Photo: author's)

Fig. 124 A stuffed 'Continental'-type panel providing substantial support for the thigh. (Photo: author's)

The Saumur, originating at the French equitation school, was narrower in the waist to allow the rider closer contact whilst still giving a relatively broad bearing surface at this crucial point. It had an extension to the panel to afford support for the knee, and usually an additional roll placed on the outside of the panel under the flap. The whole panel was, of course, cut much further forward.

   The Continental panel is similar, but with an even narrower waist and the addition of a thigh roll at the rear. In construction it closely resembles the older type of full panel very much fined down. The thigh roll is rarely evident to the rider unless it is very heavily stuffed, and its real use is to prevent the girth straps moving back off the flap. The construction of the modern tree is such that the girth straps do occasionally tend to move to the rear, a tendency that can usually be cured by regulating the stuffing of the panel to allow the head of the saddle to fit lower (without of course touching the withers) and slightly raising the rear of the saddle. *(The use of the self-adjusting girth slide, discussed more fully in the following chapter, obviates almost entirely the problem of girth straps slipping backwards. In fact, very few of the modern saddle patterns, almost all of which employ a cut-back head, exhibit this failing. It was, indeed, the practice to regulate the panel in the manner described to counter the problem and there is no doubt that it provided*

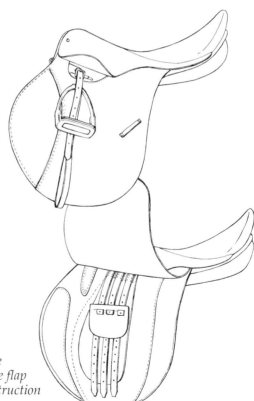

Fig. 125 The modern saddle showing the inset bar, suede flap insert and (below) the construction of the panel.

a solution, so long as the regulation was carried out by an expert. However, there was always a danger of tipping the rider too much to the front, causing the weight to be concentrated over the waist of the saddle and running the risk of damaging the horse's back.)

Occasionally with the modern dip-seated saddles and particularly with dressage saddles (Fig. 141, p.177), where the tree is sometimes relatively short, the panel of the saddle at the rear will have an inserted gusset. This allows a greater amount of stuffing to be inserted and is intended to give a bearing surface along the whole length of the panel. I call this gusset a Melbourne facing, or sometimes a German panel, but there are doubtless other names as well.

Of these types, the full panel and the short one are usually confined to the older type of saddle employing a flatter, broader tree of rigid construction, and to children's saddles. The other two will practically always be made in conjunction with a dipped tree, usually, but not always, of the spring variety. *(At the present, the Danloux panel pattern is enjoying a revival. In brief it incorporates on the sweat flap a stuffed leather squab to give support to the upper thigh and a similar squab placed to the rear, behind the crook of the*

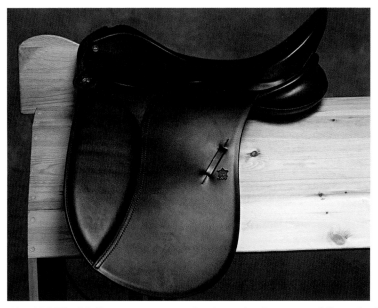

Fig. 126 The Melbourne gusset endemic to the German saddle and others. (Photo courtesy Arabian Saddle Co.)

knee, or lower, which secures the leg position. The arrangement leaves the rider's knee free from the influence of the conventional 'knee' roll. Commandant Danloux of Saumur was one of the greatest of the French horsemen in the period between the World Wars.

My personal preference is for the Saumur panel of felt/latex fitted to a slightly dipped spring tree. It provides an excellent bearing surface on the back and gives the rider the closest possible contact with his horse.)

The Modern Synthetic

While saddle development in the years immediately spanning the Millennium was replete with technological advances that would have been unimaginable in the 1970s and 80s, the success story of the industry during that period was the establishment and acceptance of the synthetic saddle as a significant element in saddle manufacture and as a powerful force in bulk marketing.

The concept of a saddle using man-made materials that was waterproof, required minimal attention and could be constructed on a semi-production line basis belongs to the Australian-based Wintec company, which is still very much in business.

Fig.127 This is the synthetic answer to the broad-backed cob-type animal who has come into fashion for general riding in recent years. It is broad enough to fit a roly-poly conformation and is available in three wide fittings. Fine tuning of the fit is possible with the help of the 'Fish' system of easy fit inserts. (Photo courtesy Thorowgood Ltd)

In the early 1990s the New Zealander Peter Thorowgood was also making synthetics on polymer trees and in a variety of patterns in Walsall – very much the lion's den of the industry. In 1993 Thorowgood's was acquired by the Hon. Rupert Fairfax LVO, an unlikely and perhaps even surprising addition to the traditional world of the Walsall saddle manufacture. A year later Fairfax became Thorowgood's Managing Director and took the firm to a modern building on the outskirts of the town.

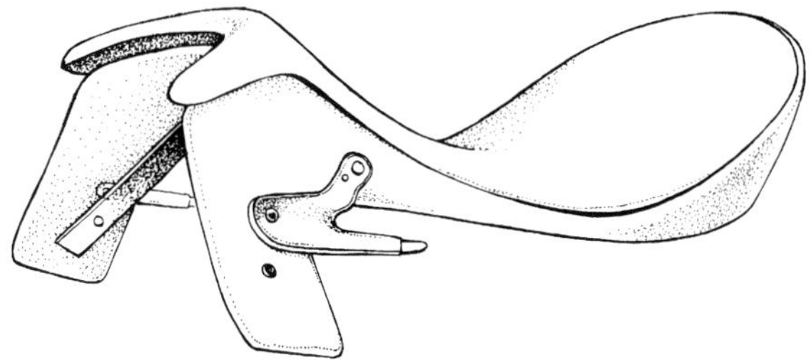

Fig. 128 The modern, 'two-way flexible' moulded synthetic tree with the foam seat in positon.

Rupert Fairfax's background is not one easily associated with running a saddle-manufacturing company on a West Midlands industrial estate. It is, one might think, more appropriate to the Brigade of Guards, the Foreign Office or a lucrative post in the City. But Fairfax brought to the industry a business expertise unrivalled in the manufacture of equestrian equipment and was, moreover, a more than competent horseman. A member of one of Britain's oldest titled families, his ancestor Thomas Fairfax was created Baron Fairfax of Cameron in 1627. His grandson, the third Lord Fairfax (1612–1671), was Cromwell's commander-in-chief of the Parliamentary Army, remodelling it into the New Model Army. Rupert Fairfax's elder brother is the fourteenth holder of the title.

Educated at Eton, Rupert Fairfax completed his studies in economics and modern languages at Madrid, Paris, Washington and Lee University, Virginia, USA.

He became one of Hanson's 'young men', working as a Marketing Manager and then as Operations Manager for Hanson Properties. From Hanson plc he was seconded to the office of H.R.H. The Prince of Wales as assistant private secretary, being much concerned with the Prince's Youth Business Trust and Business in the Community.

Leaving the Prince in 1988 he went into management consultancy and in this interim period indulged his love for polo, a passion shared with his former employer, and at one time had a string of twenty ponies, including his purchase of the whole Chilean team.

Giving up polo for Thorowgood's he appointed Vanessa Roberts, a Loughborough graduate and a successful showjumper, who is now his wife, to co-ordinate sales and design. Within a short time an adjacent factory had been acquired for the manufacture of the company's Sima-Tree on which all Thorowgood saddles are built and Thorowgood's had also taken over Prolite for the manufacture of numnahs, pads and protective boots.

Production of saddles is in excess of 100 a day and exports are made to over 60 countries.

Modern synthetic saddles are entirely symmetrical, waterproof, non-slip and superior in wearing properties to anything other than the best quality leather saddle. The finish is excellent and the latest model on the market is to all intents indistinguishable from leather.

Racing saddles, either for the flat or over fences, are almost entirely synthetic and are in every way superior to the conventional article – with the exception of the now extinct Australian Bosca of hallowed memory, which was made from kangaroo hide and was, in its day, the best race saddle in the world.

Fig. 129 The top of the range general-purpose synthetic saddle is indistinguishable from the finest leather saddles. It employs a four-strap girth system to ensure stability and is, of course, adjustable. With these saddles, saddle soap becomes a thing of the past. (Photo courtesy Thorowgood Ltd)

The principal advantages of the synthetic or fabric saddle are:

 a. Good design.
 b. Wide range of fittings, including a broad, cob range and an effective adjustability system.
 c. Lightweight, usually no more than 2.7 kg (6 lb)
 d. Instant comfort/ good adhesion.
 f. Easy maintenance and wash-down cleaning.
 g. Price. About one-third the price of a good quality leather saddle and often half the cost of a run-of-the-mill product.

Ride on Air

In the last half of the nineteenth century patent registrations were just as numerous as they are today, and far more so in the field of saddlery and harness. Even then, there were numerous 'adjustable' saddle trees, forerunners of the high-tech saddlery of our own century, and at least one registration for 'the usual padding' to be replaced by pads 'filled with compressed air', the 'india-rubber air chambers' being 'inflated by means of valves'. (E.P.A Villette of Lille, France.)

A French inflatable saddle panel was actually in production briefly in the 1970s but seems to have been more than usually subject to punctures and air-loss via the valves. It was not until the turn of the twenty/twenty-first centuries that the principle, and the product, became firmly established with the Flair and Korrector systems of First Thought (Equine) Ltd, which also produced the startlingly futuristic Wow saddle that incorporated Flair panels in the design.

The Flair system, along with the market acceptance of the synthetic saddle, does, indeed, deserve recognition as a landmark in saddle development. Many problems in training, particularly those concerned with the horse's action, can be traced to discomfort caused by the pressure of the saddle. The Flair air-bags inserted into the panel of the saddle reduce the pressure per square inch by a little under one-third and increase the panel's overall bearing surface in consequence.

Clearly, too, the system can be used to compensate for a rider's natural imbalance. Everyone distributes their weight unevenly when sitting in the saddle, the extent of the imbalance being noticeably less in the instance of the educated rider and conversely greater in the case of the novice.

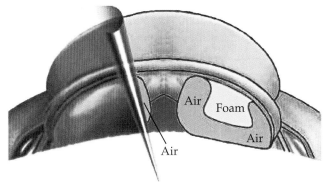

Fig.130 Cross-section of the innovatory Flair panel composed of four air-bags, two at the front and two at the rear. The air-bags can be fitted to any type of saddle. (Photo courtesy First Thought (Equine) Ltd)

(a)   (b)   (c)

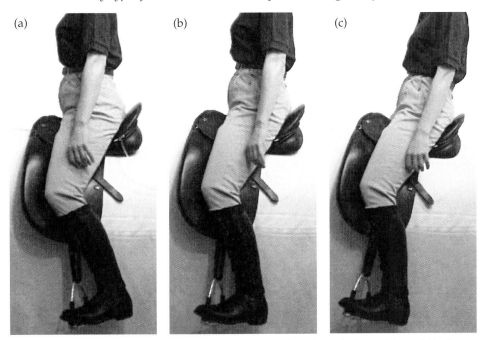

Fig.131 The Flair saddle can be adjusted to the rider's position while the latter is mounted and the horse is in movement:
(a) shows rider tipped on the fork
(b) shows rider upright and correctly positioned
(c) shows rider behind the movement.
(Photos courtesy First Thought (Equine) Ltd)

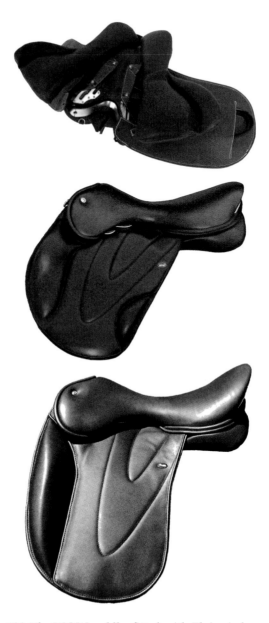

Fig. 132 The WOW saddle, fitted with Flair air-bags, with adjustable, flexible carbon-fibre tree. Flaps, seat designs and knee blocks are all interchangeable. (Photo courtesy First Thought (Equine) Ltd)

The four air-bags that comprise the Flair system can be built into any existing panel, whatever the type of saddle. Two bags are fitted at the front of the panel and two at the rear, the air content being controlled by two valves inset under the saddle skirt.

The Korrector is an independent pad using the same air and foam technology and is adjustable to fit more than one horse as well, of course, so as to correct the rider's imbalance. It is discussed in the section on numnahs in the next chapter.

17   Saddle Fitting

'Our withers are unwrung…'

Well over a century ago the principles of saddle fitting were expounded in detail and with great lucidity by a small group of cavalry reformers. These were professional soldiers, mostly British and often serving as mercenaries in the armies of mainland Europe. Among them was Louis Nolan, the officer who carried the order that resulted in the disastrous charge of the Light Brigade at Balaclava in 1854 and who was killed as the action began. Nolan, one of the most innovative thinkers of his time, was responsible for the design of the Army Universal Pattern (U.P.) saddle (Fig. 134) which is still used today by cavalry and police forces throughout the world.

Nolan's early designs involved the use of a stripped tree placed on a thick felt cloth and may have included a prototype of the later Wykeham panel. Another of the cavalry gurus, and probably the most famous, was Francis Dwyer, who came from an Anglo-Irish family and served as a major of hussars in the Imperial Austrian Service, in which Nolan had begun his career.

Nolan had been influenced by the Hungarian saddle which Dwyer adapted and on which he based his theories of saddle fitting, expounded so lucidly in his book, *Seat and Saddles, Bits and Bitting, Draught and Harness*, particularly in the expanded edition of 1869.

The Hungarian saddle was composed of two wooden bars, the angle of which could be adjusted according to the conformation and condition of the back. Between wooden arches at front and rear was stretched a 'bearing strap' laced to the bars on either side, the whole being covered with a piece of canvas. By adjusting the lacing of the seat it was possible to place the individual trooper over *'the centre of motion of the horse's body'*, where he would be the least possible encumbrance to the horse's balance and action. Dwyer calculated the centre as being over the 14th vertebra, the only one standing upright and which he regarded as the 'keystone of the arch'. (Very few modern saddles can position the rider with so little expenditure of effort with such accuracy.)

To assist the rider further in maintaining a central balance, Dwyer placed the stirrups directly under the rider, making it difficult for him to fall off sideways. 'The saddle in the centre of the back, the girths, stirrups and rider in the centre of the saddle'.

Dwyer's Hungarian saddle dispensed with the heavy flap between the horse and the rider's leg, allowing in Dwyer's words for 'the leg to be wrapped round the horse and in contact with two-thirds of its length'.

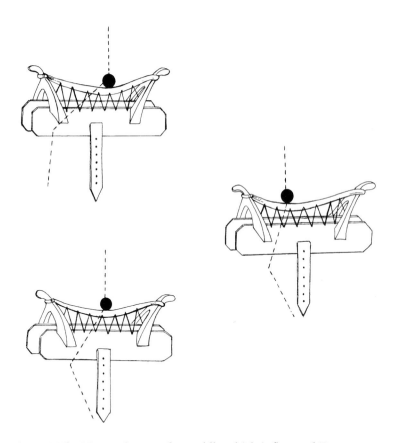

Fig. 133 The Hungarian cavalry saddle which influenced Dwyer, Nolan and McClellan could be adjusted to place the trooper over 'the centre of motion of the horse's body'. It was, perhaps, a prototype for the Flair adjustable panel of the twenty-first century.

One hundred and fifty years later, no riding manual puts it more succinctly than that. (Interestingly, the efforts of Nolan and Dwyer were against the background of poor management, much of which was concerned with the incidence of back injuries, in cavalry formations. At the battle of Solferino in 1859 the French cavalry could only field 3,500 horses fit enough for action out of a total complement of 10,206, while within two months of the action at Balaclava in 1854 the British cavalry had lost 1,800 of its 2,000 surviving horses. It was even worse after the South African War (the Boer War). Between 1899 and 1902 the British lost 326,000 horses out of 494,000. In fairness, the British learned their lesson and up to World War II the cavalry regiments maintained impeccable standards. In World War I British cavalry alone remained operational throughout while their French and German counterparts were rendered impotent for most of the time by equine casualties caused by poor management, much of it concerned with back injuries.)

When the British War Office published the manual *Animal Management, 1933*, the recommendations relative to the fitting and maintenance of saddles were based quite firmly on the principles established in the previous century.

Those principles, whatever the pattern of saddle employed, remain entirely relevant to this day, although in our own century they are not nearly so well understood nor, in consequence, are they put into practice as they should be.

A properly fitted saddle is one that is constructed so that when the rider is in position it:

a. Conforms to the shape of the individual horse's back.
b. Avoids the possibility of damaging any part of the back with which it comes into contact.
c. Affords complete comfort in respect of the manner in which the rider's weight is distributed over the bearing surfaces.
d. Does not restrict the potential for natural movement.

These are basic requirements and they are clearly interdependent. However, they are unlikely to be met fully unless the saddler fitting the saddle, and the horse-owner, has some knowledge of equine conformation and, particularly, of the back structure for which the saddle is intended.

The authors of *Animal Management, 1933* went further. They stated unequivocally that 'a sound scheme for the prevention of injuries…can

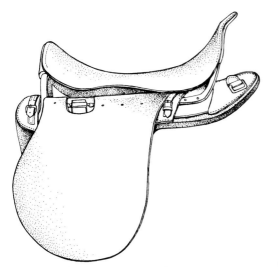

Fig. 134 The army Universal Pattern saddle pioneered by Louis Nolan.

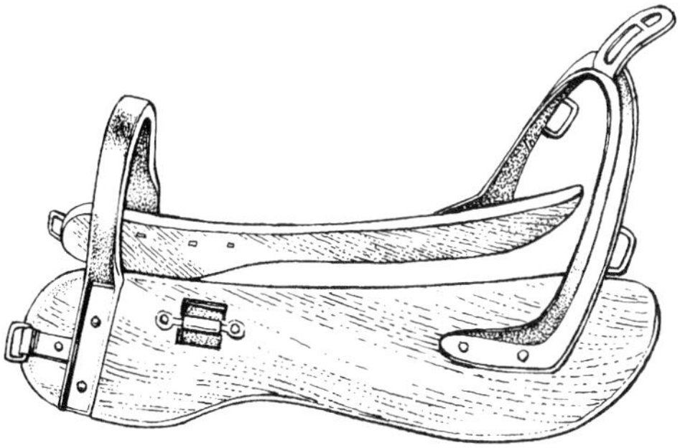

Fig. 135 The simple, robust tree of the Army Universal ensured maximum weight distribution over the bearing surface and freedom for the spinal complex. Note the fixed stirrup bar – what would the safety lobby say about that?

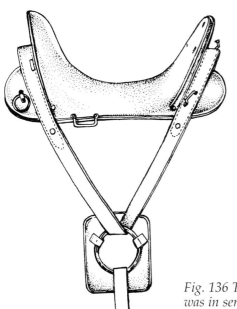

Fig. 136 The American McClellan saddle which was in service with the U.S. Army up to 1940. It was based on the Hungarian pattern, probably the ultimate light cavalry saddle.

only be laid down by a knowledge of the structure of the parts. *All else is guesswork'*.

Nonetheless, they showed their natural frustration with a task that by its nature defies a precise solution in this rueful observation: 'In the ordinary course of things, it was not intended that horses should carry a weight or pull a load, or some special protection would have been given them, whereas the structure of the back is such that it lends itself to injury, and invites trouble by its very peculiarity and delicacy of its organisation'.

It all amounts to successful saddle fitting being dependent as much on the conformation of the horse as anything else. No saddle, however good, will compensate for serious conformational defects.

For the purpose of saddle fitting, the back extends from behind the scapula to the last rib and it follows that any departure from the desirable norm in this area will make the job of fitting the saddle so that it meets the necessary requirements much more difficult.

The well-made riding horse has fairly prominent withers adequately covered with muscle. High, very fine-withered conformation is less satisfactory, rarely carrying much muscle and thus complicating the overall fit of the saddle. Low, flat-withered conformation is similarly unhelpful and is usually associated with the additional problem of upright shoulders. This conformation also encourages the natural propensity for the saddle to ride forwards.

A good riding shoulder, which facilitates saddle fitting, is that which is long and, in horsy parlance, well sloped. R.H. Smythe *(Horse – Structure and Movement)* defined the desirable inclination as being about 60 degrees when the measurement was taken from the point of the shoulder to the junction of the neck and withers, from the point of shoulder to the centre of the withers at the highest point, 43 degrees, and from the point of shoulder to the junction of the withers with the back proper, 40 degrees.

The back, in simple terms, is that area between withers and quarters which is bounded on each side by the ribs. The eight sternal ribs (*true* ribs) are attached to both vertebrae and sternum bone. The remaining ten (asternal or *false* ribs) are secured only to vertebrae. Ideally, for the purpose of riding and the fitting of the saddle, the sternal ribs will be long, well sprung but otherwise fairly flat, so that the rider's thigh and leg lie easily behind the triceps muscle. (The ribs contribute to the depth

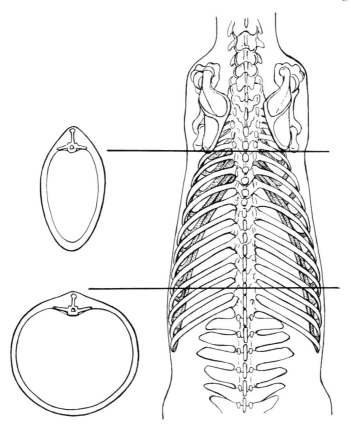

Fig. 137 For the purpose of saddle-fitting the back extends from behind the scapula to the last rib. It will be seen that the width increases progressively from front to rear. The cross-section of vertebrae (left) shows the difference in shape.

of girth, which allows room for the full expansion of large lungs.) A crucial factor is concerned with the curvature of these ribs. From the diagram (Fig. 137) it can be seen that the curve of the ribs becomes increasingly accentuated from the first true ribs backwards. The narrowest part of the body is between the first two ribs and the widest between the last of the false ribs. The shape, viewed from above, is therefore that of a triangle. Any shape departing from that outline, any notable deficiency in the rib curvature and so on, will clearly add to the difficulties of keeping the saddle in place. The asternal ribs are rounder and shorter, but if they are too short, causing the horse to 'run up light behind' like a greyhound, they cause their own problems. In the context of saddle fitting, short false ribs, which are usually inclined to be flat also, will cause the saddle to slide *backwards*.

The usual tendency is for the saddle to move *forwards* towards the point of the triangle. Low withers will certainly accentuate the tendency, as will poorly developed triceps and trapezius muscles. Wasted dorsal muscles will also, of course, contribute to the problem.

A saddle which, because of its construction and/or that of the individual back structure, puts pressure on the thoracic vertebrae forming the ridge of the backbone, or on the all-important loin, will cause injury and seriously inhibit the movement. (The loins lie between the last rib and the quarters and are composed of five bones. Out of them, at right angles, grow long thin processes that do not occur in the other regions of the spine. Their length governs the loin's width and, in consequence, its strength. The greater the width, the more effective will be the propulsive force of the quarters.)

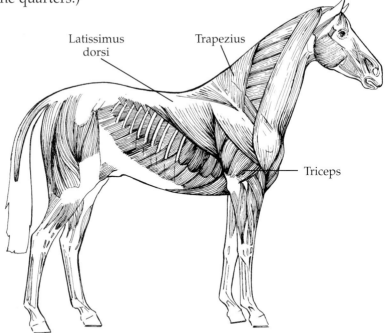

Fig. 138 The musculature of the well-developed horse allows the saddle to sit behind the big trapezius muscle.

The other crucial factor is the relationship between the forepart of the saddle and the scapula. If the slope of the latter is less than desirable the front edge of the saddle, the slope of the head and the forward inclination of the points may interfere with its movement, shortening the stride still more and possibly resulting in dangerous stumbling if the shoulder is especially upright. Similarly, a saddle with an exaggeratedly forward-cut flap and panel can also inhibit the free movement of the scapula. Inevitably, the stride shortens, the horse becomes tired more quickly and, once more, a point can be reached where the horse may be brought down.

These are some of the factors involved in fitting the saddle and it follows that they also govern its shape and the position it assumes on the back.

Clearly, the saddle must rest on either side of the backbone, the weight being over the big muscle lying over the ribs. The condition of this muscle is also, therefore, crucial. So long as it is well developed and well nourished it will prevent injury to the bones and skin. Without it, the bearing would be directly onto bone and much damage would be caused. The pressure would also cut off the supply of blood to the skin. The skin would die and severe galling would ensue.

If the Tree Fits…

If the saddle is to fit correctly it is absolutely necessary for the *tree to fit the back*. If the tree does not fit, neither will the completed saddle.

Too *wide* a tree in the forearch will put pressure on the withers; to *narrow* a tree will pinch on either side of the withers at the ends of the points (the extensions below the stirrup bars). Too *long* a tree can put inhibiting pressure on the loin; too *short* a tree concentrates the weight over too small an area, particularly when 'the joint is too big for the plate'. Those who are generously built in this respect must ensure that the tree is wide enough (and long enough) to accommodate their proportions.

It is a fallacy to suppose that too broad a tree can be adjusted by stuffing the panel heavily. In fact, it makes matters worse. As well as throwing the saddle out of balance it may, indeed, cause pressure points because the panel is so full that its bearing surface is reduced. (When a panel is overstuffed a half-moon shape is created and it is only the edge of the curve which provides a bearing surface. A flatter panel, obviously, provides a larger surface of contact.)

It will be equally ineffective to remove stuffing from a narrow-treed saddle in the hope that it will fit a broader back, since pinching at the points will still occur.

The original fit must never be altered by pulling in the forearch or forcing it outwards. It will only result in the head (gullet) being seriously weakened. The stamping of the size on the B.S.I. tree is an effective deterrent to this pernicious practice. *(The trees made with adjustable head plates go a long way towards providing a solution, but they are by no means used universally and trees of conventional construction are likely to be with us for a long time yet. Very recently a device has been put on the market which enables a saddler to alter the fitting of the forearch, making it wider or narrower – see p147.)*

Another fallacious argument sometimes put forward is that a tree with long points extending below the stirrup bars will keep the saddle in place more effectively than the more usual, shorter points, since their

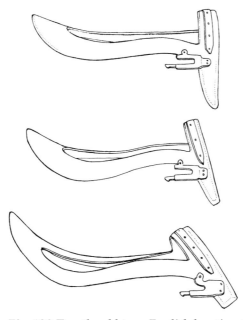

Fig. 139 Top: the old-type English hunting tree with a vertical head and the long points which limited the range of backs it would fit satisfactorily. Centre: a more modern all-purpose type with the head sloped to bring the bar further forward. It also increases the range of possible fittings. Below: a full sloped head of the type employed in the Toptani saddles.

length will prevent it slipping to one side or the other. In fact, such points cause more problems than they will ever cure. Furthermore, they seriously limit the capacity of the tree to fit all but a limited range of backs.

Given that the tree fits, so should the completed saddle, minor adjustments being made by regulating the wool flocking in the instance of a stuffed panel. Initially, a new saddle will stand somewhat high from the back, particularly at the withers, but after some use the wool settles and the panel begins to conform to the contours of the back. (*That it does so gives emphasis to the fundamental precept that each horse should have his own saddle. In the 1963 edition of* Saddlery *I wrote, having made that point:*

> *In pre-war days this was the rule rather than the exception, but today two or three horses may share the same saddle…from a saddlery point of view, if not a common-sense one too, it is wrong.*
>
> *Horses, like humans, may be similar in build but are never identical and the constant changing of a saddle from back to back does not give the saddle a chance to settle down to one particular shape…where a saddle is used on a number of horses, it may initially, if the structure of the backs is roughly the same, fit all of them reasonably well, but it will ultimately never fit one of them really correctly…*

Even today, I know folk who have a saddle 'that fits everything'. It doesn't, of course, any more than one pair of trousers would fit every man in my village.)

A new saddle should be regulated after about three months use, when the wool has had a chance to settle. It is then helpful to the saddler if a template of the back can be provided. This can be done by shaping a piece of pliable plastic (an artist's 'S' curve is ideal) so that it fits closely to the back just behind the withers in the position taken by the saddle's forearch. A further measurement can be taken at a point 20 cm (8 in) to the rear and a final one along the length of the spine. The resultant outlines can be transferred onto a stiff card and will provide a reasonably accurate guide for the saddler regulating the panel.

The Principles

The completed saddle has to observe what amounts to specific principles, the correctness of the fit being assessed when the rider is in position. The saddle itself is put on in advance of the withers and slid into place in the direction in which the hair lies. These are the principles involved:

> a. *There must be clearance of the spine along its length and across its width.*

This entails the forearch being sufficiently clear of the withers to allow the insertion of three fingers when the rider is in place. There must also be clearance of the backbone at the cantle and, of course, throughout the length of the saddle. To check that the seat at its centre does not come into contact with the spine it is necessary to stand close up behind the horse, possibly using a stool to obtain sufficient height to be able to look down the channel dividing the panel. It should be possible to see 'light at the end of the tunnel', i.e. at the head of the saddle.

So long as the channel is sufficiently wide and the stuffing adequate, clearance across the width of the vertebrae should not be a problem. However, in most instances it will need to be at least 6.25–7.5 cm (2½–3 in) in width throughout its length if it is to be broad enough to afford clearance not only to the upper spinous process but for the much wider base of the vertebrae as well. This base is, of course, deep-seated and is well protected by flesh when a horse is in good condition, but a broad channel allowing the saddle to rest upon the ribs and the overlaying muscles is, nonetheless, an essential requirement.

In cheap saddles, as well as in some expensive ones, the channel may become narrowed as the two sides of the panel move inwards. When that occurs (and it does so all too frequently and often without the rider being aware of what is happening) pressure is put directly on the backbone.

> b. *The saddle must not interfere with the free movement of the scapula.*

The causes of such interference and the serious effects it may have are discussed earlier in this chapter. However, it is as well that we should recognise the special difficulties arising with Arab horses. The Arab shoulder is not always or necessarily upright, but it is *different* in its relationship with the (often low) withers and where it meets the humerus. Because of this, special care should be taken in the choice of a saddle. It has to lie *behind* the scapula and the saddle has, therefore, to be straighter in the panel and flap than would be the case with the big, sloped, galloping shoulder of the Thoroughbred.

Of course, there are faults in the design of saddles which cause impingement upon the movement of the scapula, but for the most part the failing is with the conformation of the horse. The problem can be overcome by a straighter cut saddle or the purchase of a better-made horse.

> c. *The panel has to bear evenly upon the back in its entirety and over as large an area as possible, so that the rider's weight is distributed over the whole bearing surface.*

It is probably easier to detail the reasons why these requirements are not met rather than to attempt the opposite.

Much of the problem is caused by the imbalance of the saddle either laterally or longitudinally.

If the panel is stuffed too much at one end or the other, the weight will be concentrated at the lower end. If the stuffing is heavier on one side, the rider's weight will be concentrated on the opposite side (and, usually, the rider will be encouraged to collapse the hip as a result). In both instances the imbalance will affect the movement adversely. The horse will stiffen one side of the back to compensate for the imbalance and the concentration of weight may result in soreness and/or bruising.

A twisted tree (Fig. 140) will also cause the rider's weight to be thrown to one side and, clearly, will prevent its even distribution over the full bearing surface of the panel.

Twisted trees can be caused by an error made by either the tree-maker, in the first instance, or the saddle-maker, who may pull the tree out of shape when putting on his seat webs. The fault usually occurs in spring trees and whilst the tree-maker or saddler may be to blame, it is often the rider who is the cause of the trouble. The tree, and the springs, can easily be twisted by a rider mounting continually from the ground and assisting the process by grasping the *cantle* in the right hand and pulling himself up by this means.

If you must mount from the ground, the right hand should be placed over the waist of the seat where the rear of the flap is joined to the tree. An even better solution, unless you are possessed of an agility that allows vaulting lightly into the saddle, is to mount from a mounting block or to be given a leg up. It is really not very sensible, having put the saddle on carefully, to disturb its position, and risk irritating the horse by climbing up the side of the animal.

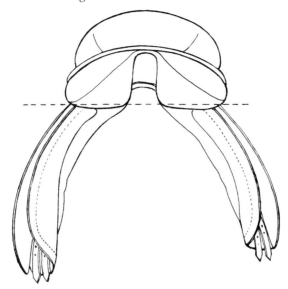

Fig. 140 A twisted tree viewed from the rear. It prevents the even distribution of the weight over the bearing surface and the rider will be compelled to sit out of balance.

Trees made with an exaggerated *dip* to the seat will cause the weight to be put forward and concentrated over the waist of the panel, which in many modern saddles is deliberately narrowed so as not to spread the rider's thighs.

The dip in a spring-tree saddle can become more accentuated over the years as the metal of the spring becomes 'tired'. But that is the consequence of wear over a fairly long period and should not be used as an argument against the use of a spring tree. Ideally, in my view, the head of the saddle should be in line with the highest part of the cantle, or not much below it. The panel will then bear on the back throughout its length. The heavy Melbourne, or German, panel (Fig. 141), gussetted at the rear to allow for greater depth is, in reality, no more than a means of correcting an overdeep seat, and its use frequently results in the saddle sitting on the back like an elephant howdah with the rider in anything but close contact as a result.

One is bound to ask why it should be necessary to seek the correction of an initial fault by the imposition of a second one. It would be much easier to employ a correctly made tree in the first place. *(The Melbourne*

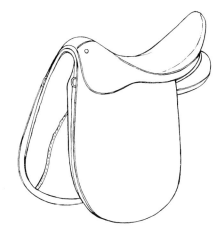

*Fig. 141 Dressage-pattern saddle fitted with
the gussetted Melbourne, or German, panel.*

*panel originated with the Australian stock saddle and was entirely appropriate
to the tree employed. It is far less satisfactory when used with European trees of
less merit.)*

When pressure is concentrated over a small area, the circulation of blood
is interrupted. Galling can occur and even if that is not immediately visible
it is likely that deep-seated bruising will have already been caused.

> d. *The panel must be free from irregularities and should offer a degree of
> resilience.*

A small lump or unevenness in the panel at once creates a pressure point
with a potential to cause injury to the back. It is like a wrinkle in a sock
or a small lump in the sole of the shoe, and is just as uncomfortable.

Panels that are flat and have been allowed to become hard will also
contribute to soreness and discomfort. On the other hand, a panel skilfully
flocked with good quality wool, or a felt panel interlaid with latex, will
provide the sort of resilience needed to ensure the horse's comfort.

> e. *Whilst conforming in other respects, the saddle should fit as close to
> the back as possible.*

If the panel is stuffed so heavily that it causes the saddle to stand high off
the back the possibility of injury caused by friction is much increased. It
becomes possible for the saddle to shift from side to side across the back,

a movement encouraged by a tired rider trying to ease aching limbs.

The *howdah* type panels will also shift forward more easily whilst obviating the desirable close contact between horse and rider.

Relevance of Condition

Obviously, condition has a large part to play in the business of saddle fitting.

A horse in poor condition with wasted musculature will be very likely to suffer injury from the saddle. When that occurs, the fault lies with the horse's physical state and, more so, with the owner who allowed the animal to deteriorate to that point. *It is not the fault of saddle or saddler.*

Conversely, it is not much more sensible to expect a grossly fat horse to work under saddle for any length of time. Fat, soft horses gall easily and it is, in any case, difficult to find a saddle sufficiently wide for them. The moral is not to subject backs that are not in hard condition to anything but short periods of pressure.

(The application of surgical spirit or even salt and water to the back and girth areas, to help the hardening process, is one to be commended.)

The state of training is also relevant. Schooled horses are also straight horses, i.e. their hind feet follow directly in the track of the forefeet, not being carried out to the side like the hind legs of a lurcher dog. The schooled horse will thus be more or less equally developed on both sides of the spine and that will facilitate the lateral balance of the saddle and rider enormously. Unschooled horses, or improperly schooled ones, almost always have a more pronounced muscular development on one side of the body. Usually, it is on the offside, which is why horses turn more easily to the left than the right. They are stiff to the right because any bend in that direction is opposed by a block of ungiving muscle.

Furthermore, schooled horses carry their weight on engaged quarters and are light in front as a consequence. The rest spend much of their time on the forehand, i.e. the weight is carried more over the front end than otherwise, and in that situation the saddle is more inclined to shift forwards. The rounded outline of the schooled horse helps the saddle to maintain its position. Conversely, the hollow-backed horse, holding his head above the bit like a camel and trailing his quarters behind, invites the saddle to slide forwards and the girth to chafe behind the elbows.

It is comparatively easy, within the natural limitations, to fit a saddle to a schooled horse of good conformation. It is very difficult to do the same for one of an opposite inclination.

Results of Bad Fitting

Any sort of discomfort is inhibiting and contributes to the formation of a stress situation which can give rise to behavioural problems. In brief, a badly fitting saddle detracts significantly from the performance potential by restricting movement and encouraging resistances, some of which will be made evident in the mouth.

Saddles that pinch in the act of jumping, when the back is rounded, may easily cause refusals in less confident and courageous horses. The bold horse, however, may quickly be turned into a dangerous tearaway, rushing at his fences and jumping hollow-backed as he anticipates the painful pressure over his withers. The sad thing is that riders, even very good ones, rarely consider that a saddle may be the cause of their problems.

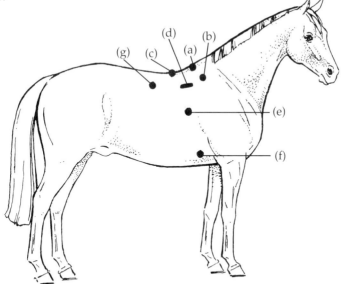

Fig. 142 Sites of common injuries: (a) front arch too wide;
(b) front arch too narrow; (b) seat sinking or tree weakened and so
in contact with spinal area; (d) saddle bearing against rear of scapula;
(e) sweat flap or girth attachment chafing; (f) girth galling;
(g) imbalance due to unevenly flocked panel or twisted tree.

Of course, back injuries are fairly frequent occurrences in the present climate of high-standard competitive sport, but just as many may be caused by saddles as by falls over fences. If there is any restriction or unlevelness in the movement; any signs of an unwillingness to engage the hind legs under the body; any evidence of uneven hock flexion (which may or may not be an incipient spavin); or if there is a tendency to carry the off-hind, for instance, away from the track of the forefeet, then have the horse professionally examined. Do the same if the animal suddenly becomes difficult in the mouth, *but do, in all those instances, have the saddle checked most carefully.*

Saddles for Children

A pony saddle for a child need be no more than a smaller version of an adult saddle, although it would be unwise to put a child into a dressage saddle which, in my view, is too restrictive for young people who have yet to acquire the specialist skill required to sit in one satisfactorily. Nor would I recommend a spring-tree saddle for children not yet in their teens. It is somewhat too much of a specialist instrument for youngsters and more likely to be damaged.

The principles of saddle fitting that apply to a horse, apply equally to ponies, but with ponies additional problems arise. I am speaking now not of the blood-type show pony whose conformation may be nearer to that of a horse, but of the good old family Dobbin kept at grass and whose figure at any time of the year approximates more to that of a barrel than anything else. Like most ponies he has practically non-existent withers and even in mid-winter his backbone is difficult to find. Fortunately, like all his type, he is exceptionally tough and a sore back is a rarity. In many cases, however, he is so broad that the problem is how to keep a saddle on his back without it, and possibly the child too, rolling under his tummy.

Another difficulty, apart from the flatness of the back, is the difficulty of keeping a girth in position. The place for the girth is in the sternum curve behind the elbows, which corresponds to a waistline. In the horse in work this curve is fairly well accentuated, but it is rarely found in Dobbin. Girths with a strip of pimple rubber set in the centre (like that used on table-tennis bats) will help to keep the girth from shifting, but it is also possible to induce a waistline by means of a roller. If the pony is put out in a roller, particularly if it is wrapped in felt and polythene to encourage sweating, some sort of waistline will appear, and you may even get a little shape on either side of the non-existent withers. The principle is much the same as that involved in wearing a belt or a corset and it does help with this particular problem!

A Saumur or Continental-type panel will also assist in keeping the panel in place because it affords greater purchase round the barrel and it is, in any case, more supportive to the rider. Short panels, still used in some patterns, are not recommended because almost invariably they allow the saddle to slip round.

An additional girth strap known as a 'point strap' and fixed underneath the point itself, which allows the girth to be fastened to this strap and to the first of the normally positioned ones, will place the girth that much farther forward and help to keep it and the saddle in place.

Where the pony is really balloon-like and the children are small, a felt pad saddle as a first saddle is probably the best. It has no tree to worry about and the felt has a pretty good grip on the pony; it is also comfortable for the child and will conform to the shape of any back. The introduction of a pony saddle made in synthetic fibre is the up-to-date solution and is very satisfactory, for the shape and overall design is good. This saddle is illustrated and discussed in Chapter 18.

A more difficult matter is when the saddle habitually rides forwards on a pony and after only a short time has slid up on to his neck. The problem is, of course, not difficult if a crupper is used, but few people will adopt this obvious solution. A certain amount can be done by ensuring that the saddle fits as closely as it can and by adding point straps and even strips of pimple rubber to the front of the panel, but the only satisfactory remedy is to use a crupper. The cause of the trouble, of course, is not with the saddle but with the pony's conformation. The pony could be improved to a degree in expert hands but that is probably neither practical nor economically viable. With a pony of this type a crupper is the only real answer, short of replacing the animal with one of a better shape.

Girth Fitting

By a long-established tradition saddles are fitted with three girth straps, though it is probable that neither the makers nor many of the riders who buy them have a clear understanding of why *three* straps should be provided in order to attach a girth which has *two* buckles.

It may be reassuring to know that a spare is available should the necessity arise but that is by no means the principal reason for fitting three straps. The position of the girth is, in fact, of enormous importance to the fitting of the saddle and the purpose of fitting three straps is to ensure that the girth lies correctly within the sternum curve. The position of the curve will obviously vary a little from one individual to another. Properly fitted, the girth helps to counter the natural inclination of the saddle to slip forwards or, conversely and less usually, for it to move in the opposite direction.

Using the first two girth straps it is possible, so long as the girth is positioned in the sternum curve, to place the saddle a little to the rear. Use the back two and the saddle is brought a little forward. *It all depends on the position of the sternum curve and the spring of the ribs in relation to the shape of the back.*

On the very well-made horse the central position of the girth can be obtained by using the first and third straps.

Fig. 143 The conventional three-strap girthing arrangement punched with oval holes to facilitate adjustment from either the ground or the saddle. The girth 'safe' protects the inside of the flap from wear caused by the buckles. (Photo: author's)

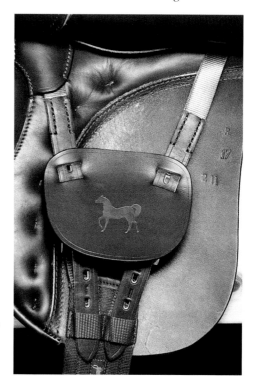

Fig. 144 The girth straps positioned front and rear to assist the saddle's purchase on the back. (Photo courtesy Arabian Saddle Co.)

Both the U.P. saddle and the eminently practical Australian stock saddle employ a surcingle passing over the top of the saddle at the waist. It is of great assistance in maintaining the saddle's position but is largely ignored in present-day equestrian circles, if, indeed, its value has ever been appreciated outside the army, the Australian continent and the racing industry, which also makes use of a surcingle. The surcingle is, admittedly, used in the cross-country phase of eventing, but is almost always positioned too far back to be really effective.

Most horses 'blow themselves out' when being girthed and it is a sound practice to tighten the girths, from the saddle, after a few minutes. If a surcingle is used then some assistance from the ground will be needed. *A loose girth is as mistaken an act of kindness as a loose curb chain, for it allows the saddle to rock on the back.*

Unhappily, saddle-makers contribute to the problems of girthing correctly and effectively; many saddles having their girth straps put on in the most impossible positions. Polo players overcome the problem by

Fig. 145 The Wellep balancing plate or 'slide' which achieves the same result as the 'humane' girth even more effectively.

using a 'humane' self-centring girth (Fig. 187, p.229), which allows the girth to be positioned in the sternum curve and holds the saddle very firmly in position. Even better is the 'slide', an oval metal plate introduced by the Wellep company, which is attached to the girth webs and straps (Fig. 145) and can be used with any ordinary two-buckle girth to achieve the same result. *(My personal choice would be to use the Wellep self-centring 'slide' with a two-buckle girth made from a plain strip of stout red buffalo hide, split to form laces in just the same way as the old military pattern girth. To complete the arrangement I would, if it were necessary, use a light leather surcingle positioned over the centre of the saddle, and made to the proven Australian pattern.)*

On the whole, saddle-makers compound the errors made in the fitting of girth straps by punching them with *round* holes instead of an *oval* hole which would allow the rider of an excited four-year-old, trying to adjust the girth from the saddle on a cold Monday morning, to accomplish the task, more easily, quicker and more safely.

Rider Considerations

Very properly, the emphasis in fitting the saddle is given to the horse, but the principles involved also have to take account of the rider. The military saddles of the last century made few concessions to the rider's comfort, but then the troopers who sat in them were young, physically fit men in hard condition. On the other hand the cavalry *gurus*, appreciating that the disposition of the weight influenced the freedom of movement, were much concerned to place the rider centrally and securely where he would be the least possible encumbrance.

That principle holds good to this day, but modern competitive riding calls for equipment of far greater sophistication. Running shoes, ski and climbing gear, tennis racquets, javelins and a whole lot more sporting items are now the product of today's high technology and they contribute substantially to the extraordinarily high performance levels. Whether the saddle can be regarded in the same light is less certain. Clearly, it can enhance the performance of horse and rider, or, conversely, if it is of poor design in respect of either party, it will detract in similar measure. Unlike the running shoe, however, the saddle has to meet the requirements of both the animal and the human being. For that reason it has to be a compromise between the needs of the two. In some respects the design of modern saddles may occasionally be weighted too much in favour of the rider, but most will also incorporate features which are of special benefit to the horse.

So far as the rider is concerned, the object of the saddle is to provide the *maximum comfort, security and control* (all interdependent) while positioning the rider in relation to the movement and, therefore, as near to the horse's *centre of balance* as possible. If it does that then it also adds to the horse's comfort and ensures that there is minimal interference to the movement.

The centre of balance in the horse at rest has been established as being at the intersection of a vertical line dropped from a point a little behind the withers through the centre of the body to the ground, and a horizontal one, drawn similarly through the body to correspond with the line from the point of shoulder to the buttock. It is a fluid point governed by the gestures of head and neck which act as balancing agents for the body mass. At speed, and in extended outline, the centre moves forward. In collection, when the base is shortened in accordance with increased engagement of the hind legs and the lowered croup, and when head and neck are held high with the face in the vertical plane, the point of balance moves correspondingly to the rear. When the horse moves sideways in the lateral movements the centre of balance shifts in the same direction, as it does when a tight turn is made.

It follows that if the rider is to be in *balance* with the horse his weight must be positioned over the latter's centre of balance – a matter made easier if the saddle is constructed with that object in mind.

The importance of positioning the rider in balance with his horse is

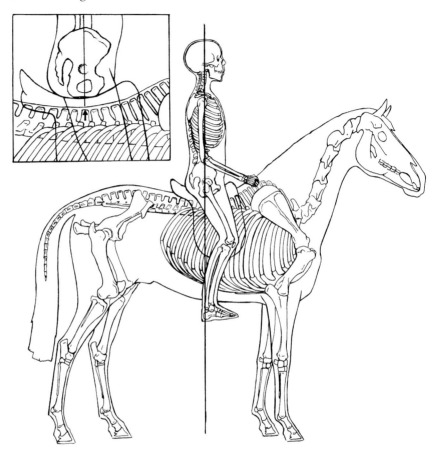

Fig. 146 A saddle fitting the horse to perfection, the rider sitting centrally in the classic position. (The weight, in fact, is over the fourteenth vertebra – the 'keystone of the arch'.) Horses of less correct conformation cannot by the nature of their structure carry either rider or saddle so well or with such comfort.

made very clear when a horse is galloping over uneven ground. If, in that situation, the rider cannot remain in balance the continual shift of the body in front and behind the movement disturbs the horse's equilibrium very seriously. Every time the rider comes out of balance the horse is bound to make a compensating adjustment so as to maintain his own equilibrium. Such adjustments require the expenditure of much additional effort and energy and are obviously tiring.

In the modern saddle the objectives are achieved by a number of design features. The rider is helped to sit comfortably, securely and in balance by:

 a. The correct positioning of the dip in the seat. (A pronounced dip is not essential but the shape of the seat must be such that it is difficult for the rider to sit other than centrally.)

 b. The provision of strong forward rolls and bars positioned so as to assist the easy maintenance of the leg position. In conjunction with the seat these two features help to anchor the lower half of the body.

 c. The employment of a resilient spring seat.

 d. The recessing of the stirrup bars so that there is no uncomfortable bulk under the thighs.

 e. The narrowing of the tree at the waist; the consequent narrowing of the panel in that area and the shaping of the side-bars to place the rider in close contact with the horse without the thighs being spread. A slim, close-fitting panel is a positive assistance to close contact.

Whether the difference between the conformation of the sexes makes it necessary or desirable to build saddles to accommodate each structure has yet to be established. At least one manufacturer makes a selling point of saddles designed specially for the lady rider but for the moment both sexes seem to manage pretty well in the unisex pattern.

There are some design details, however, which are not always appreciated by the female rider and probably one or two that are uncomfortable for the male.

An almost artificially narrow waist, whilst not spreading the thighs, is not so suitable for the female form as a rounder, flatter waist, for instance. A high pommel, on the other hand, which might be thought to cause a degree of apprehension in the male rider, is more likely to bother members of the opposite sex. It could be, of course, that heavy padding at the rear of the saddle, tipping the rider off the seat bones, is the cause of the discomfort.

(In most instances in which the rider – either male or female – complains of discomfort it is, indeed, because of the saddle's imbalance. Excessive depth in the seat or too much padding at the rear will push the rider onto the pubic bone and, of course, will also concentrate the weight over the forepart of the saddle.)

Numnahs and Wither Pads

Numnahs and wither pads are used in conjunction with saddles, but should not be regarded as permanent preventives against the effects likely to be caused by an ill-fitting saddle.

The apparent reason for using a numnah is to give added comfort to the back and to provide a further cushion of resilience between the back and the weight of the rider. Providing that the back is hard and has not suffered injury, the saddle well fitting and the panel well kept, there should be no real necessity for them and in some cases they may even become detrimental to the comfort of the back.

The reasons against the use of a numnah are that, firstly, they cause additional heating and sometimes overheating of the back, and a back constantly overheated becomes tender and is, therefore, more liable to become sore. Secondly, some types will quickly become saturated with sweat and dirt and if not kept scrupulously clean will become uncomfortable and may chafe. The acrylic type of numnah, the wool fleeces and those made from sheepskin can become knotted as well as dirty when subjected to sweat and the hard knots will themselves cause soreness. Thirdly, considering the rider only, the addition of a numnah will put him much further away from his horse when the object in the design of his saddle is exactly the opposite.

That many people will disagree with this view is proved by the large number of riders who do use them, and I will concede that there may be certain horses who require a numnah. I do, however, think that many numnahs are bought and used for no very good reason, and that many are put under a saddle to make the latter a better fit. The remedy in the last instance is to have the saddle properly stuffed. *(Thick numnahs would seem to be obligatory equipment in many riding and trekking stables and I suspect that in some instances they do save the horse's back from the damage that might be caused by both a poorly fitting saddle and a novice rider.)*

Probably because of the increasing awareness of back injuries sustained by horses in competition, numnahs, of all types and in every sort of material, are in greater evidence than ever before. Many of them claim to have prophylactic qualities, i.e. they are designed to prevent the onset of back injuries, others go further, suggesting therapeutic (healing) properties. On the whole one tends to think that the majority of numnahs are concerned with the treatment of the symptoms rather than the disease.

(The more cynical might see the large number of patterns – one American firm advertises no less than 45 varieties – as reflecting the general ignorance about saddle construction and fitting and its relevance to the back formation.)

The materials used in modern numnah production vary from shock-absorbent synthetics, neoprene and the like, to the traditional felt and sheepskin. In between are the improved man-made felts, which are non-absorbent and are not easily compressed; various forms of synthetic fleece materials; quilted polyester foams covered in a whole range of materials and probably a few more than that.

They are made usually in the traditional manner following the shape of the saddle or, increasingly, the numnah is made as a back pad, without the usual, but quite unnecessary, flap extensions, in an effort to remove the bulk from under the rider's leg.

A case can be made for the thin, quilted saddle-cloth which keeps the surface of the panel clean, and if the horse appears to appreciate a back pad and to go more freely as a result of wearing one that is sufficient reason for its employment. Possibly, a numnah, or pad, will prevent bruising, the implication being that it is the saddle that causes the problem. If that is so, why not correct the saddle? If, as a result of a fall or a strain, a horse is fitted with a pad or numnah it may ease the discomfort *slightly* although the healing process will, in consequence, be lengthened. It WILL NOT CURE THE CONDITION. That will be brought about by professional attention and *rest*, NOT by a numnah.

A very light numnah is needed for racing. It protects the back and, if cut deep enough, prevents the horse's sides being rubbed by the upper half of the jockey's boots.

Wither pads are also a racing prerogative. Few lightweight saddles can make much pretence of fitting the horse in the accepted sense, and the use of a wither pad tucked under the forearch is an essential for the horse's comfort.

With a hunting saddle a wither pad should not be necessary unless used as a temporary measure under a saddle that has begun to sink in the front. Immediately such a sinking becomes apparent the saddle should be sent to the saddler for his attention.

Wither pads used to be made of knitted wool but the pad has to be knitted right through and not just stuffed. A stuffed pad was useless since the wool worked down either side of the withers, leaving the essential part unprotected. Modern wither pads either of the gel variety or made

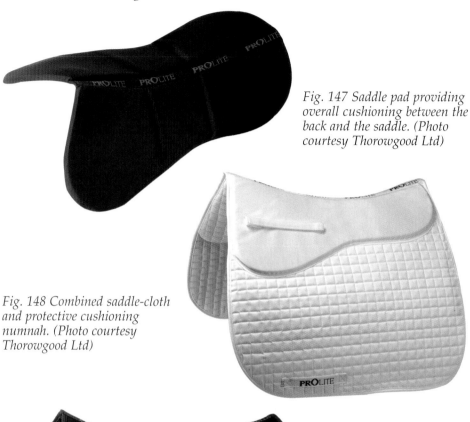

Fig. 147 Saddle pad providing overall cushioning between the back and the saddle. (Photo courtesy Thorowgood Ltd)

Fig. 148 Combined saddle-cloth and protective cushioning numnah. (Photo courtesy Thorowgood Ltd)

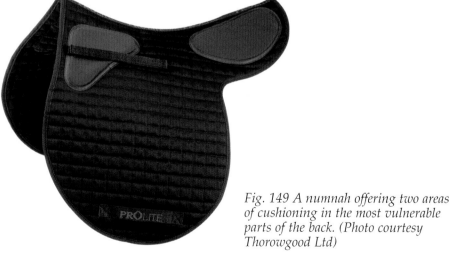

Fig. 149 A numnah offering two areas of cushioning in the most vulnerable parts of the back. (Photo courtesy Thorowgood Ltd)

from shock-absorbent material are far superior and easier to keep clean.

Numnahs tend to slip backwards with the lie of the hair, just as saddles slip forwards because the horse is narrower in front than behind. Their means of attachment to the saddle is, on that account, of some concern and should be examined carefully before a purchase is made. Equally the numnah has to be so constructed that it can be tucked up into the fore-arch of the saddle and will remain in that position. If it slips and lies flat and tight over the withers it is worse than useless since the pressure exerted is almost certain to cause chafing.finish

The New Breed

While there are still numnahs that are bought for the wrong reasons and do little good to the horse's back, there is also a new breed, so carefully designed and constructed that they have become an almost essential adjunct to the saddle. Some provide a cushioning effect through the use of a shock-absorbent gel, but many, probably most, rely on technically advanced absorbent substances that are lighter and less bulky. The new 'pads' and saddle-cloths absorb impact, spreading the weight and reducing the pressure per square inch. Moreover, they do not slip backwards after the fashion of the old, conventional numnah. There are also patterns, the 'rider-pads', that address, very effectively, the changing conformation of the back as the horse's training progresses.

Air and foam technology is employed in the Korrector pads, the air-bags (there are four of them) being inflated as required to accommodate the back conformation and to place the rider in balance.

These pads are available for all types of saddle, including race exercise patterns, Western saddles and even side-saddles.finish

People Numnahs

There are also numnahs for people. These are covers made of fleece fitting over the saddle seat and are, I understand, greatly comforting to those who, like Xenophon's 'soft-arsed Athenians' would put 'more coverlets upon the horse than upon a bed'.

(Xenophon (c.430–356 bc) was the Greek cavalry commander, historian and agriculturalist, who wrote the first manuals on horse management and horsemanship. However, he was a Spartan, who rode without benefit of saddle or breeches.)

18   Saddle Types

*'The definition of riding: 'To keep a horse
between yourself and the ground.' Anon.*

Saddle types, specifically designed to particular purposes, are clearly
defined, even though there are variations of detail between the patterns
on the market.

The extremes of the saddle spectrum are represented by the *dressage
saddle* at one end and the *jumping saddle* at the other, both attempting to
conform to the needs of the contrasting seats employed. In the middle is
the *general-purpose saddle*, the sensible choice for the majority of riders,
which combines something of both the specialist patterns. Otherwise, the
principal types, outside racing, comprise the *long-distance saddle*, owing
something to the Western saddle, the Australian stock saddle and sometimes to the Army Universal as well; the *show saddle*, American and
English, the strongly-built but otherwise unremarkable *polo saddle* and
the *Western saddle*, the latter now increasingly evident in Europe.

Dressage

The dressage saddle may be built on either a straight-headed
tree or one that is cut back. A certain dip is necessary but it should not be
so deep, or the tree so short, that the rider's ability to move is restricted.
The panel and flap are cut almost vertical, and to accommodate the
resultant long leg and straightened thigh position, placing the rider over
a centre of balance which is to the rear of that adopted by the extended,
galloping horse, it is *essential* that an *extended bar* is fitted, i.e. one that is
longer and thus places the leather and iron further back and more nearly
under the rider's seat.

Virtually every dressage saddle is fitted with long girth straps and a short
girth so as to obviate any bulk under the leg that might be caused by the
girth buckles. This girthing arrangement was first devised by Lord Lonsdale,

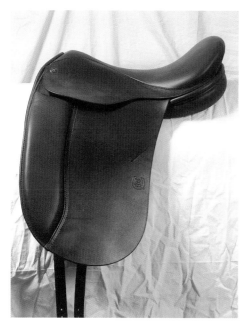

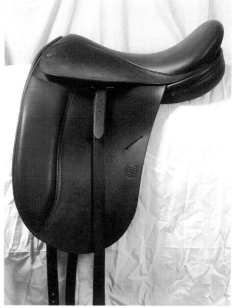

Fig. 150 The custom-made Gineta saddle by Creaton saddles is notable for the slightly flattened seat and the obvious Portuguese influence. (Photo: Mary Herbert)

Fig. 151 The stirrup leather position on the Gineta using the Wellep bar. (Photo: Mary Herbert)

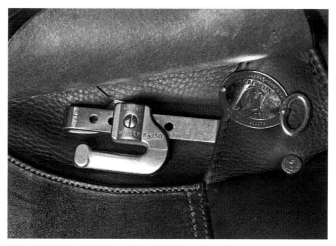

Fig. 152 The Wellep adjustable bar fitted to the Creaton Gineta. It governs effectively the position of the rider's leg (Photo: Mary Herbert)

the legendary Yellow Earl who was the first president of London's International Horse Show and filled that position for no less than 26 years from the inaugural event in 1907. Up to the immediate post-war years the short girth was referred to as 'the Lonsdale Girth' (Fig. 153).

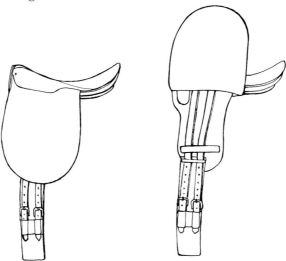

Fig. 153 The 'original' dressage girth devised in the nineteenth century by the legendary Yellow Earl, Lord Lonsdale.

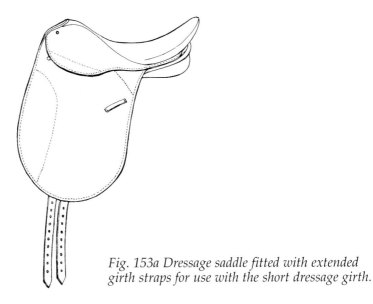

Fig. 153a Dressage saddle fitted with extended girth straps for use with the short dressage girth.

The purchase of a dressage saddle, more than any other, should be approached with great care. It is a specialist saddle for a specialist pursuit and, ideally, it should be tailored to the individual. In general, a well-designed saddle that fits the horse's back will enhance the rider's performance, but this may not be so in the case of a dressage saddle. One that suits an advanced rider, who has learnt to sit in the optimum position demanded by the sport, may do nothing for a less accomplished rider who has yet to acquire a 'dressage seat'. Indeed, it may well make matters worse and cause the rider to tip onto the fork and the front of the seat bones.

Most dressage saddles, following the German pattern, have full stuffed panels with a gusset at the rear, and some are so heavily stuffed

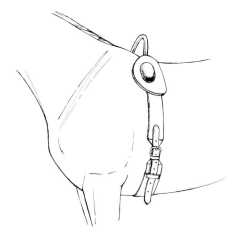

Fig. 154 The German-inspired foregirth', 'one of the more ridiculous developments in the history of riding equipment'.

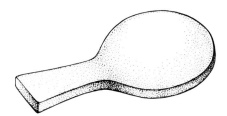

Fig. 155 The 'mind-boggling' 'seat-riser' is indicative of a disturbing ignorance relative to the application of riding equipment and to equitation itself.

that they not only tip the rider forward but have a pronounced tendency to slide to the front, a failing to which the rider adopting the ugly, driving-from-the-back-seat position contributes materially. To counter this fault in saddle design and rider position a 'foregirth' (Fig. 154) fitted with pads lying on either side of the withers in front of the fore-edge of the saddle, is sometimes employed. I have no hesitation in condemning it as one of the more ridiculous developments in the history of riding equipment. (Just as bad are the 'seat-risers' (Fig. 155) made from a firm foam and shaped so that the pad lies in place under the rear of the saddle. *'The pad'*, writes one manufacturer, *'raises cantle and lowers head of the saddle, moving the rider forward off the cantle to center of saddle seat.'* Such a piece of idiocy makes use of the old cliché 'mind-boggling' eminently forgivable.)

There are some very excellent German and British dressage saddles that avoid the principal faults in construction, etc., but otherwise the ultimate precision tool for the sport is still a long way off. (Encouragingly,

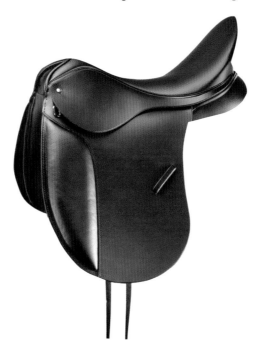

Fig. 156 The very attractive synthetic dressage saddle produced by the Thorowgood company.(Photo courtesy Thorowgood Ltd)

some use is now being made of the French panel made from alternate layers of felt and latex or from a moulded foam. Because such panels can be made thinner than the conventional wool-stuffed panel they allow the rider to sit closer and to rely upon the shape of the tree to maintain a central position, rather than on heavy stuffing of the panel. Furthermore, such panels are less prone to sliding forwards and when used in conjunction with the self-centring girth slide mentioned in Chapters 17 and 19 they allow the saddle to be anchored firmly in the proper position.)

Jumping

The classical jumping saddle is still exemplified by the Toptani pattern, particularly by the later models. It gives maximum support to the rider in maintaining his position and places him in very close contact with the horse. In recent years, however, there has been a spate of

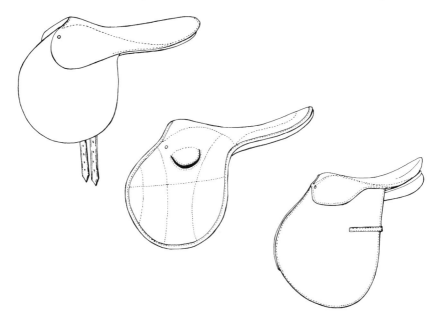

Fig. 157 Quite clearly the old race-exercise patterns (top and centre) have led to the modern close-contact saddle (below). In fact these jumping saddles offer less close contact than Toptani's classic model and are far less supportive.

so-called 'close-contact' saddles, inspired by a pattern developed by the French firm Hermès, from the old and far less satisfactory French-type jumping saddles, and popularised by the Brazilian showjumper, Nelson Pessoa and the New Zealand Olympic rider, Mark Todd.

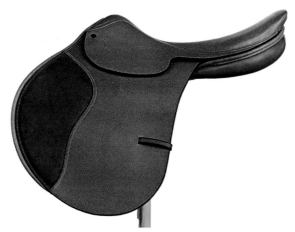

Fig. 158 The Creaton close-contact jumping saddles shows the influence of the polo saddle designed by Curtis Skene (see Polo, this chapter) in its lean, elegant lines. (Photo: Mary Herbert)

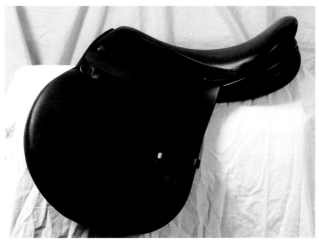

Fig. 159 A Creaton general-purpose hunting saddle of robust and restrained design. The shallow dip to the seat is noteworthy. (Photo: Mary Herbert)

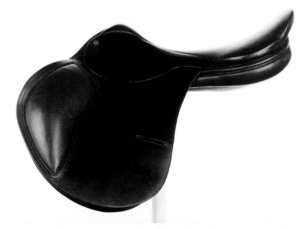

Fig. 160 A leaner, more rakish outline characterises the Creaton cross-country saddle, together with greater length in the seat. (Photo: Mary Herbert)

These saddles, made with a much smaller and flatter seat than the conventional jumping saddles following the Toptani pattern, have a lot in common with the old type of race-exercise saddle. They do give a close contact, but no more than that offered by the Toptani or a general-purpose saddle made with a felt/latex panel, but they are not by any means so supportive of the rider's position. Nonetheless, they obviously find favour with the accomplished rider. For the less expert they are usually less satisfactory and for those of us who are well upholstered the plate is sometimes woefully inadequate in proportion to the size of the joint.

General-purpose

This is the middle-of-the-road saddle which increasingly is labelled an 'event' saddle. Less exaggerated in cut and in respect of the bar position desirable in the jumping saddle, it is the obvious choice for the rider who does a bit of everything. Properly constructed, it is ideal for cross-country work and hunting; it is more than adequate as a jumping saddle and it is quite possible to school a horse on the flat in one, or to ride a dressage test at a good Riding Club level. It is also a saddle in which one can hack comfortably in the sure knowledge that the horse will be comfortable too.

The type of general-purpose saddle to be avoided is that with an exceptionally dipped seat – which will affect both the balance and the bearing surface – or with a flap and panel cut unduly far to the front. An unnecessarily forward-cut flap, apart from the risk of it impinging on the movement of the shoulder-blades, limits the degree of support offered by the forward roll and in consequence the variety of purposes for which the saddle can be employed. It will be clear that the forward inclination of the panel and its supportive roll demands the use of a much shorter leather if it is to fulfil its purpose. Employing a longer leather causes the leg to be held well to the rear of the forward roll and this removes any possibility of the leg being supported in its position.

Long-distance

There are a number of saddles designed for this purpose but increasingly the tendency is towards those patterns which are based loosely on the Western saddle and the well-proven Australian stock

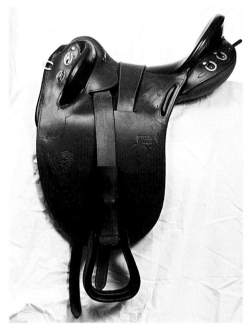

Fig. 161 The well-proven Australian stock saddle. This is the popular 'gooseneck' pattern. (Photo: Mary Herbert)

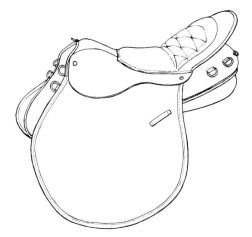

Fig. 162 The long-distance saddle is really a combination of the Western and the Australian stock saddle.

saddle. The criteria applied to the distance saddle are:

    a. A deep, very resilient panel affording the maximum possible bearing surface so that the weight is distributed evenly over as large an area as possible.

    b. A generous, fairly deep and relatively broad-waisted seat, reminiscent of that of the Western saddle, which has additional padding on the surface to ensure a comfortable ride.

The weight of the saddle is less important than the extent of the bearing surface. Most leather saddles, however, are not unduly heavy (not nearly so heavy as the Western saddle, for instance), whilst those made of synthetic materials, which appear to be a most suitable medium, are remarkably light, weighing no more than 3.1 kg (7 1b).

Close contact is not too much of a consideration – comfort, for both horse and rider is, on the other hand, a vital feature of the distance saddle.

Show Saddles

The old-time English show saddle has largely disappeared, although it may still be seen in the show-pony classes. It featured a flat seat with a straightcut flap and was fitted with a thin leather-covered felt

*Fig. 163 A relatively flat-seated English show saddle
with a thin half-panel of felt covered with panel hide.*

half-panel so that there was no visual interruption to the line of the back (Fig. 163). Necessarily, if the rider's knee was not to rest beyond the front edge of the flap, the bar had to be of the extended type. Most show saddles were also provided with a point strap, an extra girth strap fastened to the underside of the point, which helped to place the saddle just that little bit further to the rear and so accentuate the length of the shoulder in front of the saddle. It was a saddle designed to show off the horse's conformation to the best advantage, but to what extent it affected the decisions of an experienced judge is arguable. It was certainly not the most comfortable of saddles to sit in.

Today, the practical 'working-hunter' type of saddle is more frequently seen, and even dressage saddles and those general-purpose patterns not distinguished by a too forward-cut flap are not by any means unknown in the show ring.

The working-hunter saddle is really a scaled down and more elegant version of the general-purpose saddle. It avoids the lumpiness which sometimes characterises the latter; its supportive rolls are more discreet, though not much less effective, and the cosmetic touches – contrasting flap inserts and so on – are mercifully absent.

In America the flat-seated, wide-flapped Lane-Fox show saddle remains supreme in the Saddlebred and other gaited classes but there are signs of a deeper-seated saddle gaining popularity in the equitation

Fig. 164 The Lane-Fox show saddle with a full cut-back head ('cow mouth') which remains supreme in American gaited horse classes. (Photo courtesy Arabian Saddle Co.)

divisions. Invariably these saddles are made on a full cut-back, or 'cow-mouth', tree and almost inevitably incorporate extended bars. The flaps are cut very wide to prevent the rider's upper leg coming into unpleasantly sticky contact with the horse's hot flanks. The saddle design, it will be understood, compels the rider to sit well back and thus makes the wide flap a necessary feature.

Polo

Polo is a hard game for men, ponies and saddles. In consequence polo saddles are made up on strong, rigid trees which are specially reinforced. Usually, the head is straight and the seat not unlike that of the very best type of hunting saddle, for it often has something of a dip. It is otherwise fairly long and correspondingly broad. The saddle has plain flaps and the panel is either of the short stuffed Rugby pattern or it is cut with a light forward roll to give a modicum of support in that area.

Good, straightforward, polo saddles, undistinguished other than by their durable quality and old-fashioned appearance, are made in Europe, the best of them coming from Walsall. A great many players, however, will opt for the cheaper Argentine saddle, which, if one was being kind, could be described as distinctly rustic. (The saddles made of synthetic fabrics are far superior.)

Polo saddles are made in narrow fittings to suit the often knifey withers of the polo pony but the niceties of fit are sometimes blurred today by the use of heavy numnahs. Many polo saddles are, indeed, out of balance, being higher at the head than at the cantle.

(In my opinion, the best polo saddle ever made derived from the Australian stock saddle and was made in Australia just before World War II. It was designed by Curtis Skene, father of Bob Skene, the first Australian 10-goal player, and was described as 'having a short, ample seat with a high cantle…the flap cut rather straight with a small knee roll…It helps to keep the point of balance considerably further forward than is the case with the conventional English saddle…' Fig. 165 illustrates the Skene saddle which was, in fact, not so straight in its flap as the description suggests. The roll, of course, supports the front of the thigh, not the knee.

The shape of Gibson's Distas Central Position saddle of the pre-war years was, in fact, suggested by an old and broken-treed stock saddle which Jack Hance had in his tack room. There seems no reason why the Australian saddle, with its many virtues in respect of the fit and the correct positioning of the rider's seat, should not form a practical base for the development of an exceptional dressage saddle.)

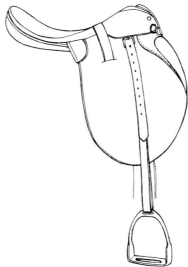

Fig. 165 *This is the Skene polo saddle, a streamlined version of the Australian stock saddle, and in the author's view one of the best saddles ever made – and not only for polo.*

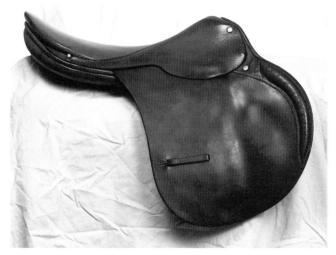

Fig. 166 The 'Kingham' saddles made for John Shedden, winner of the 1949 Badminton Trials, by F. E. Gibson Ltd. To all intents it is identical to the Skene polo saddle. (Photo: Mary Herbert)

Racing

Racing saddles from 0.45 kg (1lb) upwards (and some even lighter than that) are little more than points of attachment for the jockey's stirrup leathers (Fig. 167). Fit is not a matter of consequence since the saddle is put on over a pad; the fitting is, of course, of more importance in the so-called race-exercise saddle which today is not much more than an enlarged version of the race saddle.

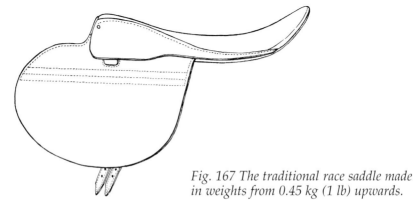

Fig. 167 The traditional race saddle made in weights from 0.45 kg (1 lb) upwards.

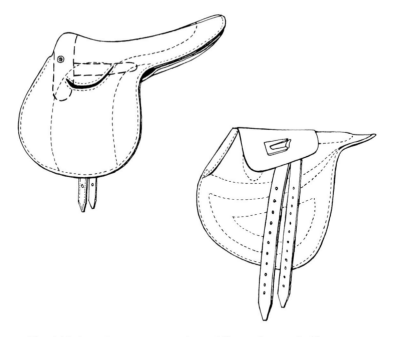

*Fig. 168 A modern race-exercise saddle made on a half-tree.
It is probably superior in terms of 'close contact' to the very
much more expensive jumping saddles which go under that name.*

Modern exercise saddles are for the most part made on a half-tree (Fig. 168) extending some 12.5–15 cm (5–6 in) beyond the bar fitting. Race saddles, usually made without bars – the leather being looped over the side-bar of the tree – are more often made on very light full-length plastic trees. Within a short time it seems likely that both race and exercise trees will be made from graphite, a material of enormous strength combined with great lightness. Already, the race saddle market is dominated by the manufacturers of synthetic saddles.

These race saddles are constructed with a one-piece seat and flap made up round a light felt panel, an arrangement which, in the exercise saddle, gives an almost bareback contact between rider and horse. Indeed, the exercise saddle, on its half-tree, is not dissimilar to the much-vaunted close-contact jumping models – you just sit even closer to the horse. It would not be impossible to imagine a jumping saddle being developed on these lines.

Children's Saddles

The child's saddle – 35–40 cm (14–16 in) long – follows the lines of the larger adult saddles, although it may not be made up in the top quality leathers or, indeed, with the more expensive spring tree. The replacement of the spring tree with the more robust rigid one is not unreasonable in view of a child's destructive potential.

One of the companies specialising in synthetics has recently filled a gap in the market by producing a really well-shaped saddle for smaller children which is sufficiently flexible to sit in balance and securely even on the roundest-backed pony. It is illustrated in Fig. 169.

In Britain the Pony Club for long supported an 'approved' saddle, which while serviceable was otherwise unremarkable. The design, etc. was, of course, approved by a committee, composed no doubt of capable horsemen and women, good and enthusiastic administrators but to all intents having minimal knowledge of saddle construction and design (and sometimes of equestrian theory, also). In the circumstances the description 'unremarkable' is to be expected.

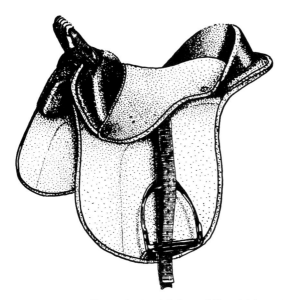

Fig. 169 An all-synthetic child's saddle which positions the rider centrally whilst giving ample support. The position of the stirrup leather is especially noteworthy.

The Queen of Saddles

Side-saddle riding in Europe and particularly in Britain has become increasingly popular in the last forty years or so and was much encouraged by the formation of the English Side-Saddle Association in 1974. Prior to the 1970s it is doubtful whether more than one or two saddles, or, indeed, any at all, were made in the post-war period. Today, however, there are craftsmen (both tree-makers and saddlers) capable of undertaking this exacting work, although many side-saddle enthusiasts rely on pre-war saddles rescued from the loft or the corner of a tack room.

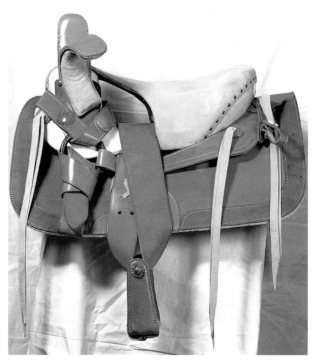

Fig. 170 The Queen of Saddles. The unusual Mexican Charro side-saddle has a stirrup fitted to the offside of the saddle as well as that on the nearside. This is so that the lady can throw her leg over to the offside if she needs to prevent her saddle slipping to the left. The saddle is used in the Escaramuza (skirmish) competitions which are carried out at the gallop and the rider is penalised should she use the offside stirrup. If she didn't and fell as a result she would be disqualified! No Health and Safety regulations in Mexico! (Photo: Mary Herbert)

Fig. 171 Doeskin seated side-saddle. (Photo courtesy Edward Stagg)

The side-saddle originated some 600 years ago in the courts of mainland Europe and it is claimed that it was brought to Britain by Anne of Bohemia, wife of the ill-fated Richard II of England.

Previously, women had ridden behind a man sitting sideways, or some might have ridden astride in divided skirts.

The first side-saddles were stuffed pads on which the lady sat at right angles to the horse with her feet resting on a small platform, a *planchette*.

The next stage was to fit a pommel to the front of the saddle, around which the lady could hook the knee and sit facing the front, or almost so. Two pommels were in use by the end of the sixteenth century so that the rider could gain greater security by wedging her knee between them. The introduction of a second pommel is attributed to Catherine de Medici, who was certainly using the arrangement in about 1580.

An important feature was introduced in the early nineteenth century (circa 1820) when the balance strap made its appearance allowing the

Nearside

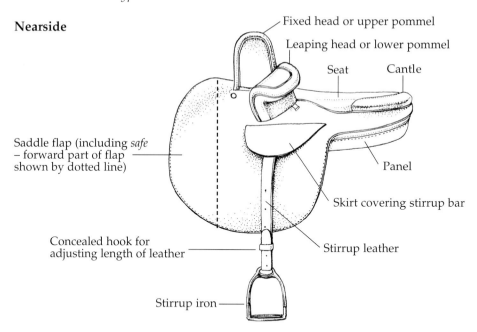

Fixed head or upper pommel

Leaping head or lower pommel

Seat   Cantle

Saddle flap (including *safe* – forward part of flap shown by dotted line)

Panel

Skirt covering stirrup bar

Concealed hook for adjusting length of leather

Stirrup leather

Stirrup iron

Fig. 172 Parts of the side-saddle.

saddle to be secured firmly without the girth being excessively tight.

Ladies did not begin to follow hounds in any number until later in the nineteenth century, although two notable exceptions were the Marchioness of Salisbury, who was a Master of Foxhounds in 1775 and who later rode in an early Champion and Wilton saddle, and the notorious Lady Lade, whose colourful vocabulary was matched only by her dash and skill across country in the early years of the nineteenth century.

Pride of place, however, has to be given to Elizabeth, Empress of Austria, who visited England and Ireland on sporting tours between 1876 and 1882. A brilliant horsewoman she was 'piloted' by Capt. Bay Middleton, one of the greatest cross-country riders of the day, and earned herself the reputation of a fearless rider who went as hard as the men. Elizabeth, persuaded from practical considerations to ride in the forward position, was largely responsible for the disappearance of the dipped seat and its replacement by the doeskin-covered flat seat which had only a barely discernible dip.

Perhaps the greatest advance in side-saddle design was made in about

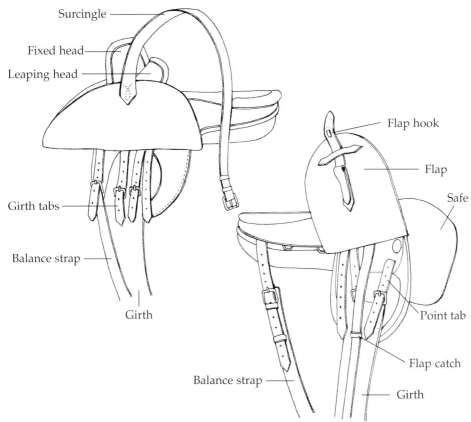

Fig. 172a Parts of the side-saddle, underside.

1830 when Jules Charles Pellier, a French riding master teaching in Paris, invented the 'leaping head' which did, indeed, allow ladies to jump with a great degree of security. (The invention is also claimed by François Baucher (1796–1873), who exhibited his art at the Franconi circus and remains as one of the great later Masters, if a controversial one. Another claimant is Thomas Fitzharding-Oldaker (1788-1820), a hunting man, who for whatever reason was compelled to ride sideways for a short period and is thought to have invented a form of leaping head as a means of greater security. (Lindsay-Smith, author of a carefully-researched treatise on the side-saddle which is included in *In the Saddle* published by the Archaeological Leather Group and Archetype Publications in 2004, suggests that all three may have 'arrived at the same

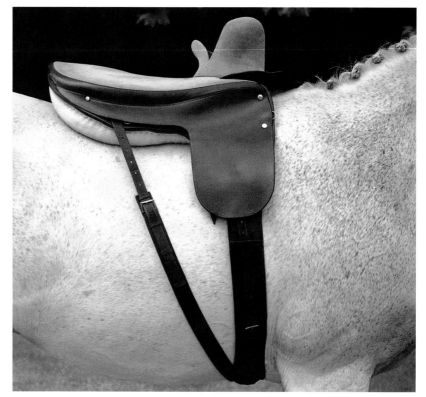

Fig. 173 The full balance girth in position. (Photo courtesy Edward Stagg)

Fig. 174 (right) Three patterns of safety irons: a & b, Latchford; c, Cope; d, Scott. All three were developed in the nineteenth century. (Photos courtesy Edward Stagg)

result at the same time …' although Fitzharding-Oldaker would necessarily have been considerably in advance of the other two with his prototype.)

The level seat, together with a cut-back head, or pommel which facilitated the fitting of the saddle, allowed the rider to sit on the right thigh with shoulders facing straight to the front, whereas previously she had had to twist from the waist in order to face forwards.

Improvements, particularly in regard to safety bars and the shape and positioning of the heads continued apace throughout the nineteenth century, largely due to the three pre-eminent English companies specialising in side-saddle manufacture. Owen, Mayhew, and Champion and Wilton

(a)
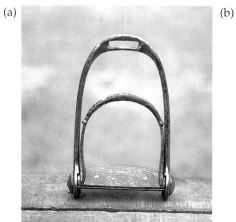

(b)

(c)
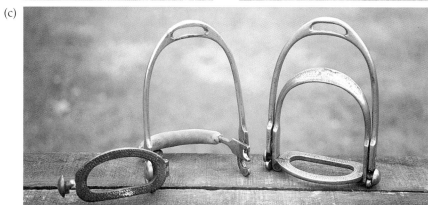

(d)
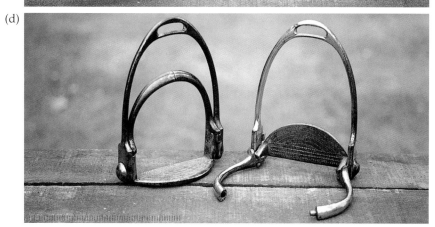

(a)

(b)

(c)

were all established in the early years of the century and all three patented safety bars. Additionally there were a number of safety irons patented specifically for the side-saddle. (Both, of course, are essential to side-saddle riding.)

Mayhew, a firm which was in business up to 1947 when Miss Mayhew died, patented Wykeham pads for the side-saddle in 1903, so as to accommodate changes in the back condition (see Wykeham panel p.145). Increasingly, due to the expertise of the London houses, the side-saddle became more functional and, importantly, lighter in weight.

Lindsay Smith postulates the period 1925–35 as that producing the best side-saddles for modern riding. However, the side-saddle was in

Fig. 176 An offside saddle allowing the rider to sit to the right instead of the left. (Photo courtesy Edward Stagg)

Fig. 175 (left) Three quick-release mechanisms: (a) was used by Champion and Wilton; (b) by Mayhew and Whippy and (c) by Owen, the four principal side-saddle makers. (Photos courtesy Edward Stagg)

general use well before that date. The First Aid Nursing Yeomanry (F.A.N.Y) is pictured riding side-saddle before and during World War 1 and women were riding point-to-point races in 1913. Between the Wars side-saddles were commonplace in the hunting field and, indeed, until well into the 1920s it was not considered, in some circles, quite ladylike to ride astride.

The Western Saddle

There are now Western Riding Clubs and societies all over Europe, offering an attractive alternative to the European riding disciplines, while the sport of reining, the Western equivalent of the dressage test and equally demanding, is recognised as an Olympic discipline.

Fig. 177 The traditional saddle of the Iberian Peninsula which was the inspiration for the Western saddle. (Photo: Mary Herbert)

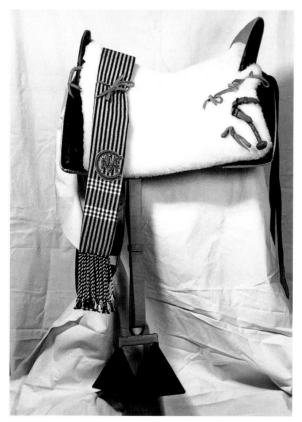

Fig. 178 Spanish saddle of the type used by the Mexican vaquero (Photo: Mary Herbert)

Western saddles and riding gear are necessarily the prerogative of the specialist outlet employing staff qualified to advise and to fit saddles. Indeed, it would be unwise to purchase equipment other than from such establishments.

The American horse culture has its roots in the horse-lore of the Iberian Peninsula brought to the American continent by the Spanish *conquistadores* of the sixteenth century, who were responsible for the re-introduction of the equine species to the Americas, after an absence of some 8,000 years.

Similarly, the Western saddle and it supporting equipment derive from the Spanish accoutrements of the period inherited, initially, by the Mexican vaquero.

Western equipment is far more complex than it would appear at first sight and is complicated further by regional differences and a variety of purposes for which it is used.

Essentially, the Western saddle was a highly practical work platform for cattle ranching and was designed to carry the cowboy and his personal belongings. It was broad, spreading the weight over a large area of the back, and it was heavy, often between 18–23 kg (40–50 lb). It was always fitted over a substantial folded blanket that could double up as a bed-roll for the rider, and usually over a sheepskin as well.

Today's saddles are lighter, the tree often being made of fibreglass, polymer and so on, but they retain much of the original character.

The 'general-purpose' Western saddle is the cowboy's stock saddle, but there are variations on that basic pattern to suit specialist pursuits: roping saddles, cutting saddles, parade and pleasure saddles, barrel racers and, of course, the reining saddle, which has the stirrups constructed to give a considerable forward swing that allows, in particular,

Fig. 179 The Western stock saddle, descendant of the Iberian patterns which remain unchanged to this day. (Photo: Bob Langrish)

for the spectacular sliding stop. It is, also, considerably lighter than the roping saddle, for instance.

Most Western saddles are notable for the high level of decorative detail that includes elaborate tooling of the leather and in the instance of the parade saddle, some very extravagant trimming with silver edging, studs and so on.

A characteristic feature of the Western saddle range is the horn to which the lariat could be tied when a steer was roped. In fact, the Mexican prototypes, although high at the pommel, did not have a roping horn. This appeared considerably later in the early nineteenth century, along with a widened and strengthened front arch that supported the thighs. Roping techniques were then in the process of development, but before that the end of the lariat had been secured to the horse's tail, a system that had inherent and obvious drawbacks.

The practice of roping revealed all too clearly a fundamental failing in the Mexican design, when the latter was, in the course of time, fitted with a horn. The problem lay with the cinches, or girths in European terms. The Mexican saddle was 'single-rigged', that is, secured with one girth round the barrel that lay just behind the elbows. Clearly, the sudden and usually violent pull on the rope via the horn had the effect of pulling the saddle forwards and tipping the cantle upwards. To counter the problem a second cinch fitted behind the rider's leg was employed. Fastened fairly loosely, it came into play when pressure was put on the horn, and prevented the saddle being pulled upwards and forwards, causing injury to the horse and possibly unseating the rider. This system, soon followed throughout the Western states, is known as 'double-rigging'. To prevent a loosely fastened 'flank' cinch swinging backwards and forwards and possible damaging the sheath of stallions and geldings, the two cinches were joined by a connecting strap positioned under the belly.

There are numerous regional variations in the type of rigging generally employed, so much so that it was said that a man's home range could be identified by his saddle rig. Five rigging positions are recognised: Spanish (rim-fire or full), ⅞, ¾, ⅝ and centre fire. (Rigging is either on-tree or in-skirt, i.e. rigging rings are either in the rigging straps on the tree or fixed in the skirt.)

The origin of the terms rim-fire and centre fire, according to Robert W. Miller, author of *Western Horse Behaviour and Training* and an accepted Western authority, lies with the manner of firing a rifle cartridge. Some are fired when the firing pin strikes the centre of the cartridge and others when the cap is struck on the edge or rim of the cartridge. In the absence of any other explanation Mr Miller's must be regarded as definitive.

Other modifications to the Mexican saddle, made in the interest of comfort as well as for utilitarian purposes, were the enlargement of the skirts and the addition of the thick saddle blanket, folded carefully to lie under the saddle.

The narrow stirrup leathers of the Mexican saddle were replaced by wide fenders or *sudadaro* (Spanish *sudar* – to sweat, to ooze) made of stout leather. Their purpose was to protect the rider's leg from chafing and prevent sweat soaking into his clothes. The heavy stirrups were attached to the bottom of the fenders and because of the weight and substance of the latter were unable to move to more than a limited degree – an advantage when roping, which calls for the cowboy to mount and dismount quickly and frequently.

The cowboy's stirrups were shaped from wood and covered with rawhide. A metal stirrup would not have been a practical option since the metal would be too cold for the feet in winter and too hot under the blazing sun of summer.

The stirrup covers, adopted from the Mexican saddle, were called *tapaderos* or 'taps' and were much the same as the 'slipper' stirrup of the eighteenth and nineteenth centuries. Their purpose was to protect the feet when riding through thorny, rough scrub country, while in winter they could be lined with sheepskin to give extra warmth.

In addition, the cowboy added sets of strings to the nearside and offside saddle skirts, to which could be attached his personal belongings. Another set of strings was usually fitted to the front to act as a *latigo* carrier. (Latigo is the leather strap that secures the cinch either by buckling or tying.)

The fit of the Western saddle is just as important as that of the European patterns, particularly as the rider may be in the saddle for long periods. Crucial to the fit are the side-bars between the forearch (fork) and the cantle. They are the weight-bearers and saddles are made in different bar widths to fit a range of back structures. Four bar widths are usually available: regular (about 14 cm [5½ in]); semi-Quarter Horse (about 15 cm [6 in]); Quarter Horse (about 16.5 cm [6½ in]) and Arabian or Morgan (about 17 cm [6¾ in]).

Too wide a saddle bears on the withers; if it is too narrow it will pinch.

In both instances the movement becomes restricted significantly, largely because of the saddle's weight and size.

Roping saddles have narrow swells to facilitate movement and usually the horn is higher than in other patterns.

On the *cutting* saddle the fork is fitted with wide swells to support the thighs and increase the rider's security as the horse makes the lightning-quick turns and pivots to control the steer. The stirrups, unlike those of the roping saddle, are narrow and rounded to hold the foot securely.

Reining saddles are lighter, with the stirrups having a pronounced forward swing ability, a necessary factor in executing the sliding stop.

Show or *Parade* saddles, apart from their decoration, are deeper in the seat to encourage a more upright posture and the stirrups hang straight, with minimal forward or backward movement. The horn is no more than an acknowledgement of convention and is low and small.

Barrel Racing is a speed event and the saddle used is very much a streamlined version of the norm. It is therefore, lighter and, additionally, the skirts are cut far shorter so as not to obstruct the movement in any way.

Fig. 180 The sliding stop of the Californian reinsman executed in a specialist reining saddle which allows a forward swing of the leg. (Photo: Bob Langrish)

Fig. 181 For the speed event of barrel racing a light, streamlined version of the workaday stock saddle is the appropriate Western pattern. (Photo: Bob Langrish)

Top quality Western saddles are constructed by lacing the outer leather layers to the tree, which is time-consuming and calls for a very skilled saddler. Cheaper saddles may have screw fittings or the outer layers of leather may be stapled or nailed on the tree.

South American saddles, especially those of the *gaucho*, differ in their construction. Allowing for the addition of the stirrups, the *gaucho* saddle is not dissimilar to those Scythian saddles preserved in the frozen tombs of Pazyryk* almost 3,000 years ago. Essentially, they are composed of two well-stuffed pads or cushions lying either side of the spine and joined by wooden arches at front and rear, or by a connecting piece of felt or leather. A sheepskin is used under the saddle and also over the seat and, of course, there is no horn as in the Western saddle, the *gaucho* using his lariat in different fashion and relying, too, on the *bolas*, the rope fitted

(*The deep-frozen tombs of Pazyryk in the Altai Mountains of Western Siberia were excavated by Dr S. I. Rudenko in 1929. They belonged to Scythian 'ranchers', one of the earliest horse peoples, and their contents were preserved in the ice exactly as they were 3,000 years ago on the day they were buried)

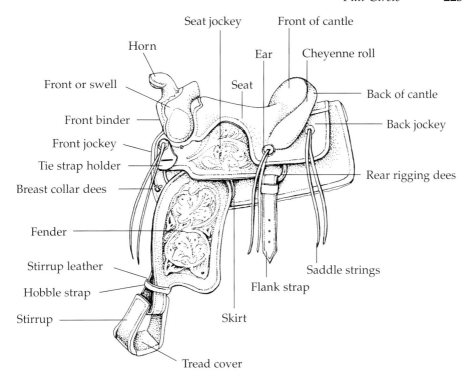

Seat jockey
Front of cantle
Horn
Ear
Cheyenne roll
Front or swell
Seat
Front binder
Back of cantle
Front jockey
Back jockey
Tie strap holder
Breast collar dees
Rear rigging dees
Fender
Stirrup leather
Hobble strap
Saddle strings
Stirrup
Flank strap
Skirt
Tread cover

Fig. 182 Parts of the Western Saddle.

with two or three balls or stones at one end which is thrown to entangle the legs of cattle and bring them down.

The Western saddle is comfortably reassuring for the novice but it is also a most sophisticated piece of equipment. Western sports and riding classes are, indeed, far more formal than their European counterparts and great attention is paid to the detail of clothes and equipment.

Full Circle

Following the domestication of the horse some 6,000 years ago the first saddles were no more than skins or pads thrown over the horse's back. In fact, the Greeks under Xenophon (c 430–356 bc), the iconic soldier, historian and philosopher who wrote the first equestrian instructional manuals, rode bareback and largely without benefit of breeches. It was not until the early Christian era that the Sarmatians, a nomadic tribe of Iranian origin, began to build saddles on a wooden frame (a tree) and introduced the concept of heavy cavalry and the shock tactic of the charge. Although the invention of the stirrup was still a long way off, the deep-seated Sarmatian saddle offered a degree of security, the horseman being able to brace himself against the high cantle at the moment of impact with the enemy foot soldiers.

The further development of the saddle was concerned almost entirely with saddles built on the foundation of a tree, but there were the odd exceptions, like the early saddles of the native American, the prototype gaucho saddle and the saddle of the Hungarian *czikos* horsemen of the Hungarian *puszta*. Then, much later in time, there were the pad saddles built for children between the two World Wars. A notable treeless saddle was the Australian Cobbar, an adult version of the child's pad, constructed of felt and fitted with a panel of the same material. It was to be seen quite frequently in jumping classes up to World War II but was not much in evidence after that time.

In our own century, many Western catalogues feature bareback pads and in the last decade there has been a small but discernible movement towards a treeless saddle suitable for modern riding disciplines.

There was an Italian saddle, 'so flexible it can be rolled up into a rucksack', which was developed for the endurance riding market and made with wool pile and layers of shock-absorbing foam. That one seems to have gone out of production, but a few years ago an American firm patented a treeless saddle, the patent being subsequently and understandably contested since there were already treeless patterns in production.

The market leader in Europe at the present time is probably the range of treeless saddles made by Heather Moffatt of Enlightened Equitation in south-west England.

Moffat's saddles, in essence a 'bag' into which a central core is inserted, can be made up by competent seamstresses, experienced in sheepskin and leather-working, without the need to employ qualified saddlers. Layers of wool felt and viscose elastic foams form the body of the saddle. Girth straps and stirrup bar webbings are passed through the body and are very carefully positioned to assist the rider's central seat.

Initially, these saddles were frequently too wide over the waist, but a change in the material used for the seat allowed the waist to be narrowed and overcame the problem.

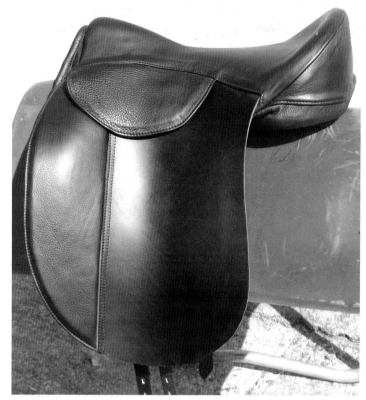

Fig. 183 Full Circle. The English Fheonix saddle made without the traditional tree. Layers of wool felt and viscose elastic foams form the body of the saddle. (Photo courtesy Enlightened Equitation)

Clearly, a saddle constructed without a tree avoids the pressures and fitting problems associated with the latter. The shock-absorbent material makes for great comfort (one would imagine for both parties): it facilitates fitting and it certainly allows for a close contact between rider and horse.

To what extent the treeless saddle will impinge on the conventional market is impossible to foresee at this juncture, but it adds another legitimate dimension as a modern version of the saddles used by the first and most significant of the horse peoples of the Central Asian steppelands; the fierce warrior tribes who were the catalyst for future civilisations – a matter of the wheel turning full circle indeed.

19 Girths and Breastplates

'A horse is a vain thing for safety…' Psalm 33 v.17

Girths

Moderately priced modern girths are made largely from nylon or cotton, often fitted with a centre of soft, resilient foam. On the whole they are satisfactory, except for the cheaper types made up wholly in nylon. They easily become hard in use, unless washed very frequently, and even then are not sufficiently soft. Furthermore, since by its nature nylon is an abrasive, nonabsorbent material, girths made from it are more likely to chafe and gall.

Surprisingly, the woven cotton girth, 8.75 cm (3½ in) wide, made from tubular *lampwick* has largely disappeared from the market. It was soft, hard-wearing, relatively inexpensive and ideal for use on fat horses, brought up from grass, as well as for any other purpose. *(On a visit to Walsall a few years ago I was given a roll of lampwick because the factory had no use for it and I suspect, indeed, were uncertain about its use. In consequence I have a good supply of excellent lampwick girths.)*

Similarly, *nylon and string cord* girths are now out of fashion. One the whole, with the exception of some German and American patterns, they were not much good and we are better off without them.

At the top end of the market are the *leather* girths. They are costly, but long-lasting and possessed of particular advantages. Treated with a good leather preparation from the outset they retain the grease content and become soft and supple as the result of contact with the horse's body.

Both the *Atherstone* and *Balding* pattern girths (those are the correct names) are shaped at the elbow to reduce the risk of galling in this area and this sensible precaution is followed by some of the nylon/cotton girths also.

Less well known is the admittedly expensive *three-fold leather* girth made from soft baghide and folded in three to give a 8.75 cm (3½ in)

226

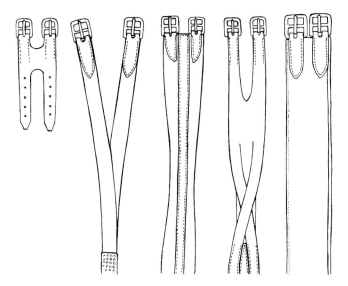

Fig. 184 A selection of girths. From left to right: girth extension; twin-web pony show girth with pimple-rubber centre; Atherstone; Balding; three-fold baghide.

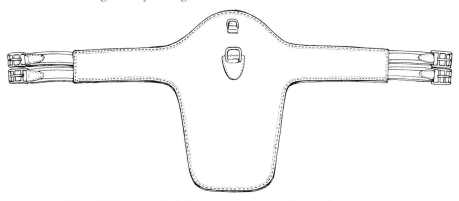

Fig. 185 Leather girth incorporating a stud guard as a protection against injury by the forefeet.

width. A traditionally made *three-fold* girth has a strip of serge cloth laid inside the fold. If this is smeared with a grease dressing before use, the warmth of the horse will melt the preparation and it will work through the leather making it wonderfully soft and supple. The rounded edge of the three-fold girth should form its front edge when it is in position so as to avoid the possibility of pinching or rubbing in the area of the elbow, and the same applies of course to a short dressage girth made up in the three-fold style. *(This is a point worth checking when purchasing such a girth. At a recent national dressage event I saw three competitors, none of them novices, riding with leather girths that had been made up the wrong way round.)*

The most effective girth, in terms of keeping the saddle firmly in position, and the one that will give the longest service, is based on the broad military girth made from a single piece of leather split in the body to form laces (like a string girth) (Fig. 186). My personal preference would be for one made from a strip of stout, red buffalo hide. Such girths, however, are not in general production and would need to be made specially.

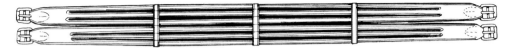

Fig. 186 *The author's personal preference. A single piece of leather split in the body to form laces on the pattern of the old military girth.*

Webbing girths are not now in general use, although they are still obtainable, and in a narrow width are used for racing and cross-country riding. They are sold in pairs, each girth terminating in a single buckle, and may have become unpopular on this score for it takes a few seconds longer to girth the horse correctly.

When web girths are used they should be made of *wool* web, not cotton which becomes hard when it has absorbed a lot of sweat and is less reliable in respect of its breaking point than the woollen types. Both wool and cotton need to be washed frequently. Web girths may not be a popular choice, but they are distinctive, for the web is obtainable in combinations of two or three colours.

Following the racing example, cross-country riders will wisely use a *surcingle* with web girths, lest one should break under the considerable strain imposed on it. A surcingle also acts as an additional means of keeping the saddle in position. A surcingle is a single piece of web fitted with a buckle at one end and a long billet (fastening strap) at the other. It is sufficiently long to be passed over the waist of the saddle and fastened over the girths under the belly. To call a surcingle a roller or vice versa is a mistake in nomenclature. A roller is wider and is fitted with stuffed pads which lie either side of the withers. Its purpose is to keep a rug in place, or it can be made up as a breaking roller for use on young horses. If it is thought necessary to anglicise a word of French origin it would be permissible to call a surcingle an *overgirth*.

For *show ponies* an excellent girth is made from two strips of narrow – about 3.2 cm (1¼ in) – tubular white web, the join at the centre being encircled with a piece of pimple rubber, like that used on a rubber-hand-part rein. The rubber grips the coat and the skin and the divided body of the girth, forming a vee, ensures that the girth and saddle remain central. This is particularly so if the girth is fastened to a forward point strap and to the last of the usual girth straps.

Dressage girths of the short *Lonsdale* type are made up from nylon/cotton materials or from leather. It is a matter of some importance to ensure that there is an adequate 'safe' (backing) behind the buckles to prevent rubbing. If the horse's conformation is such that the saddle slips forward unacceptably, a surcingle, with a billet strap on each end, passed over the waist of the saddle and attached to buckles (set on to elastic if you like) fitted at the belly of the girth will be helpful and as effective, if not more so, as the ill-conceived foregirth.

Strong elastic can be inset into any girth and allows for the lungs' and rib-cage's expansion at moments of peak effort, as well, probably, as making the girth more generally comfortable. If elastic inserts are used for racing or cross-country riding, which is sensible, and a surcingle is also employed, it is logical for the surcingle also to incorporate an elastic insert – it is surprising to see how many plain, non-elastic surcingles are used with elastic-inset girths.

The fitting best calculated to keep the girth central in the sternum curve is the vee arrangement used in what used to be called the 'humane' girths. 'Humane' or not, the twin-buckle fitting set on an oval metal ring acts to equalise the pressure, to centre the girth and to hold it and the saddle very effectively in position. Surprisingly, perhaps, it is used very frequently with polo saddles.

Fig. 187 The very practical 'humane' or self-centring girth allowing accurate positioning in the sternum curve. It holds the saddle in position more firmly than other girth patterns.

Even better is the Wellep slide (Fig. 145, p.184) attached directly to the girth straps which can be used with any two-buckle girth.

Girth extensions are a useful way of adding length to a girth when fat horses come up from grass and *girth safes*, thin pieces of leather slotted on the girth straps to cover the buckles, will prevent the latter from wearing holes in the underside of the flaps. Thick girth safes, supplied, one imagines, by manufacturers unaware of their unsuitability, will certainly save the flap from damage but will also cause an irritating bulk under the leg as well as making the business of adjusting the girth straps more difficult.

Buckles are obviously crucial to the efficiency and safety of the girth. The best buckles are those made from stainless steel and they are characterised by the firmness of the tongue setting, the end of the tongue lying neatly in the recess provided on the upper bar. Good buckles of this sort make the girth adjustment a simple matter. Bad buckles of nickel with loose, ill-made tongues, act in opposite fashion and are suspect in respect of their strength.

(For riders of small stature, owning large horses, or for the weak and feeble, there is an American girth tightener device to give greater ease of leverage. Made from 'strong fiberglass filled nylon' it is called the 'belly buster'!)

Fitting

The shape of the girth and the material it is made from help to keep the girth and the saddle from sliding forwards – when the former will be likely to chafe at the elbows. What is even more important, however, is the shape of the horse. The girth passes round the brisket lying, in reasonably well-made horses, in the convenient hollow termed the sternum curve. If there is no such curve, the girth and the saddle will ride forward. The girth has to have some purchase against the edge of the brisket if it is to stay in place.

Where the brisket runs up towards the elbow rather than down, there is usually a prominent swell to the rear ribs and a spreading belly as well. That is an impossible situation which is bound to result in a saddle slipping forwards. The same happens, of course, with a horse moving hollow-backed with the head carried above the bit. The saddle rides forward and the girth chafes against the elbows.

Chafing will occur when horses are worked in soft condition and the problem can be helped by fitting a sheepskin sleeve, or even a section of rubber inner tube, around the girth.

Breastplates

Breastplates are used to prevent saddles sliding *backwards* and may be necessary with a flat-sided horse or when operating in hilly country. Hunting breastplates need to be backed with sheepskin or a circle of soft leather at the juncture of the body strap (passing between the

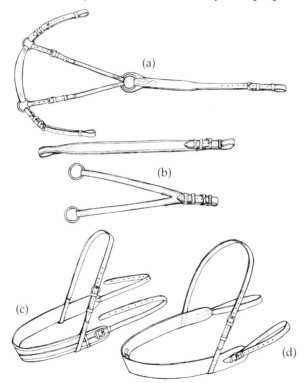

Fig. 188 (a) Hunting-type breastplate;
(b) standing and running martingale attachments
which can be used with a hunting breastplate;
(c) Aintree-pattern web 'chasing breastplate;
(d) folded leather or elastic polo breastplate.

forelegs) with the neckstrap so as to prevent any possibility of the horse being rubbed. *(It is as well to check the length of the return straps fastening to the saddle dees – they are rarely long enough on a big horse.)*

For racing or cross-country riding it is usual to employ an Aintree-pattern breastplate fastening round the chest. It is a sensible precaution because light saddles can slip, but the breastplate should be adjusted with care to ensure that it does not ride up and interfere with the wind-pipe. The Aintree can be made from web, light folded leather or from elastic. A similar type, made in leather, is used for polo but a loop is needed on the inside, in the centre of the breast part, to accommodate the body of the obligatory standing martingale so as to dispense with the usual martingale neckstrap.

20 Stirrup Leathers and Stirrup Irons

'There is room for much to happen twixt the stirrup and the ground.'

Stirrup Leathers

Stirrup leathers are made from either oxhide (usually of an 'oak bark' tannage), rawhide or buffalo hide, often known as 'red leathers'. In the first two the flesh side is made to face outwards so that the grain side, which is the tougher of the two, receives the friction from the eye, or slot, in the iron through which the leather passes, whereas in the last case this position is reversed, the flesh side this time coming into contact with the iron. This leather is so strong, however, that there is little difference in the wearing properties of the two sides. *(In our increasingly litigious age manufacturers take extra precautions by inserting a layer of nylon between the leather and the buckle bar to which it is fastened. Some leathers, indeed, are made with a nylon reinforcement throughout their length and, of course, there are stirrup 'leathers' made entirely from nylon which to all intents are unbreakable in normal use. Nylon 'leathers' are recommended for use with saddles made from synthetic fabrics as they do not mark the flap surface in the same way as the naturally greasy leather.)*

All leathers, other than those made of nylon, will stretch in use; rawhide and buffalo hide to a greater extent than oxhide. As the majority of riders place more weight in one stirrup iron than in the other, you should alternate the leathers, particularly when new, from side to side to prevent uneven stretching in either one of the pair. It is also essential to get the stretch out of a new pair of leathers before they are used for a specific event. It would, for instance, be unwise to use a new pair for the first time in a point-to-point where the rider might well find that they had stretched in the course of his journey to such an extent that he was forced to ride a good deal longer than he wished.

When a pair of leathers has been used for a considerable length of time, wear occurs where they pass through the iron. With red leathers this is not material, but in other types the leather should be shortened a little from the buckle end to allow an unworn portion to come into contact with the iron. It is helpful to have the holes on a pair of leathers numbered, and personally I like the holes punched fairly close together to enable a finer adjustment to be made. Holes so punched are termed 'half-holes' and used almost always to be present in show leathers for the greater convenience of the judge.

Of the three types of leather mentioned, the buffalo hide is probably the longest lasting. It remains supple throughout its life and is virtually unbreakable. *(I have six pairs of leathers. Four are made from the best oak-bark tanned oxhide in a 2.5 cm (1 in) width. Two of these pairs have been in constant use for some thirty years; the other two are about five years younger. The remaining two pairs are 2.5 cm (1 in) red buffalo hide. One pair was in use before the Second World War and the other is certainly forty years old. They have either Eglantine – one of the best mixture metals ever made – or stainless steel buckles.)* On account of their strength it is unnecessary for buffalo hide leathers to be wide and thick with a correspondingly large buckle to bulge under your thigh. For racing 1.6 cm (⅝ in) and 1.9 cm (¾ in) are plenty wide enough, and for hunting 2.2 cm (⅞ in), 2.5 cm (1 in) and possibly 2.9 cm (1⅛ in) for an exceptionally heavy man are the most suitable. *(In recent years, possibly again out of fear of litigation, buffalo hide leathers have been cut from hides of the heaviest possible substance and as wide as 3.2 cm (1⅝ in) and more. Polo leathers are especially wide and heavy and employ the clumsiest buckles imaginable as a consequence. Moreover, these leathers are usually badly finished. A mark of the wellfinished product, whatever the type of leather used, is that the edges should be bevelled and smoothed. This facilitates altering the length when mounted and a bevelled edge makes it easier to get the leather over the bar – or, conversely, for it to come off the bar in the event of a fall.*

These thick, clumsy leathers cause an uncomfortable bulk under the leg; they are unnecessary and even dangerous, for they do not come off the bar easily if the rider should be unseated.)

Lightweight racing saddles are frequently mounted with stirrup webs instead of leathers when weight is of paramount importance. The points of these webs where the holes are punched are reinforced with leather, but the remaining length is a plain tubular web. These are made in a 1.25 cm (½ in) width for flat racing, and 1.6 cm (⅝ in) and 1.9 cm (¾ in) for 'chasing. *(Increasingly, of course, nylon webs are used.)*

'Dressage' leathers are obtainable with the adjustment fastening

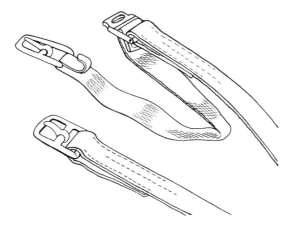

Fig. 189 'Hook-up' or extending stirrup leathers for the short of leg or non-athletic horseman.

placed just above the stirrup. The arrangement obviates the bulk of a buckle under the thigh but is not, of course, adjustable from the saddle.

For those who find mounting difficult, or who have short legs and large horses, an expanding or 'hook up' stirrup leather (Fig. 189) is available. The nearside leather is fitted with a hook and slot attachment, the two parts being joined by a piece of strong tubular web. When open this allows the leather to extend downwards for some further 15 or 20 cm (6 or 8 in), and when the rider is mounted it is a simple matter to slip the slot over the hook, when the leather is again at its normal length.

Most people, I feel, would agree that a thick leather with a large buckle is a deterrent to our sitting as close as possible to the saddle and yet the majority of us persist, almost instinctively, in tucking the loose end under the existing two thicknesses of leather to form a bulge under our thigh, whereas if we just pointed the leather to the rear (after a little while it will fall naturally into this position) and passed the end through the loop which is usually fitted to the saddle for this purpose, we should have only three thicknesses and the bulge would be reduced by 25 per cent.

When the leathers have finished stretching they can be trained to lie correctly in relation to the saddle. This useful position can be easily accomplished by taking the nearside iron and twisting it in a clockwise direction before exerting a strong downwards pull. The iron will then hang naturally at right angles to the saddle and the difficulty of feeling for the iron with the toe is overcome. The offside leather is treated in the same way but, of course, is twisted anticlockwise.

Stirrup Irons

Have your irons made of stainless steel, anything else is not worth the risk. Nickel irons are wolves in sheep's clothing and should be avoided at all costs. They are prone to both bend and break and they turn a nauseous yellow colour once taken out of the wrapping paper. *(I note that in the American market stirrup irons are offered in brass and also in coloured finishes – I still prefer stainless steel.)*

Those who go showjumping or engage in similar sports, and are fearful of losing an iron over a fence will find that a piece of black mane thread attached from the spur to the iron will help to retain it and will break easily enough should that be necessary.

(There has been some disquiet expressed recently by the safety lobby about the possibility of riders being dragged as a result of a foot becoming trapped in the iron and the leather not being released from the bar. There could be a danger but it should not be exaggerated, for there are no statistics to show that this sort of accident is other than exceptionally infrequent. However, that is no reason why sensible precautions should not be taken. It is not, as I have mentioned, very sensible to use excessively thick leathers and it is just as stupid to ride in light irons or ones that are tight on the foot. Trainers, sandals and wellies are all equally unsuitable. I ride in long-soled leather boots with a substantial heel. My irons are made of stainless steel; the tread (i.e. the base of the stirrup iron) measures 12.5 cm (5 in) in width, a good size larger than my boot, and each iron weighs 680 g (1½ lb). Heavy irons fall away from the foot should the rider be dislodged; light ones do not.)

There are *safety* irons available which are more or less satisfactory. Well established is the *Peacock*, a three-sided iron, if the tread is included, the fourth side being made up with a strong rubber ring stretched between a hook and a stud at the base of the iron. In the event of a fall the rubber ring becomes detached and the foot is freed – as long as the open side of the iron is on the outside of the foot; amazingly it often is not. There is also a particular disadvantage to the design. The tread, supported on only one side, can become bent by constant mounting from the ground and that does no good for the subsequent leg position.

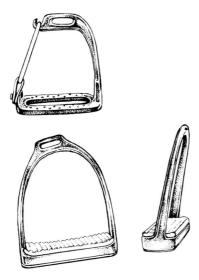

Fig. 190 Top: the overrated Peacock safety iron.
Below: the off-set Kournakoff jumping pattern.

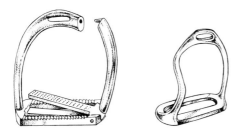

Fig. 191 Left: the hinged-spring safety iron.
Right: the Australian Simplex iron – quite simply the best of them all.

There are one or two *hinged-spring* irons about that will open to release the foot if the need arises. Their principal failing is that they will cease to operate should the spring mechanism become corroded, which is not impossible. Conversely, when in working order, the spring can open when you would rather it stayed closed.

(These patterns were in production well over a century and a half ago, appearing in the saddlery catalogues of the day. Very recently they have made a reappearance on the market, the advertising blurb heralding them as the greatest safety

breakthrough for the past 200 years – no sense of history, I fear, nor of accuracy, but a praiseworthy marketing initiative.)

Probably the most effective safety iron is the straightforward Australian Simplex with its pronounced forward loop on the outside – like the Australian stock saddle it is essentially practical.

There are three principal variations on the basic stirrup pattern. They are the *bent-top* iron, the *Kournakoff* and what might be called the *turned-eye* iron.

In the first of these the iron is bent away from the rider's instep and thus prevents the iron from wearing away the boot should the horseman ride with the foot fully home – a position not so much adopted today but which is not unknown. The shaping of the iron will also encourage a lowering of the heel.

The *Kournakoff* is a jumping iron named after its inventor Captain Sergei Kournakoff, a White Russian who settled in America after the Revolution. With his countryman, Captain Vladimir Littauer, he was co-author of a number of books expounding the merits of the Caprilli system, e.g. *Defence of the Forward Seat, Ten Talks on Horsemanship*, etc.

The iron is distinguished by having the eye offset to the inside, while the sides of the iron are sloped forward with the tread sloping upwards. As a result the foot is fixed in a position in which the toe is held up and the heel down, the sole of the foot being higher on the outside than the inside. The knee and thigh are in consequence pressed inwards against the saddle. Of necessity, the irons are marked 'left' and 'right' and one can imagine the difficulty that would be experienced if the positions were reversed. The Kournakoff may well be helpful for jumping but is less suitable for dressage riding.

The *turned-eye* stirrup has the eye set in line with the stirrup leather so that it hangs at right angles to the saddle after the manner of North African stirrups. The disadvantage is that the iron cannot be run up the leather when the horse is being led in hand. There is therefore a danger of the iron being caught up on some projection or other.

Comparative newcomers to the stirrup range are those irons which incorporate flexibility and are claimed to absorb shock to 'the back, hips, knees and ankles' while maintaining a proper foot position. Without doubt they are of good quality and constructed with great ingenuity but, of course, wear in the working parts is unavoidable.

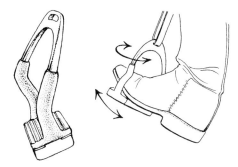

*Fig. 192 Cleverly constructed flexible stirrup iron.
It is claimed to absorb shock to 'the back, hips,
knees and ankles' while assisting the foot position.*

Rubber stirrup treads are now almost universally used. Inserted into the metal tread, they help the foot to keep its position and they keep the toes warm in cold weather. Dressage riders sometimes use a tread that is built higher on the inside. It is thought to assist the 'wrap-round' position of the leg.

(The original treads, still available in Britain, were called Agrippin and were introduced by Mrs Dorothy Popoff, a lady with strong circus connections who settled in England and was an accomplished High School rider.)

A further stirrup accessory inspired by the concern for safety is the stirrup 'hood' which clips onto the iron and will prevent the foot sliding through. They are popular with trekking centres whose clients may well turn up in all sorts of unsuitable holiday footwear. They do also, of course, help to keep the feet warm. *(These hoods are adaptations of the clog and slipper stirrups made for children and ladies in the early nineteenth century.)*

Lightweight racing irons are made in a 'cradle' pattern, often using aluminium in the interests of weight reduction. In the future they are likely to be made in graphite – a much stronger material.

In years gone by, when riding instructors might be equated with drill sergeants of the old school, shoulders were kept back and straight by the expedient of a cane placed under the upper arm and across the back. Legs that had yet to acquire the desirable quiet stillness, with the foot resting on the iron, were helped to keep their position by a piece of binder twine attached at one end to the girth and at the other to the inside branch of the stirrup iron. In the twenty-first century an

Fig. 193 Trade-named Symmetry Leg this effective device replaces the binder twine of yesteryear. The neat straps incorporate a quick-release provision and help to preserve the position of the lower leg. (Photo courtesy Equilibrium)

enterprising company has substituted a pair of neat straps, incorporating a quick-release provision, to serve the same purpose. They are marketed as a 'simple, safe and discreet way of training the lower leg'. Learning to ride, of course, will achieve the same objective but the strap fills a niche and may, indeed, be a useful aid for the novice rider.

21 Boots and the Protection of the Legs

'Prevention is better than cure.'

Boots

In simple terms boots, and bandages too, protect the lower limbs against injuries which might occur as a result of self-inflicted blows, or those caused by loss of balance when travelling or, additionally, by a horse slipping up when being exercised on the road. They may also be used to give support, particularly in respect of the tendons of the forelegs.finish

Avoiding Injuries Whilst Working

In fact, many of the common injuries which occur are the result of conformational failures resulting in an imperfect action. A good farrier is often able to correct the fault by altering the balance of the foot and ensuring that the proper foot-pastern axis (FPA) is maintained. However, that is no reason why a boot should not also be used, if only on the principle of wearing both belt and braces on a pair of trousers.

The most usual injuries requiring protective boots are *brushing*, *overreaching* and, to a lesser degree, *speedicutting*. Sometimes it may be necessary to protect shins, either in front or behind, which have been made sore by hitting an obstacle when jumping.

Brushing is when the inside of the leg, usually in the area of the fetlock joint, is hit by the opposite foot. Brushing boots should therefore be shaped (cupped) round the inside of the whole joint and they must be made of a material with a high shock-absorbent property – a thin foam, inadequately shaped, is useless: the neoprene- and polymer-lined boots are probably the most satisfactory so long as they are shaped to the joint. In some instances the injury may be sustained below the joint on the coronet and the usual brushing boot will give no protection. What is needed is a shorter *coronet* boot – Fig. 197(d) –extending from the coronet downwards over and around the hoof.

The two most simple forms of protection against brushing are the rubber antibrushing ring –Fig. 196(d) – and the Yorkshire boot. The first is a hollow, rubber ring, like that used in beach games. It is cut open to allow a fastening strap to be passed through it and is fitted below the joint, thus

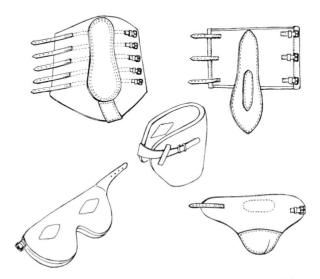

Fig. 194 Some of the huge range of brushing and fetlock boots.

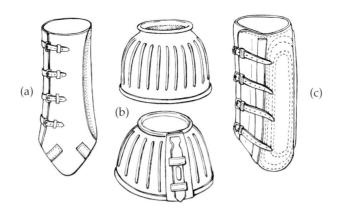

Fig. 195 (a) Heel boot; (b) overreach boots (the lower one with an easy fastening); (c) the best of all the tendon boots.

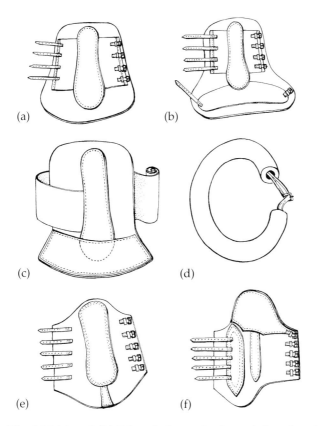

Fig. 196 (a) and (b) Felt polo boots, leather reinforced and with the fastenings set on broad elastic; (c) polo/exercise boot, bandage fastening; (d) antibrushing ring; (e) speedicut boot; (f) French-pattern 'chasing boot giving speedicut protection.

ensuring immunity from a strike in that area. A Yorkshire boot (easily made-up at home) is no more than a stout oblong piece of rugging with a tape sewn along the centre. It is tied round above the joint and doubled over to form a protective cuff. It is very effective but not much good in deep mud.

Overreaching is when the hind toes strike into the heels of the foreleg; it occurs most frequently when jumping out of heavy going, although it is common enough amongst showjumpers, too. It is a painful and disabling injury which can put a horse out of work for a matter of weeks and may need extensive stitching by a veterinarian.

The answer is a rubber, bell-shaped, overreach boot – Fig. 195(b) – put on over the hoof and extending above the heels. Once upon a time, they were made in one piece and had to be immersed in hot water before they became flexible enough to be pulled over the hoof. Today, the fitting is facilitated by some form of easy fastening.

Should the boot be subjected to a heavy blow it will, most probably, be split, and owners may be tempted to return it to the supplier complaining bitterly of poor quality and so on, an action which is quite unjustified. (*Commenting in* Equestrian Trade News *on complaints made by the public in these circumstances I was bold enough to offer this advice to retailers and I have no hesitation in repeating it here:*

> *In those circumstances, forget about the customer always being right and remember that he or she is often wrong. Reply in robust terms, telling the complainant that had it not been for the boot the horse might have been off work for two months and have been subjected to great discomfort during that time. Suggest that the hind feet had been allowed to grow too long; insist that for the horse's sake the farrier should be consulted more frequently. Cast veiled aspersions upon their standards of horse management and do not let them leave the shop without purchasing at least two further pairs of overreach boots and being grateful for the opportunity to do so.*

Well, if the cap fits…)

A more dangerous form of overreach is when the blow occurs well above the heel and the tendon is damaged. To counteract that, protection is needed from below the knee down to the joint – Fig. 195(c) – and I would use an overreach boot as well to complete the defence system. *In fairness, there has been criticism of both the overreach boot and the principles involved in the use of protective/supportive boots generally. It is worth noting but need not, I think, be taken too seriously.*

The argument that an overreach boot will not afford *sufficient* protection to avoid injury from a blow by the hind foot is not, for instance, a valid one. It *is* possible for a horse to sustain injury either from a cut or from bruising even when wearing overreach boots, but how much worse would the injury have been without the protection of the boot acting to limit the damage?

It has been claimed that continual use of leg boots for either protection or support *may* create heat that could weaken the tendon fibres of the legs; however, in what degree and how significantly has yet to be established. Many modern patterns are, indeed, made from 'breathable' materials and some are claimed to be 'self-ventilating' to reduce the possibility of the leg being overheated.

The modern range of boots, both for competition and travelling, makes use of some remarkable shock-absorbent materials and if used sensibly are very good indeed, even if the manufacturers are given to making extravagant claims. (One American manufacturer states that a specific pattern 'promotes superior hind end movement over the jump'. It doesn't but, the hyperbole apart, it is a good boot.)

Speedicutting is the name given to an injury when the horse is travelling at speed. A hind foot strikes the inside of the opposite leg well above the joint and usually just below the hock. To guard against such an injury, it follows that the boot must provide protection in that area, which those made in America and by the harness-racing saddlers of Europe do, but I have yet to find a British-made speedicut boot that relates to the specific injury or, indeed, a manufacturer who knows what kind of injury is caused by a speedicut. *(Come to that, I know precious few riders who are any more knowledgeable!)*

Shin boots – Fig. 197(a) – giving protection to the front edge of both fore and hind legs, are occasionally necessary should a horse have suffered positive injury in those areas. For myself, I prefer an open-front boot protecting the tendons and at the same time mitigating the worst effects of brushing, but without covering the shins.

The argument is that a horse wearing a protective shin guard learns to take liberties. It does not hurt to hit a fence so he gets into the habit of treating obstacles with less respect than they deserve and one day he comes a monumental cropper as a result. Wearing an open front boot – Fig. 198(b) – he quickly learns to 'tuck-up' at his fences to save himself discomfort. It would, of course, be advisable when going across country to smear the shins liberally with grease to lessen the effect of impact against ungiving timber.

Very good, comprehensive protection is afforded by a set of felt *polo boots* – Fig. 196 (a) and (b) – reinforced with leather. They have an obvious use on the polo field but they are also invaluable when working young horses who have yet to develop co-ordination of movement and are, on that account, likely to cause themselves injury.

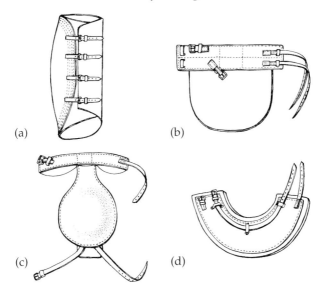

Fig. 197 (a) Shin boot; (b) jumping knee-caps;
(c) skeleton knee-cap (ideal for road work); (d) coronet boot.

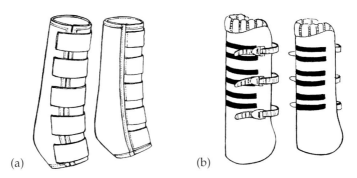

Fig. 198 (a) Modern heel-tendon boot giving good protection;
(b) open-front jumping boots.

Protection Whilst Travelling

Protective leg coverings do not stop at those designed to combat the effect of injuries sustained in active competition; they are also necessary for travelling.

Fig. 199 Ready to travel and immaculately turned out.
(Photo courtesy Thorowgood Ltd)

In either a horsebox or trailer horses will move about within the confines imposed by the partitions so as to keep their balance. Some move only a little while others are more restive. A rubber flooring under foot is the best material to save them from slipping. Straw, once used extensively, is less satisfactory and the deep, slatted floors of cattle lorries are the worst of all. The obvious areas at risk are the lower limbs, from and including the knees and hocks and extending downwards over the hoof and heels.

Common travelling injuries are caused by 'treads' when one foot strikes or treads on its opposite partner in the region of the coronary band, below the inside of the joint or on the heel. In addition, a number of horses will brace themselves by standing across the travelling compartment with a hock pressed against the outer wall or the partition. The result may well be a damaged or 'capped' hock (a soft, unsightly swelling on the point of the joint). Knees can be rubbed and damaged in the same way and it is not unknown for a horse to skin the outside of a limb if travelled without suitable protection.

The answer could be a set of full-length travelling boots with built-in hock and knee protection (Fig. 200). They are always sufficiently long to come over the hoof and, of course, Velcro fastenings allow them to be put on in a matter of seconds. They are possibly less satisfactory when used on a bad traveller who stamps and moves continually. In those circumstances they can turn on the leg or even slip downwards. My own preference is for a stronger shipping-type boot covering the leg closely below the joints and extending well over the foot. Ideally, additional protection is laid on the inside of the leg to cover the fetlock joint and a strong reinforcement over the hoof. To complete the protection one needs a separate

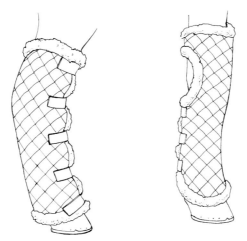

Fig. 200 Travelling wraps to protect fore and hind legs.

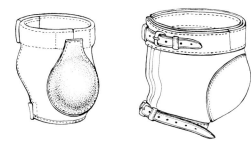

Fig. 201 Left: knee-cap. Right: hock boot.

pair of knee-caps and hock boots (Fig. 201). The knee-caps, if they are of the correct pattern and sufficiently deep, can double up as a useful boot for road riding, whilst the hock boots can be used independently on those irritating animals who insist upon supporting themselves in the stable by pressing their hocks hard up against the wall.

Materials and Fastenings

Boots made from stout Kersey cloth or from box-cloth (the same tough, weatherproof material once used to make a 'box' coat for a driving man) have now given way to modern synthetics which are in almost every way more satisfactory. Leather, however, is still used for many of the best boot patterns.

The traditional fastening method was by strap and buckle. Front boots had four straps and hind boots five. Buckle fastenings were and are reliable but they take time to put on (eighteen straps to do up with numbed fingers on a cold morning) and they must be adjusted carefully, the top strap being tighter by a hole or two than the bottom one. Otherwise, modern boots fasten quickly with Velcro straps – which wear out in time and are not suitable for other than light exercise work – or with a more satisfactory hook fastening which is often set on elastic.

A failing with the old-pattern boots was that dirt and grit adhering to the cloth could work up between the inside of the boot and the leg. In some modern boots the problem still remains, those with fleece-type linings are particularly prone to this fault, but otherwise the modern plastics are more easily kept clean.

Bandages

For the most part bandages are used for protection, support and, in the interests of good management, to keep the legs warm and comfortable – cold extremities being just as much an anathema to the equine as the human. There are, also, of course, tail bandages to keep the tail nicely shaped and to prevent it being rubbed and the hairs broken when the horse is travelling. Otherwise, there are veterinary bandages used to reduce swellings, etc.

Boots are more or less effective in all instances applicable to the legs and have the advantage of being fitted quickly. Bandages take a little longer and need to be put on with a degree of expertise, but they allow for greater accuracy and precision in their application than is ever possible with a boot.

Stable bandages, preferably made of wool and not less than 2.4 m (8 ft) in length and 12.5 cm (5 in) wide, are used following severe exertion, such as hunting, when horses often suffer extreme coldness of the limbs – and of the ears, too. The latter can be 'stripped', i.e. rubbed by hand to encourage circulation and if they are still cold you can put on a cap or hood. The legs are bandaged from below the knee and hock to envelop the fetlock joint, which is why a leg bandage needs to have extra length. It is put on over either a felt pad or over a square of the famous tissue invented by Dr Gamgee. The practice of bandaging over a pad increases the warmth, obviously, but also ensures that the tension is spread evenly so that there is no risk of the bandage interfering with the circulation.

Stable bandages need not be reserved for hunting days or specially strenuous occasions. They can be put on the stabled horse as a regular procedure each night, particularly, of course, in the cold winter months. The stable bandage will also double up as a travelling bandage if one-piece leg wraps are not used for that purpose. A travelling bandage is put on in exactly the same way, i.e. extending over the fetlock from below the knee and hock. For complete protection it would, of course, be used in conjunction with knee-caps and hock boots.

Ideally, the exercise, or working, bandage, protecting and supporting the tendons, should be 2.5 cm (1 in) narrower than the stable bandage and, since it is put on between the hock or knee joint and the fetlock, it does not need to be so long. It is made of stretch cotton material and should be put on over an impact-absorbent pad of one type or another.

Modern bandages are frequently fitted with Velcro fastenings but some still have conventional tapes. When tapes are used to secure the bandage, the knot must be tied on the outside of the leg, not on the shin where it would form a pressure point and interfere with the circulation. For competition it is usual to take extra precautions and, whether the bandage is fitted with Velcro or tape fastenings, to stitch the fastenings to the bandage with mane thread. For good measure it is then advisable to tape it over with broad adhesive tape. This ensures the bandage staying in place and will also act to repel water which could cause the bandage to shrink in use, or at best become uncomfortably heavy. In fact there are bandages now available which are both self-adhesive and water-resistant. Used with some of the latest impact-absorbent pads they give a very high degree of protection and support.

Tail bandages (usually 8.75 cm [3½ in] wide) are almost always elasticated. When used for travelling it is probably advisable to fit a tail guard as well if you have the sort of horse who braces his rear against the ramp or the side of the box. *(In my experience horses rub their tails, other than when travelling, if they itch as a result of tiny parasites or, which is just as frequent, if tail bandages are put on too tightly, in which case they are trying to get rid of the article that is causing the discomfort. Overtight bandages interrupt the circulation, break the tail hairs and can cause such pain that the poor animal is driven to kick in protest. Bandages that are left on for too long produce much the same results – a bandage put on for a couple of hours at a time is sufficient for the purpose.)*

Cold water bandages for the treatment of swellings were once made of linen, which was far less prone to shrink and tighten in use. Nowadays, there are one or two patent bandages – cold compress wraps – which are safe in that respect, much more satisfactory and longer-lasting in their effect. For the most part these wraps are applied after soaking and freezing and provide intense, sustained cold, supporting tissues and limiting swelling.

The Magnetic Boot

Magnotherapy is now featured in a range of protective boots, hock wraps, back pads and, indeed, rugs also. It provides a fruitful source of 'scientific' copy for the catalogue compilers and may, indeed, bring relief in certain conditions. After all, how many of us wear magnetic bracelets?

22　Horse Clothing

'The outside is important, but the warmth comes from what you put in his belly.'

No area of horse equipment has expanded so much as the horse-clothing industry. There are now more manufacturers than at any time in the past hundred years, all of them, in one degree or another, making use of hi-tech materials that often incorporate valuable insulating properties. Of course, in such a crowded market there will be those who have little idea of design requirement as well as the inevitable complement of cheap-jacks. However, there are many more producing goods of a far higher quality in terms of fabric and suitability for the purpose than at any time previously. Indeed, there are so many good items of clothing on the market that, although competition is keen in consequence, the purchaser is liable to be spoilt for choice and hopelessly confused by the claims made for this or that fabric or pattern.

Nonetheless, despite the *embarras de richesses* and some sensible refinements as well, the purposes for providing the domestic horse with rugs and so on, and the divisions between the various items remain substantially the same.

Rugs

The most obvious requirement for the stabled horse whose winter coat has been removed by clipping is a rug combination that will replace the lost coat and keep the animal warm.

Such rugs are known as *night* or *stable* rugs. The basic rug is made from heavy jute lined with a grey blanketing and put on over an under-blanket. Traditionally, these are fawn wool blankets with horizontal black, red and blue stripes on either side. They weigh between 3.2–3.6 kg (7–8 lb), a full-size one measuring 183 x 205cm (72 x 81 in) and it was customary for them to be sold by the 1 lb (0.45 kg) weight. These colourful blankets are still made at Witney in Oxfordshire, where they were first manufactured for the Hudson Bay Company which traded them to the Canadian Indians in return for furs.

The blanket is put on over a light cotton 'sheet', fastening in the usual way at the breast, so that the blanket is kept clean and does not gather hairs from the coat. The method employed to keep the blanket in place is to put it on high up the neck, turning back the surplus over the top rug so that it forms a comfortable collar.

The jute rug was a very serviceable item, but even better was the finer canvas or 'sail-cloth' rug which moulded itself very satisfactorily to the body outline. Rugs of this type are still used. Good ones are made with plenty of depth and should always be fitted with eyelets at the rear so that a fillet or tail string can be fitted. The fillet string prevents the rug from sliding forward.

Rollers and Surcingles

The rugs are kept in place either by a stable roller or by an arrangement of surcingles sewn on the body of the rug.

Stable rollers have largely been superseded by surcingles of one type or another, combined with a much improved tailoring of the material, the rug being shaped so that it conforms to the contours of the body.

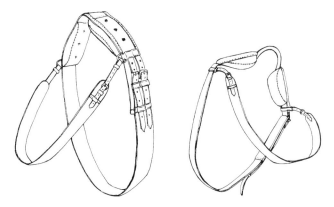

Fig. 202 Left: the stable roller with breast-girth. Right: the arch, 'anti-cast' roller. There are patterns which have the pads set on hinges so that they adjust to any back conformation.

The best rollers are made of leather; they will last upwards of half a century or more but are correspondingly expensive to buy. They are fitted with stuffed pads on either side of the spine to ensure that no pressure is placed directly on the vulnerable vertebrae. Fastening is by two straps and buckles on the nearside and the roller should always be used with a breast-girth, which will remove any need or temptation to girth up too tightly and thus cause discomfort. A popular pattern is the iron hoop or arch roller (Fig. 202) sometimes called an anticast roller because it helps to prevent a horse turning over and becoming 'cast' in the corner of his box; even more importantly such rollers cannot bear upon the spine. These hoop rollers can be made with the pads set on hinges so that they will adjust to any back conformation and are, on that account, as eminently a practical arrangement as an adjustable head plate on a saddle.

Rollers are normally made in widths between 10–12.5 cm (4–5 in) and become more affordable if made in wool web. Cheap rollers are made from hemp web and are in every way unsatisfactory; the web losing its shape and being quick to wear out.

Although it is not generally appreciated, or at least not sufficiently so, the fitting of rugs demands just as much attention as the fitting of the saddle. In fact, the latter is often blamed for rubs and galls when the real culprit is the rug and the manner in which it is secured. Rugs which are too tight round the neck (a common failing) will certainly rub the point of the shoulders but they also put continual pressure on the withers. Even rugs which are well cut, and darted or pleated at the shoulder so as

Fig. 203 A day rug kept in place by crossed surcingles.

not to restrict the latter, will need to provide some form of protection in the area of the withers; either a foam insert or a pad of sheepskin stitched on the underside. Rollers with pads which have been allowed to flatten are almost certain to cause both chafing and bruising.

By far the best method of keeping a rug in place is by surcingles sewn to the flanks of the rugs and crossed under the belly. Most modern rugs are made in this way.

Traditionally, the well-dressed equine was equipped with a 'day' rug (Fig. 203) as well as the tough night clothing which was required to stand up to hard wear. A day rug, nowadays reserved for outings and Sunday best, is a wool rug which is available in a number of plain colours, in checks or even in the striped Witney blanketing. It can be bound in a variety of colours and usually bears the owner's initials in the rear corners or, of course, a sponsoring company's name and logo. It, too, should be put on over a light sheet to prevent the hairs penetrating the cloth and it can be secured either by surcingles or a matching roller.

An All-purpose Rug

Increasingly, the modern tendency is towards a single stable/travelling rug that has built-in properties of insulation and fulfils the requirements of warmth, fit and durability without additional under-blankets, sheets etc. (Fig. 204).

Most of these rugs are built on what might loosely be termed the 'duvet' system and incorporate three compatible materials. One such rug uses a Scandinavian fabric, 50 per cent cotton, 50 per cent nylon 'as an *outer* covering. This is a very strong but *breathable* fabric'. *(Fabrics do not breathe but they do allow for the passage of air, which is what this piece of copy-writing is trying to tell us.) The lining* is a soft '12 oz pure cotton drill' and the thermal filling is described as 'the most efficient insulating filling there is'. (This particular rug and its filling were subjected to exhaustive testing at the Bristol University Veterinary School.)

The cut and shaping of this rug, and similar patterns, eliminate all pressure on the spine and obviate chafing at the point of the shoulder. It is self-righting because of the way it is shaped over the body and it is only necessary to do up the short belly band and the double-overlapping fastening at the breast secured by nylon clips. The rug is shaped to lie below and round the dock and is, naturally, equipped with a fillet, or tail,

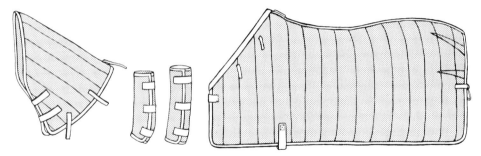

Fig. 204 The single travelling/stable rug with built-in properties of insulation has, to a large extent, taken over from the former blanket and top rug arrangement. This pattern, with an efficient thermal filling, fastens under the belly and has a fillet strap which ensures it stays in place. A neck cover and leg wraps of the same material provide full protection.

strap. To complete the ensemble and provide full protection, hoods, fitting over the head to the base of the neck, and leg wraps are available in matching materials.

Washability

A necessary feature of the modern rugs is their ability to meet the 'washability requirement' of the modern horse-owner. They can all go in the washing machine, clip fittings and all.

(The old leather chapes and brass buckles were less easily dealt with and the leather became hard and brittle if immersed in hot water. Indeed, enormous labour was expended in keeping wool-lined canvas rugs, under-blanket, etc. clean. On the other hand some of the 'duvet' type rugs are not entirely successful. I have one that is so bulky that it presents a storage-space problem. My girl groom refuses to use it because it is both too heavy and too bulky for her to get on and off the back of a big horse.)

Anti-sweat Sheets

Whilst most of the all-purpose rugs incorporate insulating materials there is still room for the anti-sweat sheet (more commonly known as a sweat sheet) based on the principle of the insulating string vest, the mesh construction creating air pockets to protect the body against the effects of either cold or heat.

Horses are said to 'break out' when they sweat heavily after exertion or excitement. Some 'break out' as a nervous reaction to travelling and hunters will frequently do the same thing hours after their return to the stable.

In the past, before the advent of the sweat sheet (first produced in Nottingham under the still familiar trade name Aerborn), the problem of breaking out was countered by the practice of 'thatching', which involved covering the back with straw and laying over it a rug turned inside out so that the moisture collected on the outside. It was an effective method to employ, but laborious. The sweat sheet put on next to the skin and under a top covering is just as effective and far quicker. Surprisingly, after over forty years, the principles involved are still not fully understood and you still see steaming horses being led about in a sweat sheet without the addition of the essential overrug which would create the insulating air pockets.

Today, however, there are also 'thermal' rugs made up from a fine cellular mesh which may act as insulators on their own account.

Coolers (Fig. 205), large woollen sheets extending from behind the poll to the dock, are still employed in America to cool-off racehorses and polo ponies gradually, the horse being walked until dry and cooled off. Wool, of course, is an excellent body insulator but these sheets may also be made from a fine cotton mesh.

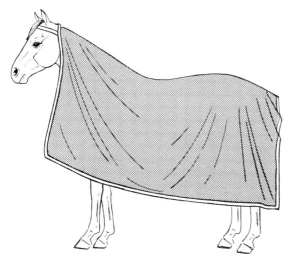

Fig. 205 A woollen cooler used to dry off horses after exertion.

For travelling in hot weather a sweat sheet worn under a linen or cotton summer sheet is sufficient to keep the horse comfortable.

Summer Sheets

The warm-weather equivalent of the day rug is a summer sheet, perfected in America and made from linen (a better and longer-lasting material) or from cotton. The American patterns of forty or fifty years ago featured cross-over surcingles to keep the rug exactly in position and British manufacturers have, for the most part, followed the American example.

Summer sheets can be made in plain colours, but the traditional cloth is a check based on the famous 'Tattersall' pattern named after the founder of the world's most famous bloodstock sales, Richard Tattersall (1724–1795). A gentlemen with a penchant for decorative waistcoats, Tattersall was the owner of Highflyer, founder of one of the great Thoroughbred breeding lines.

The use of the summer sheet under a winter blanket or stable rug has been discussed, but the sheet also serves an important purpose in the warmer months. It provides partial protection from the unwelcome attention of flies and it ensures that the coat is kept clean and lying flat – an important consideration when preparing horses for showing.

New Zealand Rugs

Increasing use is made of the New Zealand rug (Fig. 206) which is integral to the so-called 'combined system' of management. If one fact relative to these rugs emerges as being of special significance it is that only the very best will do.

The New Zealand rug is one which provides protection and warmth for the clipped horse turned out during the winter months. The practice originated, of course, in New Zealand where the design was perfected and where some of the strongest rugs are made. In Britain, this method of horse-keeping is known as the 'combined system', i.e. it involves stabling the hunter-clipped horse at night and turning him out during the day, thus combining the best of both worlds. *(A hunter clip is when the saddle patch and the legs are left unclipped.)*

Otherwise rugs may be used, and often are, on unclipped animals

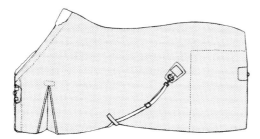

Fig. 206 *A New Zealand rug made with ample depth, non-shifting fastenings and generous pleating at the shoulder.*

whose coats are deemed to be insufficiently thick to withstand winter weather. For the working owner the system has everything to recommend it, for it allows the use of a fit horse without the owner having to spend a disproportionate amount of time looking after him. Stable work is reduced and the horse, whilst able to take continuous gentle exercise, will benefit from the mental relaxation which comes from being at liberty instead of spending most of his life confined by four walls.

There are people who dispense with the stable altogether, keeping the horse out day and night. Horses can be kept in this fashion very satisfactorily, so long as they are fed generously, but it makes severe demands on the fabric and construction of the rug, which is, after all, central to the system. To stand up to this routine the rug needs to be made of the best stout canvas, and, ideally, two rugs are needed, one to be held in reserve against the inevitable time when the rug in use becomes excessively wet and muddy. Before use new canvas rugs should be well hosed down and then left to dry. This increases the water-repellent property of the fabric by closing the cells. *(This was also the recommended practice for those splendid riding macs that preceded today's effective but infinitely scruffy waxed-cotton affairs.)*

No rug, of course, can be guaranteed to be 100 per cent waterproof, a fact which should be appreciated. It will, of course, be even less resistant to the wet if it is not re-proofed at the end of the season.

For owners operating the combined system and putting the horse out for a limited period during the day, a lighter nylon-fabric rug is probably a better choice because it is easier to handle. Again, however, two rugs per horse are almost a necessity and when alternated make good economic sense since the serviceable life of both is extended significantly.

After many years of operating the combined system the design features I consider essential in a New Zealand rug are these:

a. It *must* be shaped over the quarters, coming well down over the dock.

b. It *must* be secured by an arrangement of straps under the belly and a pair crossing between the hind legs, as in the original New Zealand pattern (Pape's pattern), *not by a surcingle* which may chafe and does not, in any case, hold the rug in place.

c. It *must* be sufficiently deep to come below the flanks, otherwise it gives little protection and is inclined to slip over to one side or the other, and it must be lined three-quarters of the way down the flanks – a full lining is not recommended since the bottom part will become wet and muddy when the horse lies down.

d. It *must* be pleated and cut generously at the shoulder to avoid rubbing and facilitate free movement, and there must be some form of protection at the withers. Additionally, the rug should give ample protection at the chest, possibly being secured with a double fastening.

I like a rug that has an extra strip of 'thatching' along the back seam to protect this most vulnerable area against water seepage.

Given a rug (two rugs) conforming to these criteria and unexceptionable in respect of the quality and weight of the fabric (as well as a paddock

Fig. 207 A stretch hood covering the face and neck saves the labour involved in cleaning the horse kept on the 'combined system'.

free from barbed wire) then the 'combined system' is the practical answer to the needs of the busy horse-owner who requires a horse in fit condition through the winter months and is prepared to exercise high standards of management to achieve that end.

One of the problems connected with horses turned out in this way is the propensity of the equine to rub the head and neck in the stickiest patch of mud to be found. Additionally, of course, the legs can become well covered in dirt, the removal of which involves much tiresome labour. These difficulties can be overcome, in part, by fitting a stretch-nylon hood (Fig. 207), or a buckle-on one of the same material as the main rug, which covers the face and extends to the base of the neck The legs can also be protected, though less satisfactorily, by long leg wraps.

Belonging, if tenuously, to the same family are rain sheets which will cover the horse from head to tail against heavy showers, for instance, whilst waiting to enter the ring.

Exercise Sheets

Exercise, or quarter, sheets were once the prerogative of the racehorse but have now spread well outside the domain of the training yard. Their purpose is to keep the horse warm in cold weather and they are usually made in wool rugging of various weights, including the Witney striped blanketing. A fillet string is an essential addition to an exercise sheet and will prevent the sheet from being blown up in the wind. The usual way of keeping the sheet in place is to put it on the back under the saddle, threading the girth through the loops provided on the

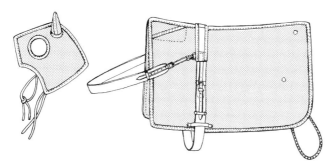

Fig. 208 A cap and paddock sheet with lightweight roller.
Caps may also be used with exercise sheets in cold weather.

bottom edge. To prevent the sheet sliding back, which, loops or not, it surely will, the front corners are turned back in a triangle and secured under the girth straps. Sheets can also be made in waterproof material and some are made to fit *over* the saddle and the rider's knees rather than in the conventional manner. Such sheets are made with an opening in the centre and a Velcro fastening at the withers. It is a clever enough idea but not very practical since the front of the sheet is easily blown up.

In very cold weather racehorses will often be fitted with a cap (Fig. 208) to match the sheet, and a cap is also part of a set of paddock clothing. The paddock outfit comprises a cap, if that is required, a sheet, cut a little shorter than an exercise rug and often made from a lighter face-cloth material, and a lightweight roller and breast-girth covered in the same cloth – as well, of course, as a fillet string.

Hoods and Tail Guards

A hood is a cap extended to cover the neck to its base and is essentially a piece of stable or travelling equipment (Fig. 209).

Tail guards of course prevent the tail being rubbed when travelling and are worn over a tail bandage (Fig. 210). In the past they were made

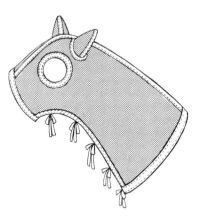

Fig. 209 A hood, a piece of clothing which covers the neck to its base.

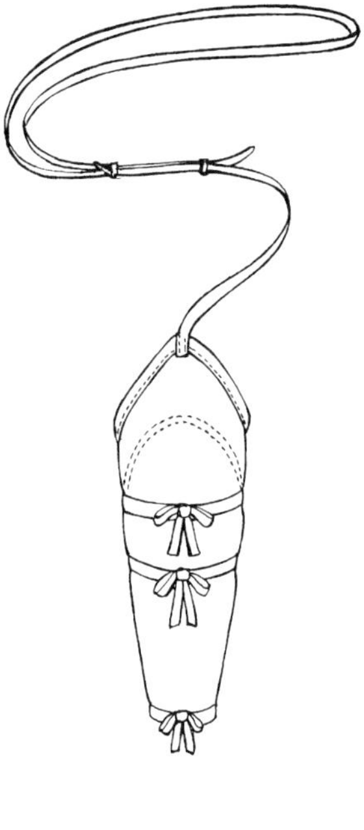

Fig. 210 A tail guard of rugging or leather is worn over a tail bandage when travelling to safeguard the tail against rubbing.

very beautifully from soft baghide with three strap-and-buckle fastenings or they were made in rugging to match the day rug. The least expensive were made of jute and fastened with tapes. They are all still available but most modern patterns wrap round and are secured with the ubiquitous Velcro fastening.

Sizes

Rugs are measured from the centre of the breast to the rug's back edge. Forty years ago a 1.8 m (6 ft) rug was the size recommended for a horse of 16.2 h.h. upwards. Today, rugs are made longer, many of them being shaped over the dock and that is an improvement. The following is a guide to the average requirement:

Hunter	16.2 h.h upwards	1.8–1.9 m (6 ft–6 ft 3 in)
		(in extremis – 2 m [6 ft 6 in])
	15.2–16.2 h.h.	1.75–1.8 m (5 ft 9 in–6 ft)
	15–15.2 h.h.	1.7–1.75 m (5 ft. 6in–5ft 9 in)
Pony		14.2–15 h.h. 1.6–1.75 m (5 ft 3 in–5 ft 6 in)
	13.2–14.2 h.h.	1.5–1.6 m (5 ft–5 ft 3 in)
	13–13.2 h.h.	1.45–1.5 m (4 ft 9 in–5 ft)
	12.2–13 h.h.	1.4–1.45 m (4 ft 6 in–4 ft 9 in)
	12 h.h and below	1.3–1.4 m (4 ft 3 in–4 ft 6 in)

1.1–1.2 m (3 ft 6 in–4 ft) would be suitable for a rug for a sick foal; such a rug is made without a front fastening and put on over the head.

Reflective Clothing

In Europe the British Horse Society, through its Safety Department, has for many years advocated the use of 'hi-viz' gear when riding on public roads. Riders are encouraged to wear fluorescent jackets and to use reflective horse clothing at all times. Fluorescent exercise sheets are the most obvious piece of equipment, but reins, boots and tail-guards are all available in reflective materials.

The use of such equipment in whatever weather conditions attracts the attention of vehicle drivers, giving them time to slow down. 'Be seen to be safe' is one of the most appropriate slogans in the campaign for road safety.

Nets and Masks

A range of cleverly designed and intelligently promoted nose nets and face masks has come on the market in recent years.

A light *nose net* fastened to the bridle is claimed to counter any propensity to head-shaking, a particularly irritating complaint for both horse and rider. Head-shaking may be the result of a number of conditions affecting the ears and sinuses. It could, also, be a deeply-ingrained habit and it may certainly be exacerbated by the presence of flies and midges.

If it is of clinical origin and long standing, a nose net is unlikely to be of much help but otherwise it is claimed that the net *improves* the condition in most cases. (Animals with pink, sensitive muzzles likely to become

Fig. 211 Fly mask for UV-sensitive horses, sweet itch sufferers, head-shakers, etc. (Photo courtesy Equilibrium)

Fig. 212 Nose muzzle for head-shakers.
(Photo courtesy Equilibrium)

sunburnt are particularly susceptible to head-shaking.) Under British Dressage rules, nose nets may be worn by confirmed head-shakers in dressage tests, with the permission of the organising committee and subject to obtaining a written dispensation in advance of the competition.

Muzzle protectors give protection from the sun's rays for animals at grass and a full-face fly mask is a useful safeguard against the attentions of flying insects. There is also available a 'full riding mask' for summer hacking, but no similar protection is offered for the rider!

23 Stable Equipment and some Stable 'Vices'

'Sufficient unto the day…'

Headcollars

As basic as any piece of stable equipment is the headcollar which allows us to secure the horse in the stable or when travelling, and provides the means for the animal to be led to and from the paddock.

The traditional stable headcollar was a splendid affair made from the best double-lined leather with brass fittings, three-row stitched on the side stays (or side pieces), fastening either end of the head strap with opulent swage buckles and often fitted with a browband of white 'buff' leather. The three rows of stitching added to the appearance and confirmed the quality of the headcollar but really served no practical purpose at all, unless it was to increase the selling price of the article. Similarly, the shaped, unadjustable, rolled leather throat piece conferred no practical benefit and was again an unnecessary expense.

For all that, a really good headcollar of that type, or for preference the even better adjustable American pattern, gives a certain style to any yard and is an item to be treasured and treated with loving care.

Field headcollars are less elaborate but need, of course, to be strong and made from materials that will stand up to outside conditions. Brass fittings give way to the cheaper 'tinned' buckles, squares and rings and in the interests of economy field headcollars can be riveted rather than sewn. The grey helvetia leather, if kept well greased, is often used in headcollars of this type, or it would be possible to make them from the very strong and naturally supple red buffalo hide.

My preference is for a stable/travelling headcollar of the American adjustable pattern, brass mounted and made from buffalo hide with the head strap lined to prevent the holes from stretching.

In fact, headcollars of this quality are now something of a rarity, their place being taken by the ubiquitous and more economical nylon headcollar,

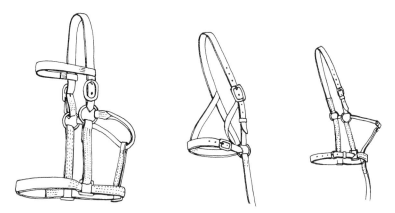

Fig. 213 From left to right: the classic stable headcollar, three-row sewn and mounted with brass swage buckles; Dutch foal slip; adjustable yearling headcollar.

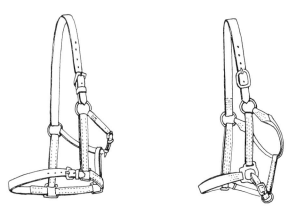

Fig. 214 Two very practical, adjustable American pattern headcollars.

offered in a range of colours varying from the almost acceptable to horrendous fluorescent baby pinks – and even worse than that. The nylon headcollar has advantages other than that of price. It is exceptionally strong, of course, and virtually weatherproof. On the other hand nylon is a harsh material that can rub unless the headcollar fits very well, and there are more than a few that do not. In my view nylon is not a suitable material for a foal collar because of this propensity to rub. Initially, a Dutch slip (Fig. 213) made of soft tubular web is more suitable for a foal, and can be fitted to the young animal easily and swiftly. As the foal grows, a lightweight adjustable leather headcollar, made very soft by repeated applications of leather dressing can take the place of the Dutch slip. *(Foal collars of either type need to be fitted very carefully indeed, lest a young animal should seek to scratch his head with a hind foot and get the hoof trapped in the collar.)*

Manufacturers of nylon headcollars place great emphasis in their promotional material on the strength of their product. Nylon is, of course, strong enough to hold an elephant but the breaking strain is not really relevant. A headcollar, whether of nylon or leather, is as strong as its metal fittings. Should a horse run back violently it is the ring or stay which breaks, and probably fortuitously since the horse might otherwise damage himself severely. In fairness, the nylon headcollar is more easily repaired by the simple replacement of the broken component, than would be the case with a leather collar when both ring and stay may have given way. *(It is recommended in official and other manuals, that the horse should be tied not directly to the wall or box ring but by a quick-release knot to a loop of string fastened on the latter, it being held that the string will break easily in the event of the horse running back and thus an accident will be avoided. The quick-release knot is an obvious and reasonable precaution, the use of the string loop could be more questionable, particularly if it is a loop of nylon baler-twine – a substance which takes a lot of breaking but is, nonetheless, much in evidence on the wall rings of the best-conducted yards. The other argument against the use of the easily broken string loop is that it may very well encourage and even confirm the horse in the undesirable habit of running back when tied. The animal learns very quickly how easily he can free himself from the restriction imposed by the tie rope and running back becomes a game played with increasing frequency.*

The answer, in my view, is to teach the horse to accept tying as part of his training when a youngster. It is not difficult and need not involve rough, tough methods. Thereafter, however, it should be a rule not to tie the horse unless the attendant is in close proximity.)

A confirmed breaker of headcollars may receive a salutary lesson (but only under observation) by being fitted with the most practical headgear of them all, the insufficiently appreciated Yorkshire halter (Fig. 215), which is unlikely to break. Made of strong, woven strands of cotton cord it is fitted with a throatlatch to prevent it being pulled over the eye (which is not so with the ordinary adjustable market halter.) The Yorkshire has every advantage as a method of securing the horse in the

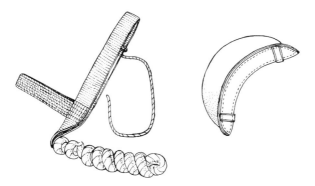

Fig. 215 Left: Yorkshire halter with cord throatlatch and rope lead.
Right: protective poll pad for travelling.

stable or the trailer/horsebox and is just as good as a lead collar. Moreover, it is not displeasing aesthetically (which cannot be said for some of the nylon products) and it is inexpensive; the lead/tie rope is, in fact, integral to the halter.

Control Halters

Largely, one suspects, as a result of the 'natural' school of horse trainers, there are a number of control or training halters on the market, mostly of American origin.

They are made from cord and a pull of the lead results in pressure being applied to all the sensitive areas of the head in salutary fashion. The pressure can, nonetheless, be released quickly by loosening the hold on the lead and is seen as a reward for compliance.

In the hands of a skilled trainer the use of these halters and of the principles involved may be effective if not universally acceptable, but otherwise they are best treated with some caution.

Poll Pads, Lead and Tie Ropes

For travelling it is sensible to provide protection for the poll in the form of a thick felt pad, slipped on the head strap of the headcollar, in case the horse should throw up his head and strike the box roof.

For leading, a *soft* cotton rope fastened to the headcollar by a shaped

Fig. 216 Left: a stable rack chain.
Right: massage or strapping pad of leather filled with hay.

eye or a snap hook is probably the best and it may double as a stable tie rope. Harsh, stiff ropes are not to be recommended. They can burn and even tear the hands should the horse pull away violently. Nylon lead reins are unsatisfactory for the same reason. *(Never, ever, of course, wrap the rope round the hand. It would be quite possible to lose the use of that necessary extremity should a half ton of startled equine seek to take off.)*

Hooks can also be a source of danger and numerous unpleasant accidents have been caused by the clip being caught up in an animal's nostril or mouth. A trigger type of quick-release hook is much safer.

For securing the horse for short periods in the stable a rack chain (Fig. 216) is often used and has much to recommend it. A tee- or vee-shaped, slip-through fastening is to be preferred to the use of snap hooks on the grounds of safety. A rack chain allows the horse to be 'racked-up' short if he is likely to bite when being groomed and it is, of course, virtually unbreakable, although it is not possible to provide for any form of quick release.

Hay Nets

Hay nets are preferable to feeding hay either from the ground or from a metal corner rack. Feeding from the ground is haphazard, as far as knowing the weight of hay eaten is concerned, and is wasteful, while feeding from a corner rack allows the seeds to fall in the horse's eyes and in any case the rack is usually so high that the animal has to imitate a giraffe to get at his hay. A net by contrast allows the owner to weigh the amount of hay and discourages the horse from bolting his food, with a consequent benefit to his digestion. *(Nylon comes into its own in the making of hay nets. The colours are still nauseous but the nets are incomparably improved on the unpleasantly sticky, tarred nets favoured in the past.)*

It is also as well to remember that a hay net should never be hung so that, when empty, it hangs low enough for the horse to get a leg caught up in it. If there is any danger of this, the cord at the neck should be passed through the wall ring until the net is as high as possible, and then passed through one of the loops at the base of the net before being secured back to the ring. In this way the net is doubled up and there is no chance of it hanging too low when empty.

Small mesh hay nets are probably preferable to any other. They keep the horse occupied for a longer time, they prevent waste and discourage bolting of the food.

Buckets, Skips and Grooming Tools

Water should always be available in the box and much as I love to see a row of painted oak buckets in a yard, that in my opinion is the best place for them. Oak buckets were heavy enough when empty and in time the inside became unpleasantly slimy. I much prefer the light, noiseless, plastic bucket which will suffer no ill effects if it is trodden on or even kicked round the box.

Plastic is also a suitable material for muck skips, and skips so made are a vast improvement on the old heavy cane types which, with age, leave a trail of dung and straw from box to muck heap; otherwise the eyeleted 'muck sheet' of stout sacking has the twin virtues of being cheap and practical.

Grooming kits, of which the brushes are an integral part, receive hard wear and like everything else will last longer if looked after. They should be cleaned carefully with a metal curry comb during and after use and should be washed regularly. When drying a brush, stand it on its bristles, not on its back, to allow the water to drain off. If the brush is left on its back the water will run down the bristle tufts and rot the wood into which the bristles are set.

All brushes, either dandy, body, or water, are either 'machine filled' or 'hand drawn'. In the former the tufts of bristle are plugged by machine into the wooden base, while in the latter each tuft is secured and wired into a base and then the wooden top is screwed on. The screws and the dividing line between the base and the top are easily discernible and although a brush of this type is initially more expensive it will give better service. The common Mexican Whisk, a vegetable fibre from which dandy brushes were traditionally made, is now almost wholly replaced by nylon tufts in an array of dazzling colours.

For those who are unable to make a hay wisp with which to strap, or massage, their horses, a convenient and efficient massage pad (Fig. 159) can be made from a chamois leather (Or an imitation of that estimable article) stuffed with hay and stitched round, and it is worth including in the grooming bag. Another excellent grooming aid is the 'cactus cloth', a rough square of string, impregnated one suspects with something like paraffin, which if wielded with vigour puts a wonderful bloom on a coat.

(Many of the modern innovations are far superior to the old items of equipment, but grooming tools are in most respects very poor in comparison, which could just be a reflection of lower standards in this area of management. The humble hoofpick is a prime example. The modern, plastic thing is next to useless and is exceeded in the non-useful league only by that ridiculous gimmick, the folding hoofpick. A stout, large metal hoofpick, if necessary knocked up by an obliging farrier, is a better tool and less likely to be lost, particularly if attached to a piece of bright ribbon.

Brushes are generally of poor quality and it is difficult, for instance, to buy a soft-bristled, leather-backed body brush. Such a brush is, nonetheless, worth looking for and though expensive is worth every penny. For a dandy brush, Mexican Whisk is still infinitely preferable to nylon tufts and a shaped, bristle water brush is something to be kept under lock and key – together with linen stable rubbers, real chamois leathers and natural sponges.)

Tricks and 'Vices'

Stabled horses may develop little tricks, or behavioural aberrations, as a result of boredom and their confinement within a restricted space. Somewhat unkindly, the horse-world defines such behaviour as a 'vice', which rug-tearing, bed-eating and occasionally the eating of droppings, crib-biting and wind-sucking are certainly not. Very occasionally one comes up against a horse who kicks or bites 'viciously' and with intent. Otherwise, a number of horses may indulge in a playful nip or nibble, which can largely be overlooked so long as it is not allowed to develop into anything more serious.

Clearly, a confirmed biter is better tied up short while being groomed or *in extremis* one may have to resort to a muzzle, which, of course, has to be removed at feeding time. The bar-type muzzle (Fig. 217) allows the horse to pick at his hay net and is probably the most useful of its type.

Most of the behavioural problems arise from a combination of

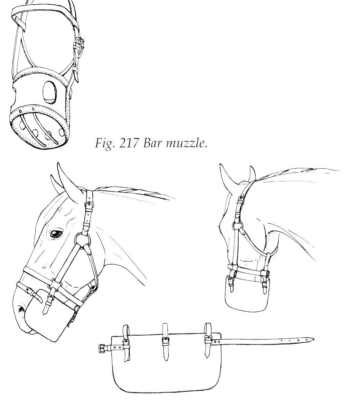

Fig. 217 Bar muzzle.

Fig. 218 Clothing bib to discourage the horse who tears up rugs for fun (or out of boredom?).

inadequate stable management and unintelligent handling and it is better to find the source of the trouble, and put it right from that point, before embarking on one or other of the artificial methods devised to combat a particular problem.

Rug-tearing is usually caused by boredom, although if you have a horse who is a confirmed tearer you may be forgiven for thinking it is just plain cussedness. A clothing bib of strong leather (Fig. 218) or plastic fastened to the three metal squares of the headcollar and bending round behind and below the chin will help in not too persistent cases, but for confirmed tearers, a bar muzzle or possibly a plain muzzle will be the answer if all else fails.

Bed-eating may be caused by some deficiency in food and if this can be traced and catered for the habit may disappear. In any case the horse should have hay always in the box. Continual bed-eating will affect the wind in time, but is easily cured by removing the bed and putting the horse on sawdust, shavings or shredded paper and hoping that no other vice will develop. The depraved habit of eating droppings is almost certainly caused by a deficiency in the diet and is the result of bad stable management.

Two other 'vices', to which a horse is prone, are crib-biting and wind-sucking, and they not infrequently accompany each other. The crib-biter grips any available fitting with his teeth, simultaneously gulping down air, while the wind-sucker swallows air without gripping a fixed object. It will be seen that by removing all fittings and protrusions from the box of a crib-biter he may then turn to wind-sucking.

A combination of both 'vices' will cause indigestion and colic with subsequent loss of condition, and crib-biting will result in rapid and excessive wearing of the teeth. The cause is usually of a nervous origin; it may arise from idleness or boredom or it may start in imitation of

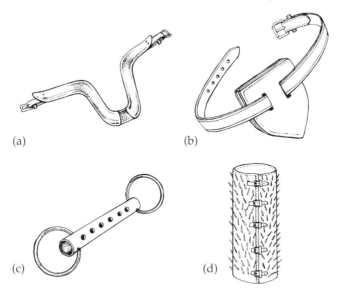

(a)   (b)

(c)   (d)

Fig. 219 (a) Meyer's crib-biting device; (b) simple cribbing strap with leather shield to fit in the gullet; (c) flute, wind-sucking bit; (d) 'pricker' boots to prevent the tearing of bandages.

another horse. Removal of all fittings from the box, a liberal supply of hay to pick at and as much work and interest as possible may curb the excesses of the crib-biter, although it may, in the end, be necessary to muzzle him except at feeding times. If, however, wind-sucking persists, then the object must be to prevent the swallowing of air and to stop him arching his neck for this purpose. A Meyer-pattern cribbing device – Fig. 219(a) – will stop it to a great extent. The device is made from vulcanite with a soft rubber centre and is strapped tightly round the gullet with a strap over the poll and fastened to the headcollar to prevent it moving out of place. The simple crib strap (Fig. 219b) acts in the same way, the thick leather shield fitting into the gullet, but is not as effective as the Meyer pattern.

A wind-sucking or 'flute' bit – Fig. 219(c) – can also be used and is probably as good as anything else. It has a perforated hollow mouthpiece which disperses the gulp of air and prevents it being sucked in.

Articles for Injuries

Occasionally, the need will arise for certain articles to cope with the treatment of injuries. A common practice is for a horse to tear at bandages on an injured leg which may be causing him discomfort, and it then becomes necessary to fit some device to prevent him doing so. The 'pricker' boots – Fig. 219(d) – studded with tacks and put on over bandages were once guaranteed a place in the stud groom's chest. Undoubtedly they discourage investigation, but they are barbarous affairs that might be a source of danger.

The wood neck-cradle – Fig. 220(a) – is more effective for keeping the head away from injuries, but it is uncomfortable and sometimes chafes. The Cheshire cradle – Fig. 220(b) – which must be used with a roller and headcollar, is a far better contrivance and is not nearly so uncomfortable.

Injury to the foot itself may necessitate the use of a poultice boot – Fig. 221(a) – and this should be large enough to accommodate a bulky dressing. The best are those made of rubber. Where an injury to the foot does not require a poultice boot and when it is desirable to be able to walk the patient out quietly, either the plain walking boot – Fig. 221(b) – or the more elaborate hinged-sole boot – Fig. 221(c) – allowing a little freedom for the frog, is a useful adjunct to a stable veterinary chest.

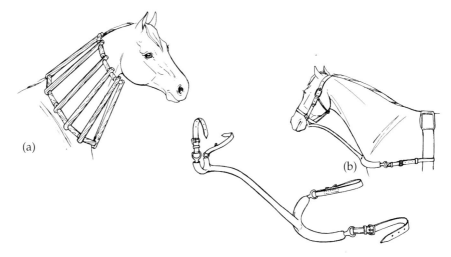

Fig. 220 (a) Neck cradle; (b) 'Cheshire' pattern neck cradle.

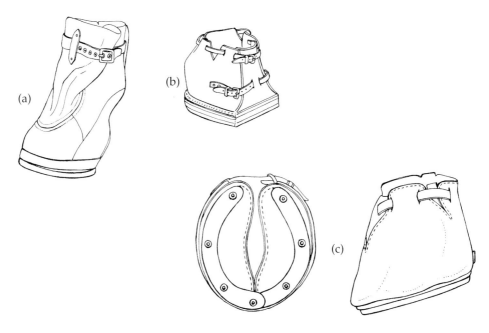

*Fig. 221 (a) Rubber poultice boot; (b) walking boot;
(c) hinged veterinary walking boot.*

A capped elbow is almost certainly caused as a result of bruising by the heel of the shoe when the horse is lying down. When horses are liable to cap their elbows a recurrence will be avoided by strapping a stuffed 'sausage boot' (Fig. 222) round the coronet and seeking the assistance of the farrier, who will usually recommend a change in the shoeing of the offending feet.

A simple 'do it yourself' leg spray (Fig. 223) can be made from garden hose with a few simple fittings and can be kept in place by a sling over the neck. There are, however, in the twenty-first century, a number of more sophisticated devices. A leg spray is invaluable for the treatment of soft swellings, strains, etc.

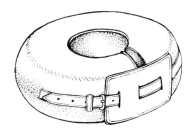

Fig. 222 The 'sausage boot' fastened below the fetlock joint to prevent the elbow being bruised by the heel of the shoe when the horse lies down.

Fig. 223 A simple D.I.Y. leg spray.

You will sometimes see, more particularly in stables which concentrate on the production of ponies, the rather strange-looking articles illustrated in Fig. 224(a). These are neck and jowl sweaters made from a heavy felt covered with mackintosh or some similar fabric. Many ponies and a few horses are so thick through the jowl and in the neck that it becomes difficult for them to flex when required to do so. In these cases recourse is sometimes made to these sweaters to assist in the breaking down of the fatty tissue.

On studs, where it is necessary to prevent the mare from kicking the stallion, hobbles of various sorts are used. Fig. 224(b) shows the most common type which fastens round the mare's neck and passes between the forelegs and attaches to the hind legs. This is frequently made with

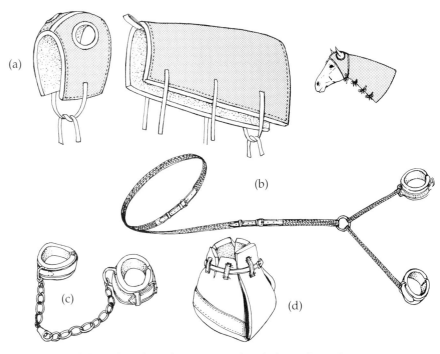

Fig. 224 (a) Neck and jowl sweaters to break down fatty tissue;
(b) service hobble; (c) simple hobbles;
(d) felt 'kicking' boots worn by the mare at service.

Fig. 225 Swales gag. The strap is
fastened to the headcollar, the coiled metal
'gag' is then inserted into the mouth to
enable examination of the latter at leisure.

a quick-release fitting in case of trouble. The simple-type hobble –
Fig. 224(c) is also employed and occasionally a kicking strap similar to
that used on cows. Many stallions are now serving mares without hobbles, but it is still sensible for the mare to wear a pair of thick felt kicking
boots on the hind feet – Fig. 224(d).

24 Breaking and Schooling Tackle

'The horse is an undisciplined force which we must strive to direct, not to extinguish.'

The early schooling of the horse is designed to:

- a. Establish a common language between pupil and trainer.
- b. Accustom the horse to the habit of discipline and, hopefully, to that of submitting willingly to the trainer's authority.
- c. Prepare the animal physically by developing and suppling the musculature in a correct form against the time when he is asked to carry a saddle and rider.
- d. Improve the balance and carriage by exercises carried out to that end.

To achieve those ends a basic set of equipment is required, comprising the following items.

Lunge Cavesson

This is an item of prime importance. It is a powerful instrument and must be of the correct design, and fitted with the greatest care if it is to be effective and not cause the horse discomfort. The ideal is a lightweight cavesson (Fig. 226) with a centre ring set on a swivel and side rings set just to the *rear* of the cheek, to which side reins or a riding rein can be attached. A jowl strap is imperative, and a browband made with a stud fastening on one side, so that the ears do not have to be pulled through the headpiece, will help keep the headpiece in place whilst getting the horse used to the feel of this necessary part of the bridle. Two further dee rings are necessary; one at the bottom of the cheekpiece on either side. From these dees it will be possible, using small bit straps or clips, to suspend a bit when the time is ripe.

The cavesson should be lined round the nosepiece to avoid the risk of

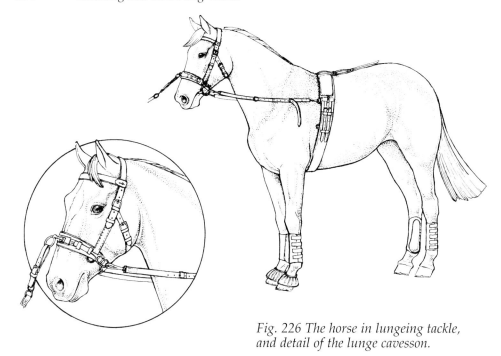

*Fig. 226 The horse in lungeing tackle,
and detail of the lunge cavesson.*

chafing and the whole thing must fit very snugly. The jowl strap, in particular, needs to be fastened sufficiently tight to prevent the cavesson being pulled across an eye.

The majority of modern cavessons are of poor design and construction and most incorporate the three-ring nose plate, which for general purposes is an irrelevant anachronism. It is, of course, ideally suited for the original purpose, when the two side rings were used to attach the horse to the training pillars in the manner still practised at the Spanish Riding School in Vienna, at Saumur in France and at the other classical schools founded on the principles of those two premier establishments. The majority of horse-owners, however, do not make use of the pillars and it is, therefore, more sensible to have side rings placed in the manner described and in a position where they can be of practical use.

A cheaper cavesson made of nylon web is obtainable, but for the most part nylon cavessons do not have sufficient 'body' to remain in place satisfactorily. Most of them tend to droop over the nose and only a few of them are of a practical design.

Lunge Rein

Nylon is similarly unsuitable for a lunge rein. It has insufficient weight to maintain an even contact with the nose, it is slippery and it will cut and burn badly if pulled through the hand. (*Gloves* should also be worn when lungeing as a precaution against the rein burning if it is pulled through the hand.) The best lunge reins are made from soft, tubular web, not more than 2.5cm (1 in) wide but certainly 10.7 m (35 ft) in length. A 5.5 m (18 ft) rein is useless, except for small ponies, whatever the material from which it is made, and it restricts unduly the size of circle on which the horse is asked to work. Too wide a web rein will hang too heavily on the nose ring and affect the position of the head.

The fastening to the cavesson ring is made either with a snaphook set on a swivel or with the clumsier strap and buckle similarly mounted.

The Roller

Rollers accustom the horse to pressure round his middle and act, therefore, as a preparation for a saddle and a girth. Otherwise they provide the essential points of attachment for side reins, the crupper and for any piece of equipment, like a Chambon, for instance, which may have to be attached between the forelegs to the centre of the belly strap. It is, indeed, the control console of the tackle.

Breaking rollers can be made from leather, which is expensive, or from web, which is less so. Whatever the material used, the best type of roller is that made in two parts. This arrangement allows the roller to be fitted with some precision since there is adjustment on both sides.

Ideally a roller should have sufficient rings to cover the differing methods employed by individual trainers. Rings, indeed, are like electric sockets – you cannot have too many of them.

The roller illustrated (Fig. 227) shows an arrangement of rings which allows for side reins to be fitted at different heights. There are also rings for long reins, a ring set on an adjustable strap on the front edge between the two panels, and a crupper ring at the back edge. The adjustable ring is useful if an overcheck is used to encourage a better head position or it can be employed when the horse is lunged from the bit with the object of putting him *in hand*. (An explanation of this advanced method is given in the author's book *Training Aids*, published by J.A. Allen). Finally there

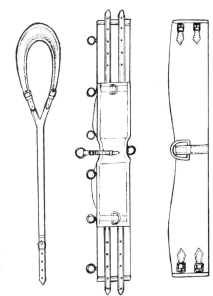

Fig. 227 Crupper and breaking roller. Rings on a roller are like electric power points – you cannot have too many of them.

is the large ring set in the centre of the belly band.

The roller has pads on either side of the withers, and, ideally, the belly band will be shaped back at the elbow to prevent chafing in that area. The pads should be fitted like a saddle and must ensure that there is no direct pressure on the spine. The roller lies behind the trapezius muscle and must not interfere with the movement of the scapula. The belly girth falls into the sternum curve and the roller should incline a little to the rear of the vertical from top to bottom edge. (There are rollers made with buckles set at an angle on the top of the pads so that the side reins can be crossed over the withers. This method is said to encourage a steady head carriage and is used to good effect by a number of knowledgeable horsemen.)

It is suggested (indeed, it is almost an article of faith in some quarters) that the roller should always be fitted with a breast-girth in the same manner as a stable roller. In fact, there is no reason at all why a roller, which prepares the horse for the saddle, should not be girthed firmly enough to stay in place of its own accord – even though it might be thought logical to anchor it in position with a breast-girth at one end and a crupper at the other.

The Crupper

The crupper does, indeed, assist the position of the roller in a small way but its purpose is more positive than that. Fitted properly, more loose than light, so that it exerts a very light pressure on the dock, it will encourage greater use of the loins and, in conjunction with the side reins 'bring the horse together' without the risk of the reins being adjusted tightly.

In addition, the crupper accustoms the young horse to accept the presence of pieces of equipment on his body, which is in itself a lesson in submission. Initially, young horses when introduced to the crupper will express disapproval by clamping the tail, stiffening the back or even indulging in a defiant buck or two. These little exhibitions rarely last for long, however, and within minutes most young horses will be going quite happily.

The crupper should be fitted so that it is possible to insert an upright hand between the back and the backstrap and its fastening. In particular, the initial fitting under the tail is made a lot easier if there is an adjustment on either side of the dockpiece. Obviously, the dockpiece should be kept very soft to prevent any chafing. *(Old patterns of cruppers had the dockpiece filled with linseed. The heat of the body, combined with the usual cleaning grease and the linseed, ensured that the leather was always kept very pliable.)*

Side Reins

Side reins come into use once the horse has learnt the rudiments of the lunge exercises and circles obediently to either hand.

Their purpose is to assist in creating a balanced outline from which it will be possible to obtain more effective movement in all the gaits. With the help of the side reins the horse is encouraged to work within a gently imposed frame, the whip pushing the horse forward at one end against the restraint of the reins at the other. As a result the reins are containing the impulsion produced to provide a rounded outline.

Trainers will vary a little in the methods they employ in the introduction and subsequent use of the reins. I use them initially from the cavesson rings, the reins being fairly loose. Thereafter, I work the horse over pole grids with the reins in place, encouraging him to take up the slack as he lowers and stretches the head and neck. He is then reaching for contact. The same method is employed when the reins are transferred from the cavesson to the bit and it is only when the horse is actively seeking contact with the bit that the reins are shortened by a little. In a perfect world the carriage is produced by the weight of the reins, the lightest of contacts resulting in an easy relaxation of the lower jaw.

If a head carriage is *imposed* forcefully by reins adjusted too tightly the horse will react by retracting the nose and becoming overbent. Inevitably this forced position leads to the horse moving with the weight on the forehand and with a shortened and restricted stride of the forelegs. There will be minimal engagement of the hind legs and no adequate flexion of the hock joints.

Since in this philosophy the *weight* of the reins is of some consequence the latter must have some body to them. Single nylon web, for instance, is too light and floats inconsequentially when the horse is in movement. If nylon reins are used they must be of sufficient substance and as stout as their leather counterparts.

Obviously, the reins must be adjustable to a wide degree. They fasten to the bit or cavesson rings either with a buckle fitting or a neat and easily operated snap-hook, which is preferable.

My own preference is for the 'classical' side reins of plain leather. I used to employ elastic-inset reins or ones inset with rubber rings, being attracted by the possibility of the soft 'give and take' on the mouth (Fig. 228). I now believe it to be a fallacious theory which may do as much harm as good. The 'give' or, more particularly, the 'take' of the rein can become an encouragement for the horse to evade the increased tension by tucking in the nose and coming behind the bit and out of contact.

Nor can I agree with the school of thought holding that the inside rein should be shorter than the outer. It sounds logical but it is, in fact, a delusory snare. The shortened rein, enforcing a bend, often causes the horse to do no more than twist at the poll and there is a pronounced tendency for the horse to either lean on the inside of the bit or retract its nose to evade the contact. In consequence the weight is thrown on the inside shoulder, the quarters are carried outwards and are thus prevented from following the track of the forefeet.

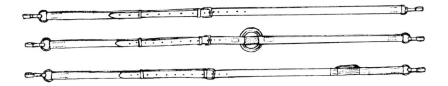

Fig. 228 Side reins with and without elastic/rubber inserts.

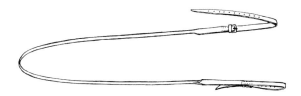

Fig. 229 The running side rein. It is fastened to the roller at each end and passes through a ring at the rear of the cavesson or, subsequently, through the bit rings.

Less well known, but probably no less legitimate, is the running side rein (Fig. 229), an unbroken rein running from one side of the roller to the other and passing either through a ring on the back of the cavesson or, in the later stages, through the bit rings. The advantage claimed for this arrangement is that it is less restrictive of the lateral movement of the head and neck.

Lunge Whip

The lunge whip should be regarded as an extension of the trainer's hand. It allows the trainer to maintain his position at the apex of the 'triangle of control', the horse making the base, and the whip and lunge rein forming the sides.

The modern whips of fibreglass and nylon are excellent. They are light, flexible and with thongs long enough to reach the horse. It is never permissible to hit the horse in anger, but one must be able to influence and maintain the movement, and that is something not possible if the whip and the thong are too short.

Long Reins

Long-reining, an extension of the lunge exercises, prepares the horse still further for the ridden work. In expert hands long reins allow the trainer to obtain obedience to the rein aid, improvement in balance and the refinement of the gaits before the horse is asked to carry an obviously inhibiting weight on his back.

The reins can be the same length and width as a lunge line but the swivel attachments are not necessary. Many trainers prefer, however, a lighter rein for 'driving' and some will use the old tapered 'plough' lines made from cotton rope.

Fig. 230 Long-reining in the English method with the reins passing through large rings on the roller.

The Importance of Good-quality Equipment

The early stages of schooling are probably the most important in the education of the young horse and are the foundation on which all the future work is based. It follows, therefore, that the equipment used in these early days should be the best available in terms of quality and design and should be selected and maintained with great care. Unfortunately that is rarely the case in practice, and whilst people are prepared to pay good money for a saddle, for instance, they are much less forthcoming where schooling equipment is concerned. Indeed, many are prepared to make do with borrowed gear of dubious merit or with their own rough improvisations. You can only assume that the parsimony of such folk is reflected in the shortcomings of their horses.

Breaking and Mouthing Bits

The traditional bit used on young horses was either a straight-bar or jointed snaffle fitted with 'keys' at its centre. The keys were thought to encourage the horse to 'mouth' or play with the bit, thus inducing saliva and a relaxation of the lower jaw. They did, I believe, produce the desirable 'wet' mouth but they have, very largely, gone out of fashion, many people preferring to use the shaped flexible mouth-pieces which may, or may not, be fitted with cheekpieces to prevent the horse evading the central action by sliding the bit through the mouth. Cheekpieces also assist in obtaining a lateral movement of the head by pressing against the cheek itself.

My own view is that, whilst it is helpful to start with a soft, one-piece, shaped mouthpiece, it should be followed, once the horse has come to accept the bit in the mouth, by a jointed snaffle of equally soft material, but more direct and decisive in its action.

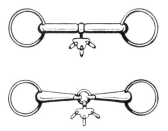

Fig. 231 Straight-bar and jointed bits with 'players' or 'keys' to encourage salivation were once used almost exclusively. Today, they are less popular.

25 Specialist Tackle

'The horse must carry his own head…'

In the early years of this current century specialist 'bending' or schooling tackle, often based on the equipment used a century ago, is still available. American and Australian saddlery concerns, the supermarkets of the trade, feature a number of these devices in their glossy, coffee-table catalogues and one must, therefore, presume that there is a demand for this sort of equipment.

In Britain less overt use is made of the less conventional tackle, probably because it is largely unknown to the majority of horse-keepers, but many professional yards, particularly those producing horses for the show ring, will have some form of specialist gear.

'Bending' Tackle

One very sophisticated schooling aid still used here and there in Britain by those sufficiently competent to operate it, is the long-established *Distas* bending tackle (Fig. 232). At one time this ingenious piece of equipment was much favoured by the producers of children's ponies. It allowed the trainer to put a pony in the required 'frame' in a way that would not have been possible using a child rider, however talented.

The tackle consisted of a bridle and bit, a roller with a backstrap and crupper, side reins, a Jodhpur-type curb chain and cord overcheck.

The bridle is fitted with a facepiece and an elastic noseband, and has a pulley on either side of the pollpiece. The bit used with the bridle is that known as a Wilson (essentially a driving bit) and has a straight bar, usually fitted with keys or rollers in the centre, and four rings. The bridle cheeks and the elastic nosepiece are both fastened to the two *inside* bit rings.

The roller is adjustable at both sides and has a large driving dee ring on the lower end of each pad as well as a ring at the belly in case a martingale is needed. The backstrap has a thick piece of elastic laid on

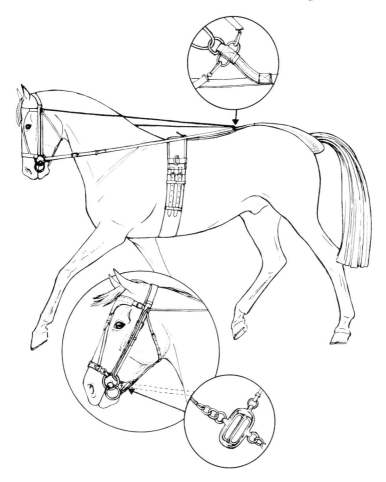

*Fig. 232 The long-established Distas
bending tackle is complex but can be productive in expert hands.*

top of it just before it joins the crupper, and this elastic has two rings on it – one fairly large and one smaller one. The side reins are adjustable and longer than usual to enable them to be clipped on to the larger ring mounted on the elastic of the backstrap.

The Jodhpur-type curb chain has two pieces of cord attached to the chain links on either side. This cord, when the curb is in position, fairly low between the two jawbones, is passed through and inside the inside bit rings up the head, thence through the pulley on the pollpiece of the bridle. The offside cord is then passed through the smaller of the two rings on the elastic of the backstrap and joins the nearside cord above the roller where they are tied together with a bow. The curbpiece is prevented from falling out of position by a lipstrap fastened to the throatlatch of the bridle.

To operate and fit the tackle, the roller is put on first, well into the sternum curve and sloping slightly to the rear. The backstrap and crupper are then adjusted (equally on both sides) with a fair degree of tension sufficient to raise the tail. When the bridle has been put on and the nosepiece adjusted reasonably tightly, the side reins are clipped to the ring on the elastic at the rump. They are then carefully tightened until the head is brought into a vertical position. The pressure to achieve this position is, because of the bridle and side reins being fastened to the inside bit rings, upon the nose and not upon the mouth. The last stage is to fit the curb chain, which acts as a head raiser and will prevent the animal from becoming overbent, the necessary head position being achieved by a careful adjustment of the tension.

It is held that when the tackle is correctly fitted it operates the whole horse, not just the forepart; the loins are brought into play and the horse must begin to bend at the poll and not in the lower third of the neck.

Obviously the final positioning of the horse had to be approached in very gradual stages and the tackle, initially, would not be left on for more than a few minutes at a time. After first accustoming the horse to the tackle in his box, it was customary to work him loose in the school or in some confined space. Later he could be driven in long reins from the outside rings of the bit.

Dumb Jockey

American catalogues still advertise Blackwell's Dumb Jockey (Fig. 233) as well as a number of 'bitting harnesses', an example of which is illustrated (Fig. 234).

The Dumb Jockey, in particular, became a controversial piece of equipment which was roundly condemned by the enlightened horsemen of the post-Caprilli period. Nonetheless, the dumb jockey was in use, particularly perhaps in harness stables, up to and after the Second World War and on both sides of the Atlantic.

Fig. 233 Blackwell's Dumb Jockey is rarely seen today but it is still advertised extensively in American saddlery catalogues.

Fig. 234 An American 'bitting harness' still used on carriage horses.

Today, one cannot think that it would find favour, but there are without doubt some variations on the bitting harness theme in evidence; the one illustrated is used in America, although principally on gaited and harness animals.

Overchecks

Overchecks governing the position of the head (and not dissimilar to the 'bearing rein' against which Anna Sewell campaigned in the famous book *Black Beauty*) continue to be seen on Hackney harness horses and ponies, although they are fastened up only for very short periods. In a much simplified form the overcheck appears as the 'grass string' (Fig. 235) used to frustrate the efforts of strong-necked and strong-willed ponies whose small riders cannot prevent their lunging into the grass to eat.

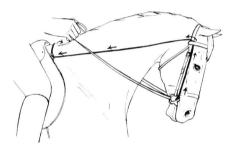

Fig. 235 A sophisticated version of the basic 'grass string' which is often made from a piece of baler twine.

The basic grass string is not more than a piece of baler twine tied to each bit ring then passed upwards through the loop of the browband and back to the saddle dees. (To what degree it is inhibiting of movement is irrelevant if it prevents the pony from behaving in this most frustrating manner and allows the child to enjoy the ride.)

The Barnum

A device used by the French, and by other schools, is the Barnum (Fig. 236). As a schooling aid for the difficult subject, it inculcates the habit of obedience and really is a simplified form of the bridle used by the American, Jesse Beary; the psychology behind its application being similar. The recalcitrant pupil is brought into the school with the bridle on and, as soon as he becomes difficult, the rein is pulled tight, turning his face to the trainer. He may continue to resist forcibly for some time, but will eventually give up suddenly and move forward to the trainer

Fig. 236 The Barnum halter is similar to the bridle used by the American horse-tamer Jesse Beary.

Fig. 237 A simple leading harness for persuading a horse to load or to teach him to lead out in hand. It derives from that used by Sidney Galvayne.

who then quickly releases the now very tight cord. Benoist-Gironière in his book, *The Conquest of the Horse*, gives a full description of the Barnum and states that by this means the horse's 'obsession of the point of resistance' is broken and the habit of straining against the rein or refusing to be led is cured for ever. More importantly the horse has learnt in one sharp lesson that the trainer has the upper hand.

Benoist-Gironière in this connection quotes Gustave le Bon:

> So long as there has been no struggle the horse cannot be totally convinced of his rider's authority. Only this struggle will convince him, and it is far better that it should take place at the start rather than later on. As soon as it is over, the animal will be disciplined and once he is disciplined in one respect, he will easily be so for all the others. The battle is won, and from now we need have recourse to nothing but kindness…a kindness which is quiet but never weak.

The Barnum, the action of which action is clearly seen in the illustration, should be made up with a soft rubber bit and not with a metal one, which might damage the mouth. The device can also be used in place of a twitch for horses who are exceptionally difficult to clip, shoe, etc.

The philosophy behind modern 'control halters' has similarities with these older devices.

26 In-hand Showing Equipment

'Fine dresses don't make fine ladies – but they help!'

Individual opinions will vary as to the most suitable tack for particular classes and the following are, therefore, only suggestions and are by no means inflexible.

A yearling can be shown in hand ('halter classes' in America) in a yearling-type headcollar with brass fittings and the addition of a white 'buff' leather browband, a bit of the straight-bar type with keys can be suspended from the headcollar squares by means of two neat straps fastened with brass buckles, and a white paddock lead rein (again with a brass buckle and about 2.4 m [8 ft] long) can then be fastened on to the offside bit ring and passed through the nearside ring into the hand; or, alternatively, a couple of one type or another can be employed. A common type is that shown in Fig. 238(a) and a better one in Fig. 238(b). This latter is called a three-way couple, the centre strap fastening on to the rear ring of the headcollar. The lead rein on the central brass ring will then be able to pull more upon the poll than the mouth, a part of the horse quite sensitive enough to give adequate control. To embrace both rings of the bit and to give an even pull on each one, a Y-couple lead rein – Fig. 238(c) – has an advantage over the usual type and is not so awkward.

A strong yearling is sometimes shown in a 'ring bit' – Fig. 239(a) – and this type may well give increased control. The Chifney 'anti-rear' bit – Fig. 239(b) is occasionally used on yearlings and stallions and can be an effective means of restraint.

Mares, if not shown in a riding bridle, can be shown in a headcollar with or without a plain bar bit. There is, however, an increasing tendency for pony mares in particular to wear what used to be termed a 'stallion bridle' – Fig. 239(c). As it is now used on everything, I prefer to call it an 'in-hand bridle'. It has neat and rather fancy brass buckles, a stitched and swelled noseband and browband, and generally shows a head off well.

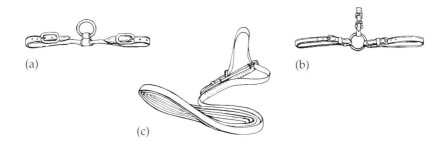

Fig. 238 (a) Simple lead couple;
(b) three-way lead couple placing pressure on the poll;
(c) Y-couple lead rein.

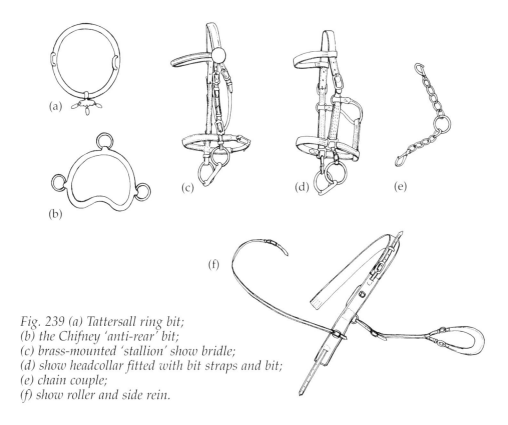

Fig. 239 (a) Tattersall ring bit;
(b) the Chifney 'anti-rear' bit;
(c) brass-mounted 'stallion' show bridle;
(d) show headcollar fitted with bit straps and bit;
(e) chain couple;
(f) show roller and side rein.

Ponies shown in this bridle often wear a straightbar bit with small and rather attractive horseshoe-shaped cheeks.

Stallions usually wear a bridle of this type or possibly a stout show headcollar, as shown in Fig. 239d. The lead rein for a stallion will often be a leather one as long as 3.6 m (12 ft) and it will be used with the chain couple illustrated in Fig. 239(e). Pony stallions (and some specified horse breeds) often have neat leather rollers with cruppers and side reins – Fig. 239(f) – an occasional variation being to have only one side rein on the offside and a leather lead rein to the hand on the nearside.

Arab breeders have developed their own distinctive showing gear, using very fine, decorative show halters to set off the beautiful heads of their charges to best advantage, or employing a genuine Arabian lead halter. Arabs, even the stallions, are rarely, if ever, shown in hand wearing a bit.

At one time the Arab showing slips became so light that they were dangerous; because they were not fitted with a throatlatch it was all too easy for a rumbustious colt to get rid of his headgear and his handler. At British shows it is now obligatory for halters to incorporate some form of throatlatch. *(Some American companies advertise show halters made entirely of light brass or white metal with the exception of a small leather poll strap.)*

Lead reins for Arab show classes are also lightweight and sometimes decorative.

27 Whips and Spurs

'A spur in the head is worth two on the heels.'

(This chapter is substantially the same as that appearing in Training Aids – In Theory and Practice *(J. A. Allen) under the heading* The Artificial Aids. *It is reproduced here, with a minor addition, because there was little more I wanted to say on this subject.)*

Whips

The whip is certainly a training aid but it is also the horseman's wand of office. In an often ornamented form it was long regarded as part of the warrior's regalia and no self-respecting steppe horseman would ever have thought of riding a horse without one.

Similarly, no driver of a wheeled carriage, from antiquity to the present day, would regard his turnout as being complete without a whip. Indeed, in the driving context, a whip takes the place of the legs of the mounted horseman and is an indispensable piece of equipment. The driver of any sort of carriage is often called a 'whip'.

The traditional material for a driving whip in western countries is holly, as it has been for centuries, but in modern riding-whip manufacture, materials like nylon and fibreglass are used almost exclusively and today's whips are probably better than those of the past; they are certainly lighter and better balanced.

In pre-plastic days, steel-core whips were common in the middle price range, but if used to correct a horse, or to encourage one in a race, for instance, they left ugly marks and weals on the body. The best of the old materials was whalebone and a good whalebone whip from a top-class maker was a much prized possession. However, whalebone largely disappeared from the market when the killing of the Greenland whale, the principal source of supply, was prohibited by International Law in 1946, and none of us will quarrel with that. Cane of all types is used to make hacking and show sticks and one old and well-tried favourite is still available – the racing or jumping whip made from twisted nettle vine. The riders of the Spanish School carry the long birch whip of classical equitation. It is used, certainly, as a practical aid but it also serves as a symbol of the rider's humility, which is a pleasing thought.

Lunge Whips

The purpose of the lunge whip is to act as an extension of the hand, pushing the horse from behind into contact with the cavesson rein. It is usually swept along the ground behind the horse although it may on occasions be applied, tactfully, below the hock as a mild stimulant. Should the horse 'fall in' towards the centre of the circle, the whip, pointed at the shoulders, corrects the fault. It is never used, or should never be used, to hit the horse, but it may be cracked to tell the sluggard to mend his ways.

To meet those requirements and to fulfil its function as a training aid used from the ground it needs to be sufficiently long and to be fitted with a thong that is a good bit longer than the stock.

Finally, the thong has to culminate in a lash made of whipcord or something similar. Without a lash it is impossible to crack a whip.

Hunt Whips

Whether a hunting whip (never a crop, which is either part of a chicken or the produce harvested from a field) is a 'training aid' or even an 'artificial aid' is doubtful, except when it is used *in extremis* to persuade a horse to take on some hairy obstacle. It is, however, cracked by hunt servants when checking or rating hounds and is therefore equipped with a heavy thong and a strong whipcord lash. (A hunt servant's whip has a stock of white braided gut and a white thong – otherwise hunt whips have a brown leather stock and a brown thong.)

(The addition of a lash is entirely practical on both a lunge and a hunting whip but why it should have persisted, even in a shortened form, on the end of cutting, dressage and polo whips, when it serves no useful purpose at all, is something of a mystery and the only explanation obtainable from whipmakers is the time-worn and very unsatisfactory: 'It has always been made like that'.)

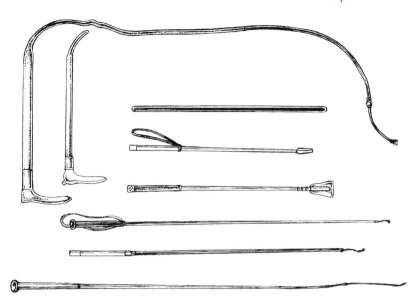

Fig. 240 A selection of whips and canes including, second from top, the child's 'twig', a potentially dangerous whip.

Dressage and Schooling Whips

A dressage whip should be long enough to be used from the saddle without taking the hand from the rein, or to be used as a schooling whip on the ground when leading in hand, teaching the horse collection from the cavesson, etc.

From the saddle, it reinforces the leg by being tapped on the flank, or it may be used in a tap down the shoulder to encourage greater effort or to counter resistances in that part. Obviously, too, like all whips, it may be used, judiciously, for the purpose of correction.

Once more, however, it needs to be long enough, otherwise the horse may be jabbed in the mouth when the whip is applied behind the rider's leg. Furthermore, it needs to be fairly rigid, more rigid, in fact, than flexible. If it is too whippy it is likely to beat a tattoo on the animal's side rather than delivering a single, decisive tap.

Sometimes, you will see a rider with an extra long whip, long enough to be able to touch and activate the hock. In fact, this rider, unconsciously,

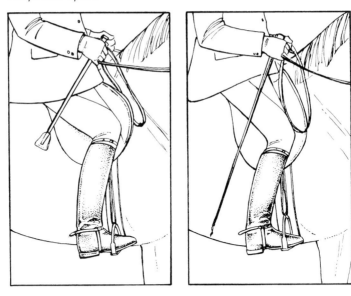

Fig. 241 Left: the jumping whip held correctly. Right: the dressage whip.

is using a type of driving whip, in effect a 'buggy' whip, but if it serves the purpose, despite being more whippy on account of the increased length, there can be no argument against its use.

Whips of this sort are always carried in the inside hand when riding in an arena or school, i.e. left hand on the circle left and vice versa. This is because the emphasis is on the inside, driving leg; we are, in fact, riding from the inside leg into the outside hand. If the whip is to support the leg, it has, therefore, to be carried in the inside hand.

Another practical reason for carrying the whip in this way when riding in a school is to prevent it from hitting the wall, something it would surely do if carried in the outside hand.

Polo Whips

Polo whips, covered in plaited kangaroo hide, with a stout button on the top and a wrist loop – both to ensure that it does not slip from the hand – are purely pragmatic in their nature. They are carried to make the pony put his legs to the ground as fast as he can.

Jumping and Racing Whips

These whips are much shorter than schooling whips, the permitted length of a jumping whip being 75 cm (29½ in). Usually, the whip terminates in a broad flap that will make a satisfactory slapping noise when applied but will not cut. This whip is used to deliver a crack down the shoulder or, when greater effort is required, a swipe behind the saddle which, of course, entails the rider removing the hand from the rein.

Such whips are almost exactly like those carried by the fierce, steppe horsemen, who were the terror of the settled communities of their day, and who often used their whips in very much the same way.

Cutting Whips

A 'cutting' whip, a term not now much used, is longer than the aforementioned, although not as long as a dressage whip. Usually it is an altogether more elegant piece of equipment, although it is still practical enough.

For the side-saddle rider such a whip can substitute for the inactive right leg.

Hacking Whips

A useful hacking whip is a stout type of cutting whip fitted with a horn handle, like a hunting whip, in order to facilitate the opening and closing of gates. A practical accessory to the handle is a small brass screw fitted into the base end. It gives greater purchase when pushing a gate and prevents the handle from slipping.

Canes

For hacking and showing, a 'cane' is carried, which can be leather-covered or plain. A half-round, leather-covered cane, i.e. one that has been split so that one side is flat, is thought to lie more easily in the hand. More distinctive is the 'switch' (stick) of holly, cherry or birch, carefully cut and nicely dressed and polished.

Children's Whips

In the trade these are called 'twigs'. My own description for these ridiculous and potentially dangerous items is 'tooth-picks', although they would be equally as useless if asked to perform that function!

The objection to these riding 'twigs' is the hand-loop fixed at about the three-quarter mark so that the top of the whip projects by a good 15 cm (6 in) above the rider's hand. In the first place, the whip, as a whip, is then rendered useless because it is now too short to be used. Second, and more important, it could be dangerous when jumping or if, for some reason, the rider lost balance or seat, even if only temporarily. In these circumstances it is possible for the end of the whip to stick upwards into the face or, worse still, into an eye.

So why are such whips manufactured? 'We've always made them like that!' My advice to parents would be to cut the wrist loops off.

Spurs

The purposes of the spur in practical terms are:

a. To sharpen, or refine, the horse's response to the very lightest action of the leg.
b. To reinforce the leg's action.
c. To act as a correction when that is required – *which should* be infrequently.
d. For a purely cosmetic effect – a boot is always set off to better advantage when fitted with a spur.

Properly used, by an educated horseman, spurs become no more than an extension of the leg. They are then a quite legitimate aid, and entirely humane, far more so than those vulgar, bruising kicks. (Indeed, the object is to make less and less use of the spur as the horse's schooling progresses.)

Whatever type of spur is worn, unless it be a dress spur, which snaps into a spur 'box' on the heel of a uniform boot, it is worn on the counter of the boot, i.e. where the boot's foot meets the leg.

The most common pattern of spur is the Prince of Wales, which has a relatively short, drooped and blunt neck. The length of the neck is governed by the rules of showjumping, but more latitude is allowed outside that sport. In practice long-legged riders will need to wear

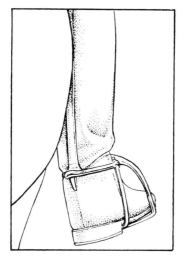 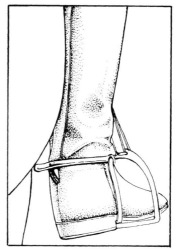

Fig. 242 Left: the spur fitted correctly on the counter of the boot. Right: the spur in use.

long-necked spurs, if the latter are to be effective, while riders of an opposite conformation need only short-necked spurs.

The neck can, of course, be straight, which increases the potential severity, and some European spurs have squared necks, culminating in a point. In my view these are no more acceptable than the neck that is set on the inside of the heel.

Sharp points (i.e. inset with a rowelled wheel) will clearly be more severe and could be used to abuse the horse. Blunted rowels, despite their fearsome appearance, are probably not as severe as they seem – as long as the leg is an educated one.

The leg aid, whether applied with or without a spur, is made with a *forward* squeeze in a slight rolling manner that can be emphasised to the point where the foot moves a little outwards. The action causes the arm of the spur and, if it is continued, the neck itself, to brush against the lie of the hair. The horse is sufficiently sensitive in this area for that to be quite enough to obtain the required response. When the leg is laid flat against the horse to control the shift of the quarters, only the metal arm of the spur comes in contact, unless the foot be turned a little outwards.

Gimmicks, euphemistically termed 'innovations', are necessary adjuncts to the saddlery trade. They encourage interest and development, but, inevitably, there will be one or two that overstretch the bounds of credibility. As an example, catalogues in recent years have featured 'spur grips' or 'spur protectors'. They are, in fact, a rubber sleeve covering the arms of the spur and are variously claimed to protect the spur (against what?), to protect the boot or to 'assist the grip' (curiouser and curiouser). A more appropriate name might be 'nonsense cover'.

Surprisingly, the horse-peoples of Asia never employed the spur, relying entirely on their whips.

Both Greeks and Romans, however, employed a short, prick spur worn on the heel. By the Middle Ages, long-necked, hugely rowelled spurs were in favour and were necessary if the mounted knight of Western civilisation, who turned his horse by the leg, was, first, to reach his mount's flanks and, second, to stimulate animals that became increasingly heavy and common.

It was, nonetheless, the spur that came to symbolise the ideal of knightly chivalry (*cheval* = horse, *chevalier* = horseman), and was central to the ceremony of knighthood in an age when the knight was the embodiment of the Christian virtues. He 'won his spurs' after a night-long vigil spent in prayer and even now the spur retains much of its symbolic status within ceremonial regalia. Its practical use should likewise be in keeping with the courtesy of chivalry.

Index

Note: Page numbers in **bold** refer to illustrations